Reviewing the AFL's Vilification Laws

This book is the outcome of an Australian Research Council (ARC)-funded project titled *Assessing the Australian Football League's Racial and Religious Vilification Laws to Promote Community Harmony, Multiculturalism and Reconciliation*, which investigated the impact of the Australian Football League's anti-vilification policy since its introduction in 1995. With key stakeholders the Australian Football League, the AFL Players' Association and the Office of Multicultural Affairs (previously the Victorian Multicultural Commission), the book gauges the attitudes and perspectives of players and coaches in the AFL regarding Rule 35, the code's anti-vilification rule. The overarching themes of multiculturalism, reconciliation and social harmony in the AFL workplace have been the guiding ideals that we examined and analysed. The outcomes from the research vectors look at and engage with key issues about race, diversity and difference as it pertains to the elite AFL code, but also looks at the ongoing international conversation as it pertains to these themes in sport.

This book was previously published as a special issue of *Sport in Society*.

Sean Gorman is a Senior Research Fellow at the Curtin University, Perth, Australia, who specialises in Australian Indigenous Studies. He has studied and worked in the Indigenous Studies field for 20 years and is affiliated with both the Centre for Aboriginal Studies and Minority Corporate Counsel Association (MCCA). His latest book *Legends: The AFL Indigenous Team of the Century* is a collection of life stories of the indigenous players chosen by an expert AFL panel spanning the years from 1904 to 2004. Gorman's work draws on social history, sports history, local history, memoir and memory, and gives insight and voice to contemporary indigenous society and people.

Dean Lusher is a lecturer at Swinburne University, Hawthorn, Australia, and is a social network analyst with expertise in the application of statistical models for social networks. He recently co-edited *Exponential Random Graph Models for Social Networks: Theory, Methods and Applications* (2013).

Keir Reeves is a professor and the Director of the Collaborative Research Centre for Australian History at Federation University Australia. His current research concentrates on cultural heritage, regional development and history. He is also committed to exploring how these trajectories can be applied to regional development policy to ensure viable communities in regional settings particularly in central Victoria. He recently co-edited *Battlefield Events: Landscape, Commemoration and Heritage* (2015).

Sport in the Global Society: Contemporary Perspectives

Edited by
Boria Majumdar, *University of Central Lancashire, UK*

The social, cultural (including media) and political study of sport is an expanding area of scholarship and related research. While this area has been well served by the *Sport in the Global Society* series, the surge in quality scholarship over the last few years has necessitated the creation of *Sport in the Global Society: Contemporary Perspectives*. The series will publish the work of leading scholars in fields as diverse as sociology, cultural studies, media studies, gender studies, cultural geography and history, political science and political economy. If the social and cultural study of sport is to receive the scholarly attention and readership it warrants, a cross-disciplinary series dedicated to taking sport beyond the narrow confines of physical education and sport science academic domains is necessary. *Sport in the Global Society: Contemporary Perspectives* will answer this need.

For a complete list of titles in this series, please visit https://www.routledge.com/series/SGSC

Recent titles in the series include the following:

Junior and Youth Grassroots Football Culture
The Forgotten Game
Edited by Jimmy O'Gorman

Gender in Physical Culture
Crossing Boundaries – Reconstituting Cultures
Edited by Natalie Barker-Ruchti, Karin Grahn and Eva-Carin Lindgren

DIY Football
The Cultural Politics of Community Based Football Clubs
Edited by David Kennedy and Peter Kennedy

A Social and Political History of Everton and Liverpool Football Clubs
The Split, 1878–1914
David Kennedy

Football Fandom in Italy and Beyond
Community through Media and Performance
Matthew Guschwan

Numbers and Narratives
Sport, History and Economics
Wray Vamplew

Healthy Stadia
An Insight from Policy to Practice
Daniel Parnell, Kathryn Curran and Matthew Philpott

Young People and Sport
From Participation to the Olympics
Edited by Berit Skirstad, Milena M. Parent and Barrie Houlihan

Reviewing the AFL's Vilification Laws
Rule 35, Reconciliation and Racial Harmony in Australian Football
Sean Gorman, Dean Lusher and Keir Reeves

The State of the Field
Ideologies, Identities and Initiatives
Edited by David Kilpatrick

Reviewing the AFL's Vilification Laws

Rule 35, Reconciliation and Racial Harmony in Australian Football

Sean Gorman, Dean Lusher and Keir Reeves

Routledge
Taylor & Francis Group

LONDON AND NEW YORK

First published 2018 by Routledge

2 Park Square, Milton Park, Abingdon, Oxfordshire OX14 4RN
52 Vanderbilt Avenue, New York, NY 10017

Routledge is an imprint of the Taylor & Francis Group, an informa business

First issued in paperback 2019

British Library Cataloguing in Publication Data
A catalogue record for this book is available from the British Library

ISBN 13: 978-1-138-65794-6 (hbk)
ISBN 13: 978-0-367-87834-4 (pbk)

Typeset in Times
by diacriTech, Chennai

Publisher's Note
The publisher accepts responsibility for any inconsistencies that may have arisen during
the conversion of this book from journal articles to book chapters, namely the possible
inclusion of journal terminology.

Disclaimer
Every effort has been made to contact copyright holders for their permission to reprint
material in this book. The publishers would be grateful to hear from any copyright holder
who is not here acknowledged and will undertake to rectify any errors or omissions in
future editions of this book.

For Professor Niall Lucy

Father, husband, friend, Fremantle FC member

1956 – 2014

Contents

Citation Information

The chapters in this book were originally published in *Sport in Society*, volume 19, issue 4 (May 2016). When citing this material, please use the original page numbering for each article, as follows:

Introduction
Introduction: the AFL's Rule 35
Sport in Society, volume 19, issue 4 (May 2016) pp. 472–482

Chapter 1
Understanding the importance and context of vilification
Sport in Society, volume 19, issue 4 (May 2016) pp. 483–500

Chapter 2
Overarching findings
Sport in Society, volume 19, issue 4 (May 2016) pp. 501–537

Chapter 3
Abacus Football Club
Sport in Society, volume 19, issue 4 (May 2016) pp. 538–548

Chapter 4
Bravo Football Club
Sport in Society, volume 19, issue 4 (May 2016) pp. 549–556

Chapter 5
Charlie Football Club
Sport in Society, volume 19, issue 4 (May 2016) pp. 557–564

Chapter 6
Delta Football Club
Sport in Society, volume 19, issue 4 (May 2016) pp. 565–572

Chapter 7
Echo Football Club
Sport in Society, volume 19, issue 4 (May 2016) pp. 573–581

For any permission-related enquiries please visit:
http://www.tandfonline.com/page/help/permissions

FOREWORD

This collection of papers arose out of an Australian Research Council project that examined Indigenous and multicultural diversity and masculinity in the Australian Football League (AFL). With key stakeholders, the AFL, the AFL Players' Association and the Office of Multicultural Affairs (previously the Victorian Multicultural Commission), we have gauged the attitudes and perspectives of players and coaches in the AFL regarding Rule 35, the code's anti-vilification rule. The overarching themes of multiculturalism, reconciliation and social harmony in the AFL workplace have been the guiding ideals that we examined and analysed. All stakeholders were keenly aware of the socially transformative capacity of the AFL to inform and change internal AFL perspectives and public attitudes given football's central role in Australian society, a game for all Australians.

Sean Gorman

Dean Lusher

Keir Reeves

Introduction: the AFL's Rule 35

Sean Gorman, Dean Lusher and Keir Reeves

This introductory paper lays the foundation for this important work. This is the first time that a multidisciplinary, systematic study has been conducted into the Australian Football League's (AFL) Rule 35[1] – the first code of conduct introduced by an elite sporting organization in the world to deal with racial, religious and sexual vilification. Social and sport history in Australia will be discussed to further contextualize the importance of the research.

Introduction

> Michael Long said: 'The AFL's racial and religious vilification rule doesn't just cover Indigenous players; it's for everyone of all colours, races, and religions. It doesn't only apply to football: it's the way we must live'. (Demetriou 2005)

On 25 May 2013, the AFL[2] had scheduled the Indigenous themed round to take place in Round 9. For the AFL, themed rounds have become big business as they promote key Australian dates such as ANZAC day,[3] as well as the contribution women, Indigenous and multicultural players have made to the code of Australian Rules Football over time. In 2013, the Indigenous round was a special fixture for a very simple reason. It was the 20th anniversary of Nicky Winmar famously raising his guernsey in 1993 to a hostile Collingwood crowd at Victoria Park, Collingwood's home ground (Klugman and Osmond 2013). Just as the photograph of Liverpool champion John Barnes kicking bananas off the pitch at Everton in 1987 has historically come to represent race issues in the English Premier League, the image of Winmar raising his jumper has provided Australians with a starting point in regard to race relations. It quite simply is the watershed moment in Australian sporting history regarding race relations.

For the 2013 series of Round 9 matches, the AFL had spent weeks in the lead-up promoting the Indigenous round. It seemed that everywhere one looked, be it on television or in the print media, there were advertisements of current Indigenous AFL players emulating Winmar's stance by raising their jumpers with pride. It was a powerful tribute to Winmar personally, a homage to his bravery as a player and strong recognition as to how far the AFL, as a code, had come from the days where gratuitous verbal abuse was 'part of the game' (Gorman 2011, 1–10; Hess and Stewart 1998, 242–243).[4] With the traditional flagship game at the MCG, the AFL's hallowed turf, scheduled for the following night, Saturday 25 May, between Essendon and Richmond with the 'Dreamtime at the G', the Friday night game between Collingwood and Sydney was guaranteed to set the tone for the anniversary. The game had all the hallmarks to be a great showcase and celebration of the contribution of Indigenous Australians to the Australian game. Furthermore, it was also an opportunity to acknowledge the AFL as arguably the biggest agent for social change in the country – because it literally is the biggest game in town (read: the biggest game in the country).

Late in the game, with Sydney all but having won, the two-time Brownlow-medal winner and AFL superstar, Adam Goodes, kicked the ball along the boundary line right in front of the Great Southern Stand at the MCG. Goodes was so close to the crowd that they could almost touch him. What happened in the next few seconds would change the tone of the Australian sporting and political landscape as discussion, argument and debate would rage for the next few weeks to determine what actually took place and, more specifically, what it meant.

The footage shows Goodes stop and momentarily look towards the crowd. Just as quickly he looks down to a member of the ground staff who has been sitting against the fence. Goodes then beckons the employee to get to his feet and then points to the crowd again. He is clearly agitated. He gesticulates some more and goes to run off. He then stops and turns back, again pointing, clearly saying something to someone.

Goodes then ran off and headed for the bench, removing himself for the rest of the game. He did not take his place in the on-field team celebrations or the team song, which become a feature of televised games. Goodes had starred with a best-on-ground performance, making his absence all the more telling. News reports several months later would detail how Goodes was feeling at the time.

> It just sort of all hit me once I was on the boundary line … yeah I just didn't want to be out there anymore. (Dalton 2013, 15)

The drama, captured on television, continued deep in the bowels of the MCG change rooms. Goodes remained agitated. The room started to fill up with players and Sydney coaching staff. Collingwood President Eddie McGuire, in an unorthodox post-game act, can be seen moving through the Sydney dressing room and making a beeline to Goodes. McGuire's body language is that of a man who is determined. His gaze is stern and fixed on Goodes. Goodes and McGuire then walk around and out of sight of the camera.

It came to light in the hours after the game that Goodes had been called an 'ape' by a 13-year-old Collingwood supporter and he felt deeply aggrieved. He had requested her removal from the oval by security staff, to which they complied, and she was held for questioning by police for a few hours. It should be noted that while Rule 35 deals directly with player-to-player vilification or people employed by the club, such as coaches and trainers, spectators also are subject to rules and regulations regarding racial abuse and anti-social behaviour. In the aftermath, McGuire understood that a transgression had taken place and he assured Goodes that the opinion expressed was that of a minority, something Collingwood had moved on from. Over the next 48 hours, the Australian media went into hyper-drive. What was meant to be a celebration had turned into a fiasco and a farce. McGuire was interviewed, saying he had spoken to Goodes and placated him, imploring Goodes not to let one ignorant supporter undo all the good work he and his club had done regarding racism in sport. McGuire reiterated to the public that Collingwood has a 'zero tolerance for vilification' and that 'we have come such a long way'. What McGuire meant was that football and Australian civil society's understanding of issues around racism have become more enlightened and, as a consequence, we are better off for it.

Four days later, McGuire was wearing his other hat – as media man and co-host of Triple M radio's 'Hot Breakfast' panel. Ex-AFL player Luke Darcy was with him on air. General banter ensued until discussion turned to the greatly anticipated stage musical *King Kong* that was about to premiere in Melbourne. As part of the promotion, a huge fake gorilla hand was suspended outside Melbourne's tallest building, the Eureka Tower, which had certainly got people talking, including those in the Triple M studio:

> Luke Darcy: What a great promo that is for *King Kong*.
> Eddie McGuire: Get Adam Goodes down for it, you reckon?
> Luke Darcy: No wouldn't have thought so ... No absolutely not.
> Eddie McGuire: You can see them doing that, can't you?
> Luke Darcy: ... Who?
> Eddie McGuire: Goodesy?
> Luke Darcy: What? ... That?
> Eddie McGuire: You know, with the ape thing, the whole thing. (Wilson 2013)

Needless to say, the 'joke' fell flat and all of the good work McGuire had done in the aftermath of the supporter's transgression on Friday night, not to mention his long record in promoting reconciliation and Indigenous causes, was quickly compromised. Goodes tweeted: 'Morning Australia this is what I have woken up to', referring to McGuire's *King Kong* gag, as his aggrievement took another turn, making a complex situation even messier. As the day wore on, McGuire tried to qualify himself and repeatedly apologized but this just seemed to make matters worse. Even AFL CEO Andrew Demetriou was forced to reconsider the AFL's position: earlier in the day, he had tried to play things down by stating:

> He knows he has said the wrong thing because he has apologised. It is very 'un-Eddy' and you saw it on Friday night and his actions straight after the Adam Goodes' incident. He is the last person with a racial bone in his body. (Thompson 2013)

By that afternoon, the AFL had reconsidered their position and charged McGuire under Rule 35, the AFL's anti-vilification rule. With this, McGuire became the first club president in AFL history to be cited under Rule 35 (Dampney and Noakes 2013).

**

Daniel Southern was by any measure a tough footballer. An uncompromising defender for the Western Bulldogs and known for his 'rough and ready' look, Southern had a football style that befitted it: rugged and reliable. Despite this, Southern's career was beset with injury and he finished his career in 2000, after being recruited by the Bulldogs in 1994, having played just 103 games. After training one night, Southern drove two of his teammates home. One was Mark West, a brilliant young Torres Strait Islander recruit, who, like Southern, would have his career cruelled by injury. The other was a young Anglo player who remains anonymous. As they drove through the streets of Footscray, a Melbourne suburb known for its predominately Asian working class, the Anglo player said, 'Look at all these Asians. What are they doing here?'

When they reached the Anglo teammate's destination, they dropped him off and drove away. West spoke up, clearly unsettled about his teammate's perspective. 'I wonder what he says about me. I'm black, I'm different. If he is saying something racist about Asians, what is he saying about me?' (Lane 2011).

In 2011, an incident occurred during the AFL home and away fixture involving the Western Bulldogs' Justin Sherman and Joel Wilkinson of the Gold Coast Suns. Wilkinson, who is of Nigerian heritage, was playing his first game in the elite competition. At some stage during the second quarter of the game, Sherman (a forward) kicked a goal on Wilkinson (a back), who was playing on him. Inexplicably, Sherman then proceeded to racially vilify Wilkinson. Astoundingly, Sherman kicked another goal while playing on Wilkinson and repeated the insult. By Saturday night, a complaint had been drafted by the Gold Coast Suns and by Sunday morning it was lodged with the AFL. By Monday, the conciliation process had been successful and Sherman was fined $5000 dollars and suspended for four games. The last reported incident of racial vilification of an on-field nature was in 1999, where St Kilda's Peter Everitt abused Scott Chisholm of Melbourne. Everitt was found in breach of Rule 35 and donated $20,000 to a charity of Chisholm's choice and voluntarily stood down for four weeks. When asked how he felt when he was abused by Everitt, Chisholm said: 'I felt like I didn't want to be there',[5] a sentiment echoed by Goodes 12 years later.

But in order to understand these incidents, one needs to understand the two previous events that set the scene regarding race relations in Australia particularly in relation to sport and especially in the AFL. The first reported incident culminated in 1993 from a hard fought victory by St Kilda at Collingwood's home ground, Victoria Park. Spectator anger from Collingwood supporters saw this Round 4 fixture become famous when Indigenous St Kilda player, Nicky Winmar, contributed a best-on-ground performance along with fellow Indigenous teammate, Gilbert McAdam, and was a key catalyst in St Kilda winning the match. Both players had experienced significant crowd abuse over the course of the game, and so it was that, after winning the game, Winmar raised his jumper to a hostile Collingwood football crowd and pointed to his body (Klugman and Osmond 2013). For the broader community, this pivotal incident sparked great debate about racism in football and society at large. Collingwood President Allan McAlister said at the time that Winmar and teammate Gilbert McAdam would be respected, 'As long as they conducted themselves like white people'. This spoke largely of the paternalistic attitudes that many non-Indigenous Australians harboured towards Blackfellas.[6]

Another critical incident occurred in 1995, with the vilification of Michael Long. During a highly anticipated ANZAC Day match, Collingwood ruckman Damian Monkhorst, who was being tackled by Long at the time, implored that, 'Someone should get this black cunt off me'. Long and fellow Indigenous teammate Che Cockatoo-Collins could hardly believe their ears. Long refused to let the media spotlight drop and pursued the AFL on its lack of protocols. Ross Oakley, AFL CEO at the time, tried to gloss over the incident by appearing at a press conference with Long and Monkhorst, refusing to let either speak, and declared the incident had been resolved (Klugman and Osmond 2013, 75–76). Yet, Long was not satisfied with this glossing over and continued his fight over this issue, which ultimately led to the introduction of the AFL's racial and religious vilification rules: Rule 35 (Gorman 2011). Now, because of Long, all who play the game have it legislated that abuse on the grounds of race or religion will not be tolerated and they are protected from it. All the players undergo education and awareness programmes as part of being a professional sportsperson.

Intent of this collection

What this volume aims to address is the importance of the AFL's Rule 35 as a policy designed to protect, respect and value the involvement of footballers from across a range of social, cultural, religious, ethnic, racial backgrounds, as well as sexual orientations. During the past 20 years in Australia, the AFL has been at the vanguard of institutional change designed to eliminate racism and intolerance, in all of its forms, from its code. It has done this with the introduction of the Racial and Religious Vilification Laws, more generally known as Rule 35. The AFL's Rule 35 states:

> No person subject to these Rules shall act towards or speak to any other person in a manner, or
> engage in any other conduct which threatens, disparages, vilifies or insults another person

4

('the person vilified') on any basis, including but not limited to, a person's race, religion, colour, descent or national or ethnic origin, special ability/disability or sexual orientation, preference or identity. (Australian Football League 2013a, 145, 2013b)

Rule 35 provides the legal and administrative framework that assists in the regulation of harmony in the AFL, which is one of Australia's largest employers per capita of Indigenous (10%) and multicultural (14%) people. This framework enables the players, coaches, administrators, members, fans and spectators to come to terms with, and understand the impact of, racism and intolerance in the community more holistically. To reinforce its message to the football community that such behaviour is not acceptable, the AFL updated Rule 35 in 1997. This was done to include new conditions for conciliation, education and confidentiality. The rule had new penalties, and its provisions extended to employees of AFL clubs with on-field access, as well as players. In 2009, this rule was expanded from prohibiting vilification on the basis of race, religion, colour, descent or national or ethnic origin to also prohibit vilification on the basis of a special disability (which includes a disease or illness) or sexual orientation, preference or identity. Subsequently, the new areas covered by the rule were added to the AFL's vilification education programme. Under the amended rule, an umpire, player or club can raise a complaint. Initially, the matter is dealt with through confidential conciliation between the persons involved, but if it cannot be resolved in that way, it is referred to the AFL Tribunal or the AFL Commission for determination. After a first offence, the AFL Complaints Officer may send any complaint about a player straight to the Tribunal or the AFL Commission.

Specifically, Rule 35 enables the AFL to refine its professional development and support processes for its players and clubs by providing cross-cultural education and by integrating the principles of that education into daily work practices. This is done in the hope the players will transition out of the game with greater awareness and tolerance and clubs become more than just sites of elite sporting pursuits but social centres of excellence.

**

Rule 35 was implemented by the AFL in 1995. At that time it was called Rule 30 and basically dealt with issues around race and religion; since then, it has been broadened to include a range of characteristics. The basic premise of this collection and the research that has informed it is to gauge the efficacy of Rule 35 in combating racism and intolerance in the AFL. Ostensibly, this has been in regard to player-to-player vilification, but more nuanced forms of racism and intolerance have also been considered. To do this, the project considered the role of education in professionally developing the players and what they took away from this education process in relation to their clubs, their teammates and their everyday lives as professional athletes. Consideration was also given to what the players individually brought to their clubs in terms of their domestic backgrounds and lives before football. We were not specifically interested in the implementation of the rule itself; our primary consideration was in what understanding the players have of Rule 35, given the evolving nature of the game and the fact that players have different social, ethnic and racial backgrounds.

The perspectives of the players about these issues and the rule itself were crucial to an assessment of its impact in addressing these significant issues. This was important because the AFL has become, and continues to be, a major agent for social change in Australia. As the AFL's CEO Andrew Demetriou's quote implores, 'It is the way we must live'; with these words, he positions the AFL in the vanguard of that social and cultural change.

As previously mentioned, there are now several themed rounds that the AFL promotes to highlight issues around multiculturalism, diversity, community harmony and reconciliation. Furthermore, one has only to go onto the AFL's website to see just how active the AFL has been in raising awareness of a number of community-based issues. In this way, the AFL ceases to be just a game but becomes a conspicuous organization at the forefront of cultural, social, racial, sexual and ethnic acceptance and understanding in Australia. Perhaps one of the major highlights for the AFL in this regard was their recognition in 1995 by the United Nations Association, and in 2001, their winning of the National Corporate Anti-racism Award (AFL 2005). As a trickle-down effect, football can provide for many of us a means to deal with and mediate complex and difficult issues. Whether it has been the rise of migrant and Indigenous players in the game or issues around the treatment of women or gay rights, drugs or gambling, the AFL is perceived to be at the vanguard of the big discussions in Australia. These positive messages of social and economic responsibility are filtered through the game and its identities; millions of people in Australia are engaged by these messages for one simple reason: football means something to them.

If football can be such a force for good in the social and cultural landscape of Australia, how effective has Rule 35 been in influencing and educating the players and its employees, in this regard? How well do the players understand issues around intolerance and prejudice and what do these things mean to them in real terms?

The AFL's Rule 35 is such an intriguing starting point for a project like this because one can see how effective it has been in the most popular football code in Australia over time. In this way, the AFL is a unique organization that has made significant changes and has led the way for many other sectors to follow suit. More specifically though, one can ask hard questions of players and coaches who have the benefit of playing/working alongside teammates from a variety of ethnic and racial backgrounds and who benefit from the AFL's and AFL Players Association's inductions and professional development around these issues. In many cases, this is the perfect space to conduct this type of research given the professional development and education the players receive but also because of the outside societal pressures and individual choices that elite AFL players will make. This type of research with this specific cohort of people is therefore a unique opportunity to measure the efficacy of the rule and the understanding of it by the AFL's employees to see what has worked under the auspices of Rule 35 and what needs improving.

Reviewing Rule 35

Rule 35 was a groundbreaking innovation in Australian sport designed to stop on-field vilification and negate negative attitudes towards ethnic minorities playing the game at the elite level. By way of comparison, since the introduction of Rule 35 in 1995, there have been 85 Indigenous players in the AFL. In 2008, Indigenous players made up 10% of AFL team lists (Harcourt 2008). In 2009, the figure rose to 70 players, with the inclusion of 12 rookies making a total of 82 AFL players (McGrath 2009, May 25. "Personal Correspondence."). According to the AFL's Community Development website, there were 68 Indigenous players listed in the 2013 and 2014 seasons. This represents 9% of AFL players, significantly higher than the national population of Indigenous and Torres Strait Islander people, which stands at 2.3% (Australian Bureau of Statistics 2014).

With this in mind, the AFL is the highest non-mining corporate employer of Indigenous Australians. In addition to the growing Indigenous cohort, increasing numbers of players from a variety of racial and religious backgrounds are becoming involved in the game. These include Irish and Muslim players (most recently Zach Touhey [Carlton] and Bachar Houli [Richmond], respectively, who are now AFL players), as well as growing numbers from the Horn of Africa refugee and Pacific Island communities. The AFL has also recently launched the Multicultural Ambassadors program to help highlight community engagement across Australia. Some of these players include Nic Naitanui (West Coast), Majak Daw (North Melbourne), Alipate Carlile (Richmond) and Lin Jong (Western Bulldogs) (AFL Community Club 2014).

However, despite this, questions emerge from a more open dialogue about race, identity and football. These include: has the AFL successfully addressed the issue of racial vilification? Does the AFL have the resources and programmes in place to deal with an increasing diversity of players from a wider range of social, socio-economic and cultural backgrounds? What has the AFL learned from its experience of combating vilification that might benefit the broader Australian community? Furthermore, has the collective player body learned from the programmes that have been introduced by the AFL not just to combat on-field vilification but also to introduce those guiding principles from the game into its players' everyday lives? In part, the answer to these questions lies in the extensive way that Rule 35 is now applied as a formal management policy throughout all tiers of the AFL. This is an important consideration due to the status and agency that AFL footballers have in the Australian community as elite athletes, public figures and celebrities.

It is our contention that AFL players occupy a unique position in society to instil positive racial perceptions, interactions and behaviour into the broader community. However, it is also through the players' experiences that many of us can perhaps take stock of what it means to be a person of colour or ethnic difference in Australia. For many, the issue comes down to the difficulties in changing people's general perceptions about the suite of racisms that are manifest in society from direct, overt, institutionalized, systemic, enlightened and casual racism. As ex-Richmond and Collingwood small Indigenous forward Andrew Krakouer recalls:

> I have walked into a shop and a lady has walked in with her trolley and she has a bag and she grabs her bag tighter, or something like that, like I might be trying to steal her bag . . . There is a security guard and I walk into a shop and all of a sudden they start following me around because of the colour of my skin. I don't see any other reason why they would follow me. (Pierik 2013)

These sentiments echo the experience of Krakouer's ex-teammate Leon Davis, who is also Indigenous, who reflected on his time as a footballer, where his identity was a constant issue for others:

> There is a level of racism that is constant. Even in Melbourne I felt racism every day . . . You would go in a shopping centre and the security guard would come straight up and follow you around, or shop attendants would watch you. I was playing for Collingwood and I was an All-Australian and it was happening. But then they would realise who I was and they'd ask for an autograph or for photos and I was always like, 'Five minutes ago you thought I was going to steal from you, now you want my autograph'. (Pierik 2013)

**

The implementation of Rule 35 in 1995 has arguably been the single biggest act of reconciliation by any sporting code in Australian history. Perhaps more important is the manner in which the introduction of Rule 35 and associated media campaigns have directly fed into a number of debates about tolerance and diversity so that there has been a discernible shift in public opinion in the Australian community. This is not to suggest that things cannot be improved upon but we have seen great progress in public awareness.

For example, culturally and linguistically diverse footballers are no longer a novelty but a feature of game at the highest level. The Indigenous and multicultural rounds are now a highlight of the annual AFL and Australian sporting calendar, and Australian society is moving towards a more mature understanding of the need for racial and ethnic harmony in the community.

Despite conscious moves by the AFL to address racism in Australian Rules Football, there continue to be incidents of direct and indirect racial vilification and intolerance. The most problematic example of that intolerance in recent times involved Adelaide Crows Football Club's recruitment manager, Matthew Rendell, in 2012. Rendell commented to the National Community Engagement Manager for the AFL, Jason Mifsud, and AFL Multicultural Manager, Ali Fahour, that he would only be prepared to draft an Indigenous player if the player had one white parent (Pierik and Kokher 2012).

This, as a comment, is one that smacks of deficit theories, paternalism and layers of intergenerational ignorance. The comment by Rendell shows how opinions can influence decision-making based on the most fraught of all characterizations: the stereotype. This can have major ramifications for all stakeholders, not the least Rendell, who lost his job for his utterance.

> In terms of the Rendell issue, the AFL were correct in following up on indigenous welfare officer Jason Mifsud's claim … The reason why the AFL needed to do this was because the comment strikes at the heart of what any sport in Australia relies upon: opportunity and participation. (Gorman 2012a, 2012b)

It is these two concepts of opportunity and participation that drive junior sport, which is the incubator and nursery that leads to elite competitions. If people abandon these sports because they believe that inequity or prejudice, either perceived or real, is a prevailing feature and they cannot tolerate it, then that sport will become socially diminished and culturally impoverished. For example, there has only been one Indigenous player to play at test level cricket in Australia, Kamilaroi man Jason Gillespie. It would be impossible to think that the AFL would have a near total absence of Indigenous players playing in its elite competition, yet for cricket, the reality is that at a certain point, Indigenous players at junior levels turn away from Australia's national summer game.

By way of comparing AFL and cricket, the Western Australian Imparja Cup captain Matt Abrahamson, a Yamatji man, spoke of moving through the cricket grades in Perth, Western Australia, and the challenges he faced. For him, cricket ceased to be just a game but a contested site where race and identity played a major part.

> I played A Grade WACA cricket at Gosnells and we were playing another team in the pennant competition. The other side had a particular player (who was Indian) and his nickname was 'Boonga'.[7] If you walked up to an umpire and say, 'I am taking offence at that', you don't know how the system is going to respond if you raise it as a concern. So you think, 'I might be best keeping my mouth shut'. (Gorman 2011)

In this way, we can see how issues of intolerance and abuse can manifest to make a totally negative experience, with the addressee humiliated and the addressor morally diminished.

Conclusion

The implementation of Rule 35 in 1995 has been the single biggest act of reconciliation by any sporting code in Australian history. It has seen changes in participation rates, which is indicative of the institutional change that has taken place throughout the AFL. Since 1990, when the Victorian Football League (VFL)[8] became the national AFL, the game has had many challenges, but racial vilification presented itself differently from the myriad financial and administrative issues that the new competition faced. The reason for this is that vilification was seen as an intrinsic part of the game.

Despite conscious moves by the AFL to address racism in Australian Rules Football, there continue to be, at worst, incidents of high-profile vilification and, at best, ignorant racial stereotyping in the code. These range from Sherman in 2011 to the Rendell incident. Both of these incidents are revealing but it was Rendell's comments that are a subtler and much harder issue to read given they are of the institutionalized variety. Rule 35 also covers issues around sexuality and other issues, and therefore other aspects of difference. The recent coming out by champion Olympic Australian swimmer Ian Thorpe and the recent change of AFL clubs of Heritier Lumumba due to his concern about homophobic comments within his club highlight that Rule 35 may indeed be very important in influencing when the first AFL player does indeed come out – which at the time of writing this collection of papers still has not occurred, but no doubt will at some point in the future.

Despite the official policy of racial harmony and tolerance in all major football codes in Australia, there remains a long way to go in eradicating racial vilification and changing attitudes within sport and throughout the Australian community. These issues are not confined to Australia but are discursive constructions that seem to play out as the backdrop to professional sport globally. Thea Lim (an American journalist who has written about racism) observed that despite America being racially aware, 'The response remains the same' towards minority sportspeople who are, in effect, essentialized because of their talents but still subjected to racist epithets (Lim 2012). Which brings us back to the question: how far have we come?

Perhaps we need to consider the actions of significant sporting figures to answer that question. A great example is the American champion Jesse Owen, who ran in the 1936 Berlin Olympics, winning four gold medals. Who can forget the calm look of resolve on Owens' face as he was surrounded by Nazis at a lost to explain how their Aryan 'supremacy' could be beaten by an 'untermenschen', the son of a sharecropper whose only means of improving his lot in the world was to run faster and jump further than anyone else. But if we think that the lot of Owens was to be improved on his return to his homeland, with his Olympic triumph, the sad reality is that his skin colour was still seen as problematic. On Owens return to the USA, he was reported to have said:

> When I came back to my native country, after all the stories about Hitler, I could not ride in the front of the bus … I could not live where I wanted. I wasn't invited to shake hands with Hitler, but I wasn't invited to the White House to shake hands with the President either. (Lapchick et al. 2008, 426)

The same aching irrationality can also be observed in modern Australia where, despite government policy and landmark initiatives by key sporting codes (particularly the AFL), racism and intolerance are still prevalent in many forms. The challenge remains to change not only institutional policies towards minority sportsmen and women in key codes but also attitudes in the wider Australian community and across sectors. It is only when this is done can the question of 'how far have we come?' be truly answered.

This collection

In the remainder of this collection, we present a comprehensive analysis of Rule 35 as it is understood by players, coaches and other staff in nine, and thus half, of the teams in the AFL. Our data comes from in-depth interviews and surveys in an attempt to understand what sort of impact Rule 35 has had. We interviewed 99 people and surveyed some 370 players and staff to this end. We present some overall findings of what we found in paper "Overarching findings" (doi:10.1080/17430437.2014.1002974, in this collection), followed by nine case studies, one for each of the clubs, in separate papers. Paper "Understanding the importance and context of vilification" (doi:10.1080/17430437.2014.1002973, in this collection) gives some further contextual and historical background to the issues surrounding Rule 35.

Acknowledgements

This project took seven years from the time it was conceived until its completion. The authors would like to thank the following people for their work, support and advice over that time. Garry Robins, Cory McGrath, Nick Hatzoglou, Kelly Applebee, Pippa Grange, Matt Finnis, Paul Oliver, Nadia Taib, Shane McCurry, Rod Austin, Colin McLeod, Ali Fahour, Patrick Clifton, Colin Gallagher, Tony Hedges and Norwich City Football Club, Antoinette Dillon, Monique Laves, Jo Tropea, Ann Dillon, Megan Ponsford, George Lekakis, Wayne Ludbey, Andrew Demetriou, Hakan Akyol, Sue Clark, Ciannon Cazaly, Jess Coyle, Caitlyn McKenzie Tony Birch, Robert Hillman, Andrew Reeves, Barry Judd, Lionel Frost, Annette Gorman, the Australian Football League Players Association, the Australian Football League, the Office of Multicultural Affairs and Citizenship, Paul Leonard, Hugh Thorn, Jolanta Nowak, Andrew Gunstone, Chris McConville, Yorgos Tserexidis, The Wesleyanne, Museum for Australian Democracy at Eureka (MADE), Ed and Al Brunetti and Noel Fermanis. Thanks also to Clare Hall Cambridge, The Menzies Centre for Australian Studies at King's College London, Curtin University, Melbourne University, Swinburne University, Monash University and Federation University Australia and the Australian Research Council Linkage Projects Scheme for providing time and resources to undertake reviewing Rule 35 project research.

Disclosure statement

No potential conflict of interest was reported by the authors.

Funding

This work was funded by the Australian Research Council Linkage Projects Scheme. Partner Organizations The Office of Multicultural Affairs and Citizenship Victoria, The Australian Football League's Players Association and the Australian Football League. Grant Number LP100200093.

Notes

1. In 2013, due to the expanding nature of the initiative to encompass a range of themes and issues around vilification, the AFL updated the rule, known as Rule 30 since its inception, and in 1995, it became Rule 35. The difference between AFL 'Rules' and AFL 'Laws' is this: the rules relate more to the administration of the game, whereas the laws refer to the actual game itself (i.e. umpiring decisions).
2. The AFL is the administration body for the game generally known as Australian Rules Football or Aussie Rules.
3. ANZAC stands for the Australian and New Zealand Army Corps. Anzac Day is commemorated on the day ANZAC troops landed at Gallipoli in Turkey, 25 April 1915. ANZAC Day is a day of national significance, afforded a national public holiday and is equivalent to Remembrance Day in Europe.
4. At AFL matches across the country today, electronic broadcasts to all patrons are played before each game stating that racial vilification at the ground will not be tolerated and will result in fines and/or ejection from the arena.
5. The authors Gorman and Lusher have made multiple requests to the AFL to supply this information over the last four years, asking only for a listing of the *number* of incidents that had gone to mediation and the *number* that had been successful and that needed to be arbitrated. This information had not been provided by the AFL at the time of going to press.

6. The term 'Blackfella(s)' is a generic colloquial term in Australia that refers to pan-Aboriginality. It is not an insult or a pejorative term.
7. The term *Boong* is a highly derogatory word aimed mainly at Indigenous Australians; it is similar to the use of the pejoratives *coon* and *nigger*.
8. The Australian state of Victoria, in which the VFL was based, was the premier state for Aussie Rules in Australia. In 1990, it changed to become the AFL, incorporating teams from Victoria and also other states of Australia.

References

AFL Community Club. 2014. "Australia Post AFL Multicultural Program Ambassadors." http://www.aflcommunityclub.com.au/index.php?id=638

Australian Bureau of Statistics. 2014. "Estimated Population by Sex, by Age Groups." http://www.abs.gov.au/ausstats/abs@.nsf/0/1CD2B1952AFC5E7ACA257298000F2E76?OpenDocument

AFL (Australian Football League). 2005. *Respect & Responsibility Policy*. Melbourne: AFL.

AFL. 2013a. Making a Stand – Joel Wilkinson. http://www.afl.com.au/video/2014-02-25/making-a-stand-joel-wilkinson

AFL. 2013b. *Rules*. Docklands: AFL House.

Dalton, T. 2013. "Adam Goodes and the 'Matter of Choice'." *Weekend Australian*, January 18.

Dampney, J., and C. Noakes. 2013. "O'Brien Slams McGuire for On-Air Gaffe." http://www.afl.com.au/news/2013-05-29/obrien-slams-mcguire-for-onair-gaffe

Demetriou, A. 2005. The Glue that Brings Us Together: Combating Racism in Sport, December 9. https://www.humanrights.gov.au/sites/default/files/content/racial_discrimination/whats_the_score/pdf/afl.pdf

Gorman, S. 2011. *Legends: The AFL Indigenous Team of the Century*. Canberra: Aboriginal Studies Press.

Gorman, S. 2012a. "Voices from the Boundary Line: The Australian Football League's Indigenous Team of the Century." *Sport in Society: Cultures, Commerce, Media, Politics* 15 (7): 1014–1025.

Gorman, S. 2012b. "What if Indigenous Australians Didn't Play Footy?" *The Conversation*, http://theconversation.com/what-if-indigenous-australians-didnt-play-footy-5964

Harcourt, T. 2008. "And the Big Men Fly ... All Over the World." http://www.austrade.gov.au/Default.aspx?PrintFriendly=True&ArticleID=7817

Hess, R., and B. Stewart, eds. 1998. *More than a Game: An Unauthorised History of Australian Rules Football*. Melbourne: Melbourne University Press.

Klugman, M., and G. Osmond. 2013. *Black and Proud: The Story of an Iconic Photo*. Sydney: NewSouth Publishing.

Lane, S. 2011. "Southern Discomfort." *The Age*, April 14.

Lapchick, R., J. Bartter, J. Brenden, S. Martin, H. Ruiz, and M. Sedberry. 2008. *100 Pioneers: African-Americans Who Broke Color Barriers in Sport*. Morgantown, WV: Fitness Information Technology.

Lim, T. 2012. "Jeremy Lin row Reveals Deep-Seated Racism against Asian Americans." http://www.guardian.co.uk/commentisfree/cifamerica/2012/feb/21/jeremy-lin-racism-asian-americans?INTCMP=ILCNETTXT3487

Pierik, J. 2013. "Off-Field Racism Rife in Melbourne, Says Krakouer." *The Age*. August 6.

Pierik, J., and A. Kokher. 2012. "I'm No Racist, Says Rendell." *The Age*, March 18.

Thompson, M. 2013. "McGuire Apologises for Gaffe Linking Goodes and King Kong." http://www.afl.com.au/news/2013-05-29/mcguires-king-king-gaffe

Wilson, C. 2013. "Swans 'Bewildered' by McGuire's Gaffe." *The Age*.

Understanding the importance and context of vilification

Sean Gorman, Dean Lusher and Keir Reeves

This paper looks at the context with which the research for the collection came out of. It draws on recent examples in the media and football and connects that up to the examples in the past particularly the incidents in the AFL that involved Nicky Winmar in 1993 and Michael Long in 1995 and the introduction of Rule 35. This paper sets the scene from which the rest of the collection positions itself.

Context of the research

In order for this research to have specific relevance, it is important to recognize that racism and race politics have become a national blight in Australia. An example of this, and one of the most publicized events in the last decade, is the 2005 Cronulla race riots in Sydney. The riots raised significant issues about Australian values of fairness, equity and authenticity, pitting the locals against recent arrivals (read: boat-people/queue jumpers) with slogans like 'We grew here, you flew here' (sic). Other examples include the incarceration rates, education and health outcomes of Indigenous Australians. These continue to be at odds with how Australia likes to see itself. For Indigenous Australians, the legacy of colonization is one that aligns with the international narrative of colonized peoples. The reality is that Indigenous people internationally 'remain on the margins of society: they are poorer, less educated, die at a younger age, are much more likely to commit suicide, and are generally in worse health than the rest of the population' (United Nations Permanent Forum on Indigenous Issues 2005). The life expectancy gap between the Aboriginal and Torres Strait Islander population and other Australians is estimated to be 11.5 years for males and 9.7 years for females (Australian Institute of Health and Welfare 2011a). The social and economic reality for many Aboriginal and Torres Strait Islander people has been described as being 'by far the most "outsider" group in Australian society' (Angelico 1993). Social exclusion associated with colonization, oppression and historical and contemporary racism continue to create barriers for this group to participate in education, training and the national economy (Hunter and Jordan 2010, Paradies et al. 2008, Reading and Wien 2009).

These overt societal issues have run parallel to race issues in sport. In the National Rugby League (NRL) in June 2010, assistant coach of the NSW Blues, Andrew Johns, used racial slurs to bolster team spirit in the lead up to the State of Origin clash. This caused Timana Tahu to remove himself from the NRL showpiece, a significant action, given that state selection is often deemed a greater honour than national selection. This mirrors incidents in the EPL in the 1990s: specifically when

12

black striker, Nathan Blake, refused to take to the pitch for Wales after team manager Bobby Gould had racially vilified and disparaged opponents in the team dressing room. As it is discussed:

> This incident was particularly revealing, as initially Gould was incapable of understanding that he had voiced racist sentiments, or, at least why this should upset one of his own players. (Gardiner and Welch 2011, 229)

More recently, in the AFL a serious development saw senior Adelaide Crows recruiter and past player Matthew Rendell resign after allegations that he would only pick Indigenous players with one white (read: Anglo) parent, given the 'problems' that he and the Adelaide Crows had experienced with Indigenous players and their perceived lack of professionalism (Rucci 2012). This follows from Emma Quayle's observations in her book, *The Draft*, where Rendell's comments regarding Hawthorn champion and Tiwi Islander, Cyril 'Junior' Rioli, in 2007 at the AFL's Draft Camp were quoted.

> Junior's best 20-metre time was 2.96 seconds. He was quick, but some recruiters were still dubious. 'I'm not sure how hard you're trying, Junior …' thought Matt Rendell. 'I reckon you're a bit quicker than that'. (2008, 229)

The assumption from these examples is that Indigenous people were unreliable and lacked the discipline to deal with the rigors of the elite AFL environment. Through these examples we are able to grapple with difficult issues around ethnic differences, social and sexual diversity, community harmony and reconciliation in Australia. This is important because, just as these attitudes were ingrained 20 (and more) years ago, we would suggest that stubborn vestiges of these attitudes still remain, as is evidenced by Rendell, Sherman and McGuire as examples of stereotyping, overt and casual racism.

However, with this in mind, it must also be acknowledged that the socio-political landscape is changing in regard to these matters. According to Dr Tim Soutphommasane, the Race Discrimination Commissioner in the Australian Human Rights Commission, the issue of racism is more nuanced now:

> Decades ago, it may have been commonly assumed that some races were superior to others; few would have batted an eyelid at racial abuse in public places. Today, things are much different. Old attitudes have largely given way to more progressive sensibilities. But the challenge of combating racism is no longer confined to fighting old fashioned bigotry. Because racism isn't always violent. And it doesn't have to be motivated by fear or hate. Quite often, the harm caused by prejudice comes from casual racism. (2013b)

The gag by Eddie McGuire about having Adam Goodes promote the *King Kong* musical is an excellent example of casual racism. Many of us have heard this type of thing before at the dinner party or the barbeque about 'tea-towel heads', 'camel-jockeys', 'boongs' and 'chinks'.[1] Many of us do nothing about it. It is just a joke we tell ourselves, nothing was meant by it. A qualification of the impact of 'casual racism' was explained by Collingwood premiership player, Heritier Lumumba (formerly known as Harry O'Brien), who spoke out against his president Eddie McGuire in an extended tweet. Lumumba did this to help contextualize the issue of racism as he sees it:

> It doesn't matter if you are a school teacher, a doctor or even the president of my football club I will not tolerate racism, nor should we as a society. I'm extremely disappointed with Eddie's comments and do not care what position he holds, I disagree with what came out his mouth this morning on radio. To me Eddie's comments are reflective of common attitudes that we as a society face. To me Australia is very casual with racism, I would argue that many people in this country would not think what Eddie or the 13 yr old girl said last Friday is 'bad'. In my opinion race relations in this country is (sic) systematically a national disgrace and we have a

long way to go to reach a more harmonious and empathetic society. (Dampney and Noakes 2013)

Lumumba was quick to go on cable TV with McGuire soon after this tweet to point out the various issues that he, as a player of colour, faces on a day-to-day basis. Sadly a lot of what Lumumba had to say had limited impact as comments from members of the public on talk-back radio and social media suggested that both he and Goodes should 'harden up' and stop complaining about jokes (from McGuire or whomever) and comments from minors. These things were irrelevancies for many people, presumably white, especially on talk-back radio, who said, 'What's wrong with calling someone an ape?', 'Sticks n stones will break my bones …'(720 ABC Perth 2013). And so it went.

This incident seemed to mirror the highly insensitive comments made by Jason Akermanis (2010) when he said homosexuals in the AFL needed to stay in the closet. Akermanis said that the 'world of AFL footy is not ready for it' (read: homosexual players). The insensitivity was so great that it prompted both former NRL player Ian Roberts and retired Olympic swimmer Daniel Kowalski to describe Akermanis as an 'ignorant knucklehead' and 'beyond old school' (Ritchie 2010). More recently, Lumumba's split with Collingwood over homophobic comments being written on a poster of two club players within the club also shows that race is not the only issue within clubs, and further that people are recognizing these different forms of vilification and discrimination as related.

This collection addresses the importance of the AFL's Rule 35 as a policy designed to protect, respect and value the involvement of footballers from across a range of social, cultural, religious, ethnic, racial backgrounds and sexual orientations. Therefore, one can begin to see that sport, in this case the AFL, plays a significant role in enabling us to gauge how tolerant we are as a society and what things need to be done to improve the situation where needed.

How far have we come?

As the gag by Eddie McGuire has shown, issues around Australian society's understanding and negotiation of racism (i.e. what is deemed as racist or intolerant) have changed. Just as racism used to be perceived in the AFL as a normal part of the game to get a psychological edge over an opponent, the way we now engage with issues of race and racism is much more sophisticated. This is a measure of how Australian society can be seen to have matured. One has only to consider the way television sitcoms in Australia from the 1970s and 1980s (many of them imported from the UK) can, in retrospect, be seen as overtly and gratuitously racist and sexist. For example, a sitcom like *Until Death Do Us Part* (1966–1975) and its Australian equivalent, *Kingswood Country* (1980–1984) were very popular because racial minorities were not only ridiculed but vilified and derided. This sort of behaviour was perceived as a type of national past time, just as 'Paki bashing' and calling someone a 'wog'[2] was seen as normal.

A much more disturbing facet of the Australian show revolved around one of the 'characters' known as 'Neville the concrete Aboriginal'. Neville, a garden statue and the type of ornament that was popular in Australian gardens at the time, was positioned outside in the garden (read: bush). Neville could not speak and was constantly referred to in his absence. This was an overt reflection of the status quo of many Indigenous Australians who are still locked out of national debates and are deemed as irrelevant or invisible by Australian society, although it may be argued that by showing racism, and indeed sexism, such a show was trying to bring to the attention of Australians via the comedy genre the issues of racial and ethnic intolerance along with overt sexism. We do not see this as the case but rather view the show as employing stereotypes to garner some cheap laughs. There is little if any social critique in *Kingswood Country*.

Kingswood Country was therefore a document of its time. By comparison, one cannot countenance that a show like *Kingswood Country* would be conceptualized and produced, let alone rate with today's television audience. But McGuire's gag does pose many questions about the current state of issues like race and ethnicity in the AFL. Some of these questions include: What have we learnt in the last 20 years around these issues? What policies and processes are in place to deal with these things when they occur? Where are the gaps? Where to from here? Why has the mainstream media taken so long to identify and critique casual racism? These questions are asked because, as we have seen in the UK regarding racism in sport as mediated through the lens of the EPL, the overarching narrative of sport as a driver of attitudinal change is central to the recent Australian rules football experience. One only has to see the recent interview of Rio Ferdinand and Adam Goodes in Australia to begin to appreciate the power that football in Australia and the UK have and how they have the agency to set the agenda (Burdsey and Gorman 2014).

Since 1995 in Australia, the AFL has been at the vanguard of institutional change designed to eliminate racism and prejudice, in all of its forms, from its code through Rule 35. Rule 35 was the precursory rule that dealt with racial and religious vilification that has led to other anti-vilification rules that the AFL now has in place, covering colour, descent or national or ethnic origin, special ability/disability or sexual orientation, preference or identity. This includes, for example, being disparaging of a player's speech impediment. This then provides the legal framework that assists in the regulation of racial, ethnic and community harmony in the AFL. This framework enables the players, coaches, administrators, fans and spectators to understand the impact of racism (and associated prejudices), even casual racism, in the community more holistically. Specifically, it enables the AFL to refine its professional development and support processes and to lead the way on these issues, given that racism and racial intolerance is never far from the media spotlight, as the Eddie McGuire example can attest.

The background to Rule 35

It cannot be denied that the names of Barassi, Jesaulenko, Daicos and Dipierdomenico have become some of the most recognizable and celebrated in the AFL. What can also be equally argued is that players from multicultural and ethnic backgrounds have suffered the cruel barbs of vilification on the football field. However, one could also argue that this recognizability and acceptance on the football field has mirrored the general integration of post-war migrants in Australia and the building of Australian society into the dynamic and rich society it is today (Cazaly 2013). As more players from different ethnic and racial backgrounds make their way into the elite AFL, it will remain to be seen if the type of integration seen in a post-war Australia will also see players from African, Egyptian, Asian, Fijian and Lebanese backgrounds take up the game in numbers and become household names in doing so.

In many respects, the struggle of Indigenous and multicultural players on the football field is the one that many people from Indigenous and multicultural backgrounds face every day. In the Indigenous context, the struggle has a long history with players like Sir Pastor Doug Nicholls, Polly Farmer, Syd Jackson and Norm McDonald (Gorman 2011; Judd 2008). Arguably, the racial struggle has been epitomized by the indelible image of

Nicky Winmar and his defiant reply to the hostile Collingwood crowd in 1993 (Klugman and Osmond 2013). This, combined with Michael Long's stance, has enabled Australia as a nation to look at racism at many levels. It is the Indigenous Australians who have been at the vanguard of that push, as was mentioned in the paper "Introduction: the AFL's Rule 35" (doi:10.1080/17430437.2014.1002972, in this collection) (Gorman 2013). The struggle, in many respects, has come down to what the colour of one's skin has represented, as the history of Indigenous and non-Indigenous relations has a long and difficult past; it is a past that we are still grappling with today. As historian Colin Tatz explains, this is a matter of history and our perceptions of it:

> The phrase from 'plantation to playing field' expresses the history of black American sport ... Aboriginal history has been the reverse. They went from relative freedom, albeit in an era of genocide, to the isolated and segregated settlements and missions which were created to save them. (Tatz and Tatz 2000, 8)

At AFL matches across the country today, electronic broadcasts to all patrons are played before each game stating that racial vilification at the ground will not be tolerated and will result in fines and/or ejection from the arena. However, despite the fact that this type of behaviour seems to be occurring less and less, it does still occur, as the Adam Goodes example and the recent incident involving Majak Daw in the AFL pre-season competition in Tasmania 2014 attest (Australian Associated Press 2013).

The backdrop of sport

Sport has long been part of the Australia's central narrative. One only has to think of the way the Melbourne Cup horse race is the 'Race that stops a nation'. Similarly, one can recall the heady days after the America's Cup win when Prime Minister Bob Hawke suggested that any boss who had a problem with employees taking a day off to celebrate the win 'was a bum'(Channel 9 1983). The 2000 Sydney Olympics was at the time declared as the best Olympics 'ever' and the Boxing Day cricket test and Australian Tennis Open are marquee international events on the world sporting calendar.

However, just as sport provides us with the basis for promoting positive values and social codes and behaviours, it also provides us with the basis to understand the contested nature of lived experience and history in Australia. One only has to do a little bit of research to consider the lives of the Indigenous men who took part in the 1868 tour of England: to perhaps step back and consider what their motivations were given that they were not paid a cent to travel to the other side of the world to a fate that was uncertain. Then there were the protests around the Springbok Rugby tour to Australia in 1981 at a time when apartheid in South Africa was in full swing. The rebel Australian cricket tours to South Africa in 1985–1986 and 1986–1987 also generated great debate about international social justice and equity issues, with Australian Prime Minister Bob Hawke saying that the players were 'traitors'. Then, in 2008, there was the racial controversy between Australian test cricket all-rounder Andrew Symonds and Indian spinner Harbhajan Singh, when Symonds alleged that Singh called him a 'monkey'.

In this way, sport enables us to see the many overlapping themes of politics, race and history. Tatz, for example, looks at key Australian incidents, such as Cathy Freeman cloaking herself in the Aboriginal flag at the 1994 Commonwealth Games. This created a furore in the Australian media: many commentators claimed that Freeman should have refrained because Aboriginal Australia is not recognized as a sovereign nation. However, as Tatz responded, 'Those who deplored her "un-Australian" behaviour have no understanding of Aboriginal history' (2001). What he meant is that media commentators equally failed to acknowledge that no Indigenous Australian has ever formally signed an agreement that they have 'given up' their land to anyone.

Evonne Goolagong, perhaps the most internationally famous Indigenous sportsperson in Australia before Cathy Freeman, also experienced racism. During the 1980 Wimbledon tournament, a senior Victorian politician at the time said he hoped she 'wouldn't go walkabout like some old boong' (Tatz and Tatz 2000). It seems incredulous by today's standards that such a thing would ever be uttered. Hopefully, measures to penalize vilification within sport can help break down these attitudes elsewhere.

It needs to be acknowledged that the argument of this collection is not unique – many organizations and social sites face the dilemma of moderating the space between avowed policy declarations (no discrimination, no vilification) and actual behaviours, dispositions and practices. The novelty and innovation of this collection lies in subjecting these policy ambitions to analysis and then absorbing that analysis into applications that can show a very rich snapshot of the perspectives and understandings of professional athletes. This, then, can lead to innovations in organizational and professional development and research-to-practice reforms, with the ultimate the desire to see an impact on public policy and, eventually, the day-to-day social practices across all sectors.

The state of play

Racial and ethnic discord in Australian society cuts across many different sectors of the community and has done so at various times during the nation's history. These include Indigenous and non-Indigenous interactions as well as exchanges between, and amongst, other ethnic minorities. Accordingly, any institutional change in managing and confronting racism by promoting diversity and tolerance in the AFL must be understood as part of a broader pattern of social change in Australia. This has particularly been the case during the past 20 years.

Internationally, Australia's record on effective multiculturalism has been eroded in the last 10 to 15 years. In part, this has been driven by a hardening of immigration policies, which reached a nadir in 2001 with the Tampa (Mares 2007) and 'the children overboard' crises (Marr 2006); these incidents occurred at the commencement of the so-called 'War on Terror'. Seemingly, since the turn of the century, immigration and international terrorism have become significant federal election issues in Australia. The two issues are regarded as co-dependent. One only need to recall the paranoia surrounding suspected misbehaviour in the case of the Indian doctor Muhamed Haneef, or the unlawful detention by the Australian government of German national and Australian permanent resident Cornelia Rau, to realize that the key narratives around them were couched in the rhetoric of 'queue jumper' and terrorist discourses and were shaped by notions of skin colour, religious affiliation and difference. What the Haneef situation showed specifically was that racial profile influenced how one was treated in Australia. Suspected of aiding terrorists due to a distant relative, Haneef was to become the longest held detainee without charge in recent history. All charges against him were dropped and he was given compensation, reported to be substantial, for his time in detention.

Other incidents of racial anxiety and discord include the previously mentioned Cronulla riots, off-shore processing of 'boat people' at Nauru and the excision of islands in Australian waters, such as Ashmore Reef, from the Australian Migration Zone. One could also include on this list the 2005 Redfern riots and the riots on Palm Island after the death in custody of Indigenous man Cameron Doomadgee in 2004 (Hooper 2008) as examples of

Indigenous civil disobedience. Further to this, during the term of the Howard Government (1996–2007), the Australian people saw the scaling back of Indigenous land rights, the rejection of every key recommendation from the Council for Aboriginal Reconciliation, the refusal to offer an apology or negotiate a treaty and the dismantling of the Aboriginal and Torres Strait Islander Commission.

More recently, and in a more banal context, the spate of race-related attacks and abuse on Australian public transport has been quite alarming. These would not generally be given any airtime in the media except that they were captured on civilian mobile phones and uploaded to social media platforms. They are disturbing because they show how close people come to real physical conflict and the aching irrationality that racial and ethnic intolerance can create. This would not be as much of an issue if it was not running concurrently to the election vow by the Abbot Government to repeal section 18C of the Racial Discrimination Act, which makes the issue of offence, insult and humiliation based on race and ethnicity (Swan 2014).

In light of these broader socio-historical events, evaluating the AFL vilification rules is important. This is because the AFL is a key driver of social change in the Australian community through its extensive Indigenous and multicultural outreach programmes. To put it simply, the AFL is a very strong part of the social fabric of much of Australia. Moreover, this social fabric has been created by long-term sustained local, state and federal government policies. These policies, in turn, have been boosted and enhanced by the AFL since its introduction of Rule 35 in 1995.

One pattern of social change has been the increased emphasis on the need to acknowledge the culturally and linguistically diverse (CALD) nature of the Australian community. For some, 'multicultural society' is a divisive term. Despite multiculturalism in Australia being an official government policy, it is also a term that is both ambiguous and contested. For some it represents a richness of diversity and cultural practices – as Macintyre (1999) suggests, 'the tolerance and pluralism of the reconstituted nation'. Some, not all of whom are necessarily conservative, have been offended by the self-conscious political correctness that has emerged from it (Macintyre 1999). This overcorrection to a great extent was driven by the prevalence of racially and culturally intolerant attitudes in some sections of the Australian community (Hage 1998). This transition was, and has continued to be, a contentious one in recent Australian society and in a sense makes the political and social significance of implementing Rule 35 all the more pressing and timely.

Australian multiculturalism has been intimately linked with the issue of immigration. Clearly, Australian identity and the country's place in the world have been determined by immigration patterns. By the 1980s, Australia faced the consequences of the abandonment of the White Australia Policy that had happened only two decades earlier. This transition was, and has continued to be, a contentious one in recent Australian society. Yet, in considering Rule 35, we are looking at a set of public policy and social outcomes that have direct implications for all Australians. It is our contention that Rule 35 represents a major shift in sports management in Australian rules football and has the potential for further sporting, corporate and community-based organizations to consider a similar policy framework in their policy and governance structures.

While the social value of a diverse and harmonious Australian society is clearly apparent, new research also indicates how 'ethnoracial discrimination (racism) has serious health, social and economic consequences' (Paradies et al. 2008). The importance of relations between differing racial and religious groups is of national significance, as was evidenced in the 2008 National Apology by the Australian Prime Minister Kevin Rudd, the 2005 Cronulla riots, the reaction to 11 September 2001 in Australia and the spate of attacks on 'Indian' taxi drivers. This last situation escalated to a point where a large gathering of predominately Indian taxi drivers staged a protest for days outside Flinders Street station in the heart of Melbourne's CBD in May 2008, protesting about being bashed and stabbed by customers (Herald Sun 2008). This was, and is, an ironic situation, given that Victoria, the heartland of AFL football, is one of the world's most CALD communities (Victorian Multicultural Commission 2008). Furthermore, with 130,000 migrants arriving in Australia each year (Department of Immigration and Citizenship 2007), CALD communities are increasingly relevant to contemporary Australia.

While our position is interested in the impact of Rule 35 upon the players and staff in the AFL, we are acutely aware of the potential 'trickle down' effects that may contribute to long-lasting community interaction, harmony, multiculturalism and reconciliation across Australian society. Accordingly, what is significant about Rule 35 is the governance, cross-cultural awareness and intercultural education that has possibly led not only to a greater level of tolerance towards other communities with CALD backgrounds but also towards successfully promoting an enduring idea of harmony throughout Australian society via sport, specifically the AFL.

Indigenous football history

Ex-AFL legend and Collingwood premiership captain Tony Shaw is noted as saying, 'It's a business out there. I'd make a racist comment every week if I thought it would help win a game' (Wilson 1991). Shaw added, 'It's no different calling a bloke a black bastard than him calling me a white honky and it only lasts as long as the game' (Wilson 1991). One could strongly assume that Shaw's comments would now be somewhat less strident and, in hindsight, he probably wishes he had never said those things. Perhaps we need to see them as a comment of their time and how far we have come. However, it was not that long ago that vilification of Indigenous and multicultural players was employed to gain a 'psychological edge' (Gorman 2008).

In saying that, absent from Shaw's reasoning is the broader context of inequality between non-Indigenous and Indigenous Australians, an inequality that renders some racist taunts more insidious and hurtful than others because it

> is not simply a matter of the abuser uttering an anachronism, or of being unconsciously held or fixed by the past. It is about words with the power to wound; words that can open old sores and perpetuate stereotypes – language of bad race relations. (Gardiner 1997)

When we view sport, particularly AFL, we can get a greater context of the 'bad race relations' that Gardiner speaks of when we look at the stories of Indigenous and multicultural players in the AFL. For many Indigenous players, uncertainty was constant and the odds were stacked against them. What cannot be disputed is that the coming of the Krakouers and Maurice Rioli to the VFL/AFL in the early 1980s created massive media interest that changed the landscape of football forever. This landscape was believed to have had its genesis with Joe Johnson, a 55-game defender, who played in Fitzroy's 1904–1905 premiership team in the VFL. However, this assumption has proven to be incorrect, as Albert 'Pompey' Austin played for Geelong in 1872, debuting against Carlton after arriving from Framlingham mission in the south of Victoria (see Ruddell 2008). In many ways, it was not just Austin or Johnson who can be seen as the Indigenous pioneers of the game. The reason why this is suggested is that, since the 1930s, the game has only seen a few Indigenous players in the VFL in each era: Doug Nicholls (Fitzroy: 1932–1937), Norm McDonald (Essendon: 1947–1953), Polly Farmer (Geelong: 1962–1967) and Syd

Jackson (Carlton: 1969–1976). In a sense, then, these players were all pioneers as they each created a space so that others might follow.

The increased exposure of sport in the media in the 1980s also coincided with the arrival of the Krakouers to North Melbourne and Maurice Rioli at Richmond: they turned the football world in Melbourne on its head. An example of this comes from respected journalist Martin Flanagan, who wrote at the time:

> Rioli is perhaps the most elegant player in the game [and] plays a fairly classical game. … Both Rioli and Jim and Phil Krakouer have that special ability to be by themselves a lot, to sense where the ball is going to be, how a passage of play is going to unfold. But it's in the imagination, the understanding of the possible futures that the Krakouers stand out. (1985)

The Krakouers and Rioli established themselves quickly as champions in their own right and VFL/AFL recruiters began to look far and wide to try to lure Indigenous players from all over Australia to Melbourne. However, with this also came stereotypical media reportage concerning 'Black magic' and the explaining away of Indigenous players' 'skills' as 'natural' without due recognition of the hours of training and application that they had endured. This attention also brought with it a contradictory situation that was both hostile (from the opposition) and celebratory (from fans and members) and culminated with the advent of the West Coast Eagles arriving in 1987 with the likes of Phil Narkle, Wally Matera and Chris Lewis. Here, the 'racial' complexion of the AFL really started to change. In the 1980s, to have a cohort of three or four Indigenous players on a team list was not common and football fans and the media grappled with the status, exposure and dynamism that Indigenous players brought with them. Today, not having a cohort of Indigenous players on a team list would be deemed extraordinary. Hence, with time, these sporting situations began to aggregate and gain momentum; so by the early 1990s a social, sporting and political alignment was possible, culminating in 1993 with Nicky Winmar.

The reason that Winmar's stance has transcended the realm of sport and football is because it was socially, culturally and politically important: it tapped into a national discussion that needed to be had. Winmar's defiant reply to the hostile Collingwood crowd in 1993 is so powerful – it is the image that helped start the conversation around racism in sport. It is Australia's Tommie Smith/John Carlos/Black Power moment from the 1968 Mexico Olympics. This, combined with Michael Long's stance, has enabled Australia, as a nation, to look at racism at many levels and try to come to terms with the struggle of what it means to be a person of colour in the country of the 'fair go' and being 'fair dinkum'. To remain silent is no longer an option despite great resistance to this, as Burdsey and Gorman explain:

> The insinuation that it is the responsibility of the player who receives racism to just 'get on with it'. This is an ingrained discourse from the political Right, which suggests that talking about racism makes the problem worse: 'If only you'd just be quiet, then the problem would go away'. (2014)

Long's actions and words led to the introduction of Rule 35 and a concerted effort by the AFL to change attitudes, not just about Indigenous players but also about players from different backgrounds. The AFL and clubs like North Melbourne, Richmond and the Western Bulldogs have also sought to build upon these ideas and embrace and include new migrant communities through multicultural programmes, as evidenced by North Melbourne's Huddle and Indigenous programmes at Richmond's Korin Gamadji Institute and the Western Bulldogs (AFL Community Club 2014).

The then AFL Chief Executive Officer, Andrew Demetriou, has publicly stated his desire to see Australia become a 'compassionate, welcoming and generous nation' and, under his stewardship, the AFL has played an active role in promoting harmony and diversity (Demetriou 2005). Within this social and historical context, much can be learned from an examination of the impact and implications of Rule 35. In this way, these examples in sport enable us to see the many overlapping themes of sport, politics, race and history.

Multicultural football history

There is a popular narrative that Australian society experienced multiculturalism as a direct result of mass migration following the Second World War. From this narrative, the Australian rules football story emerges that non-English men (usually Europeans of Mediterranean extraction) were able to excel playing football in the then VFL from the 1950s onwards and that this, in turn, provided an entrée into what was then regarded as mainstream society. While this is certainly the case, multiculturalism in Australia began almost a century earlier, during the Victoria and New South Wales gold rushes of the 1850s, and arguably even earlier. In other parts of Australia, such as Darwin and Cairns, as Henry Reynolds, Cathie May and others have observed, multiculturalism has been the norm since the earliest colonial times (May 1984; Reynolds 2003). The nineteenth-century movement of people followed a pattern of chain migration and was usually centred on people from the same religious affiliation, country or area of origin. This meant that the gold rushes resulted in a level of multicultural diversity unimaginable in Australia prior to the gold discoveries.

Clearly Australian identity, and in turn, the country's place in the world, would be determined by its immigration pattern. From the late 1960s the Australian Labor Party (which historically gained much electoral support from its advocacy of the White Australia Policy) moved to a position of racial equality and, by the early 1980s, firmly advocated a multicultural platform similar to that promoted by the Fraser Government. One practical outcome of this policy was the increase in Asian immigrants, particularly those from Vietnam as a result of the conclusion of the Vietnam War. Today, many of these immigrants can be found supporting the Richmond Football Club, as the suburb of Richmond is home to many Vietnamese migrants (Dugald 2013). The end result of the changes in political attitudes and government policy was the formal end of the White Australia policy. Clearly this was a desirable thing but the damning fact is that it had taken 75 years to dismantle the White Australia policy, and for much of that period Australian considered itself as a nation with a tolerant civic culture that acted consistently as a good global citizen. This new vision of Australian society has been a key.

Andrew Demetriou, former AFL chief executive officer and footballer, like former Australian Prime Minister Bob Hawke politically, promoted multiculturalism as a key plank of social policy despite initial community aversion. However, in promoting multiculturalism, Hawke commented, with a mixture of realism and desirability of such a situation, that

> We are a country of just over 15 million in a world of seven and a half billion but in a region of billions of people. We have to understand as Australians that is where our future lies. (Aly 2010, 59)

Implicit in Hawke's broad assertion was that Australia needed to engage with Asia, and in doing so, its immigration programme would have to reflect that reality. In turn, he advocated multiculturalism as policy directive. This was mirrored in certain parts of Australian society and in the Australian rules football community.

In 1984, Geoffrey Blainey's response to multiculturalism began at the Warrnambool Returned Serviceman's League in the Western District of Victoria (Goodwin 1984). He argued that the government had adhered to an immigration policy that made an Asian takeover of Australia inevitable. He argued that the policy switch from the White Australia policy to a multicultural one had been too swift and that the interests of the nation would be better served if the rate of Asian immigration were slower. He also claimed that national guilt over the Vietnam War and international criticism over national issues drove this anti-British policy, resulting in apologists running the government.

The response to Blainey by his critics was predictably one of indignant moral outrage and in many quarters he was branded a racist. It was not so much that he wanted a return to White Australia. Instead he queried whether Australia's future identity was as a 'nation of all nations' (Blainey 1991, 47).

Part of the problem about national identity lay in the confusion surrounding the meaning of multiculturalism and what it meant for Australia's place in the world both in practical and symbolic terms. It also meant that culture was regarded, as Macintyre has commented, as 'little more than a euphemism for race' (Macintyre 1999). Subsequently, the already polarized debate became increasingly confusing: the opponents of multiculturalism attacked its political correctness while the supporters of multiculturalism strongly advocated something they couldn't adequately define.

In the mid-1980s, Howard led the Coalition attack on multiculturalism and tapped into a sympathetic vein in the Australian community. Blainey continued to argue that it was necessary to rebalance immigration and settlement public policies to benefit the national interest. Clearly, the conservative Federal Coalition was a house divided and faced a political conundrum over its stance on multiculturalism. Although many were advocates of international trade with Asia, they failed to grasp that the internationalization of the economy also meant the internationalization of Australian society, particularly the creation of a large Asian community primarily in the eastern seaboard capital cities. During this period, the AFL began its formal embrace of championing ethnic diversity, largely as a result of having a number of players and supporters who came from a non-Anglo-Celtic background. Later, when the Howard Government from 1996 onwards rejected multiculturalism, choosing instead to embrace a different narrative of Australian identity, the AFL was seen by many as a proxy standard bearer for promoting multiculturalism as a public policy in the absence of an official Commonwealth response.

For Australian society, the policy is so significant that in the second decade of the twenty-first century it is now impossible to disassociate race from government policies such as assimilation and multiculturalism. At a football level, one need look no further than the concerted present-day efforts of many AFL clubs, including notably North Melbourne's outreach to the Sub-Saharan and North African community in inner Melbourne. This is driven by the Huddle, an educational and social hub that emphasizes club staff engaging with the community and people not usually attracted to Australian rules football to get them to participate in the sporting culture. One of the successful initiatives has been the African Warriors football club, which is made up of refugees and migrants from Africa. This may be an optimistic reading of the role of multiculturalism in Australian society, and indeed of the transformative potential of Australian rules football. Or indeed of the AFL as an organization to drive social change, promote social harmony and increased socially diverse community participation and becoming part of a racialized notion of Australian national identity. Dan Burdsey examined this theme in an English context with his theoretical study of English minority groups in the seaside (Burdsey 2011). As some, including historian Tony Birch speaking about Australian society during the past 20 years, have ventured to suggest, in many respects Australia is still in a colonial phase of its societal development. Others, such as Soutphommasane (2013a) in his recent book *Don't Go Back to Where You Came From,* have made a staunch defence of multiculturalism as a key social policy plank of Australian society and linked it as a policy with human rights concerns.

The idea of participation and belonging is a powerful one in the Australian sporting narrative. However, as Cazaly (2013) soberly points out in *Playing the Game: The Experiences of Migrant- Background Players in Australian Rule Football*, there is almost a total absence of recorded migrant or ethnic experiences when it comes to sport or football. In this way, it is difficult to map the impact migrant players have had on the game, given the challenges they have faced. As Cazaly states, 'There is no systemic discussion of sport and little critical analysis of migrant participation in Australian sport more generally' (49).

In this largely historical vacuum, there are stories that do pique the spirit of diversity and tolerance in Australian football. Hence, it could be assumed that there are many experiences across many different parts of Australia where playing football was not just about having fun or staying fit but gave one a feeling of camaraderie, not just on the field but off it. As the Indigenous umpire in the VFL Glenn James explains about growing up in the Goulburn Valley in the 1960s:

> As I got a bit older, like towards grade 5 or 6 you started to understand that this was an us-and-them situation. We became quite friendly with all the Italians and the Macedonians and the Greeks … We got on because they were being treated like we were. (Gorman 2011, 94)

Similarly, Northern Territory-based football historian, Matthew Stephen, in his book *Contact Zones,* states:

> Darwin's Coloured community acted as a 'connecting hub' between supposedly separate ethnic groups. The publicly contested site, the location where the multiracial community identity was forged and racial stereotypes continually challenged, was Darwin Oval and Australian football. (2010, 169)

Any discussion of the role of Indigenous footballers in Australian rules football begins, politically speaking, with the stance of Winmar and Long in the mid-1990s, as these two moments define the modern era of the past quarter of a century. The same cannot be said of the multicultural narrative in Australian rules football. This is much harder to track, given the slow but inevitable acceptance of multicultural Australians into contemporary society.

For Cazaly, Australian rules football is seen as a conduit for tracing the movement from marginalization into acceptance for post-war migrants, but it was also a way for migrant Australians to employ a modicum of autonomy also.

> Migrants found that sport was one way to demonstrate and maintain their own culture … Italian and Greek surnames came to be among those listed on football team sheets from the mid 1950s when players like Sergio Silvagni, Tony Ongarello, John Bennetti and Alec Epis were beginning to become stars of the Australian game … These first pioneers were not themselves post-war migrants, instead they were the sons of earlier generations of migrants, growing up in Australian schools with white Australian culture … Through their participation, the football field was beginning to reflect the increasingly diverse Australian community. (Cazaly 2013, 75)

A multicultural society – the elusive to define, and for some, divisive term – aims to celebrate cultural diversity. The AFL's stance during the past quarter of a century has been in keeping with this inclusive positive embrace of that diversity. From the 1980s onwards, multiculturalism was an official federal government policy. Arguably, this was reflected and was as a novelty at its highest point with what has been called the 'Irish Experiment'. As Cazaly points out, the 'Irish Experiment' came about through discussions between Ron Barassi (Melbourne coach and legend of the game) and Richmond administrator Alan Schwab looking at the similarities of Gaelic football with Australian rules football and the potential for recruiting Gaelic football players into the Australian game. An advertisement in several Irish newspapers managed to recruit several young players, amongst them Sean Wight and Jim Stynes, with the promise of providing a football scholarship and a chance to play with the Melbourne Football Club. In the following three decades, this has seen players like Tadhg Kennelly, Setanta O'hAilpin, Marty Clarke and Zac Tuohy amongst many others get their chance to play in the elite AFL, thus enabling a greater story to be told about the AFL.

However, multiculturalism is a term that has been, and continues to be, contested in Australian society. For some, it represents a richness of diversity and cultural practices: as Macintyre suggests, 'the tolerance and pluralism of the reconstituted nation'. Perhaps it is because multiculturalism has been closely linked with the issue of immigration. This debate, unfortunately has been reduced by some commentators in the media to infer that immigrants from certain parts of the world (read: Middle Eastern) are 'queue-jumpers' or 'boat people'. While the large numbers of asylum seekers arriving in the aftermath of Vietnam were initially under fire politically, this time from the Labour Party, there was eventually bipartisan support not to play politics on this issue by both sides of Australian politics (Rodd 2007). It has been fascinating to see the racial and ethnic discourses within football evolve as players from marginalized ethnic backgrounds have had entrée into the AFL. Players such as Bachar Houli, Majak Daw, Nic Natanui, Ahmed Saad and Lin Jong have all come from what would be considered to be new multicultural demographics.

Houli, despite being born in Melbourne, playing junior football and then going on to play with Essendon Football Club and now Richmond, has the distinction of being the first practising Muslim in the AFL. This has required his clubs and also the AFL to reconsider such things as the service of alcohol at club functions, assisting him through Ramadan during the season, the provision of a prayer room for team supporters and practising Muslims at his club and venues where games are played. Then there is the ruck-cum-forward Majak Daw. Daw was born in Sudan but he and his family were forced to flee to Egypt due to the Sudanese civil war. He and his family remained in Egypt for three years and then made their way to Australia. He became the first player of Sudanese descent to make it onto an AFL team list.

The rise of multiculturalism has led to a reconsideration of the relevance of established themes of Australian identity. Furthermore, modern Australian lifestyles are more diverse and the country is a harsher place than national myths would have us believe. Multiculturalism is certainly embraced by the AFL as official policy and amongst the elite playing groups. What are harder to discern are the attitudes about multiculturalism in grassroots football clubs or amongst the supporter base of large AFL clubs. It is unlikely that the broader football community has embraced the message of participation, social harmony and diversity in the manner of an increasingly erudite and informed elite playing group.

It has taken these difficult and complex moments concerned with racism in the AFL to reconsider the way we think about race and ethnicity in Australia and how it relates to sport and society more broadly. Yet, this could only be done if one viewed not just the game differently but also the space on which it was played. With increased sponsorships and professionalism, the MCG ceased to simply be an oval where sport was played and, with the introduction of Rule 35, it became a workplace. In this way, vilification was seen differently because we, as Australians, were looking at it through a different prism.

Sexuality and gender

Most of this collection is focused on issues of race and ethnicity, primarily because these were the issues that instigated Rule 35 as a result of Michael Long's stance. However, we note that the focus and definitions of Rule 35 have been expanded by the AFL over time to include a range of other issues around which vilification is deemed unacceptable.

We have had much less to say about the issue of homophobia in this collection because no player in the AFL has as yet identified as gay. There has, however, been much written and researched on issues of sexuality in sport, and in 2000 the Australian Sports Commission published *Harassment-Free Sport: Guidelines to Address Homophobia and Sexuality Discrimination in Sport*, which have been touted as highly regarded internationally.

As previously noted, Akermanis (2010) stated that homosexuals in the AFL needed to stay in the closet and that if they came out that it 'could break the fabric of a club'. Former NRL player Ian Roberts and retired Olympic swimmer Daniel Kowalski, both gay men, described Akermanis' comments as outdated and, indeed, unhelpful at the very least. In the AFL, Heretier Lumumba's reported request to move from Collingwood was sparked over homophobic comments on a poster of two players at the club. The comment was 'Off to the Mardi Gras then boys?' (O'Brien 2014) – a specific reference to the Sydney Mardi Gras, which is a celebration of lesbian, gay, bisexual, transsexual and queer intersex ways of life and ideals. This has further raised the issue of homophobia within AFL clubs. As at the time of writing this collection of papers, no current AFL player has yet 'come out', which is probably why homophobia as an issue has been less discussed in the AFL, in contrast to the high-level community and media discussion surrounding the vilification of Adam Goodes in May 2013 and onwards. However, country footballer Jason Ball gathered a significant amount of publicity and support for coming out, and for campaigning the AFL to do more on tackling homophobia. During the 2012 final series, 'Say No to Homophobia' advertisements were aired, which indicates that it is salient and 'on the radar'. Yet, until an AFL player does come out, it is not known how varied community and media reaction will be. In the case of retired Olympic swimmer Ian Thorpe, there appeared to be little fuss, generally speaking.

Furthermore, while not specifically related to Rule 35, because AFL at the elite level has only male players, the issues of gender and, in particular, attitudes and behaviours towards women have been significant for the AFL. The AFL has done significant work in this regard with its Respect and Responsibility Policy (AFL 2005), which is 'commitment to addressing violence against women and to work towards creating safe, supportive and inclusive environments for women and girls across the football industry as well as the broader community' (AFL 2014). It was introduced in 2005 following a number of allegations of sexual assault involving AFL players but also other incidents involving NRL players (Davies, Beck, and Read 2004; Murphy and Sproull 2004; Niall, Blake, and Ker 2003). Former Saints player Andrew Lovett was charged with rape in February 2010, but was later acquitted, although not before his contract was terminated. Additionally, former Saints player Stephen Milne faced court late in 2014 on charges of indecent assault after rape charges were dropped following a second investigation into an incident that occurred some 10 years earlier. Milne avoided conviction and was fined $15,000 (Cooper 2014).

Issues around sexuality and gender are explored in this collection particularly as they relate to club cultures. The survey data have much to say on these issues, indicating how 'playboy' attitudes and also attitudes about homophobia, violence and strict gender roles, are related to popular and influential players within the team. Although the interviews in this collection of papers focus specifically on race and ethnicity issues, by extension themes around masculinity do crop up nonetheless as important and salient to AFL players, the clubs, the code and the management and education of young men in a hyper-competitive male-dominated space.

Conclusion

As has been previously been mentioned, the AFL's implementation of Rule 35 in 1995 was the single biggest act of reconciliation by any sporting code in Australian history. This has seen a broad range of changes occur, from the implementation of Indigenous and multicultural rounds, to the drafting of players from an increasingly wider range of migrant, ethnic and racial backgrounds and the amendment of the rule to include disability and sexuality as well as religion and race. All of these things are demonstrative of the institutional change that has taken place throughout the AFL and also how the AFL has, in many respects, led the way for social changes to occur. Since 1990, with the VFL becoming the national AFL, the game has had many challenges, but racial vilification presented itself differently to the myriad financial and administrative issues that the new competition faced. Vilification, as validated by Tony Shaw's comment 'that he would make a racial comment every week if it meant winning the game', was seen as an intrinsic part of the psychology and social fabric of game.

Despite conscious moves by the AFL to address racism in Australian rules football, there have continued to be, at worst, incidents of high profile vilification, and at best, ignorant racial stereotyping in the code. These range from Justin Sherman in 2011 and the Matthew Rendell incident to Eddie McGuire's 'gag' in 2013. All three of these incidents are revealing and for many they are the tired and banal views of a time that has passed us by. But perhaps football (read: sport) reveals to us regularly that, just as we think we have reached the optimum, something or someone else will take it to the next level and we stand there and marvel about just how good 'our sport' is. This is also true of how any number of issues associated with sport can help us learn about our society and about ourselves. If sport is able to do that, it becomes something greater than that which is played on a Friday night or a Saturday afternoon: it becomes a teacher and the lessons we can learn will be life-long.

Disclosure statement

No potential conflict of interest was reported by the authors.

Notes

1. These are pejorative terms that refer to Muslims/Lebanese, Afghan, Aboriginal and Asian people, respectively.
2. The term 'wog' in Australia is equivalent to the term 'wop' in the UK, and therefore quite different from the UK use of the term.

References

720 ABC Perth. 2013. "Sports Talk." *ABC*. http://www.abc.net.au/perth/

AFL. 2005. *Respect & Responsibility Policy*. Melbourne: AFL.

AFL. 2014. *Respect & Responsibility Policy*, AFL, November 28, 2014. http://www.afl.com.au/news/game-development/respect-and-responsibility

AFL Community Club. 2014. "Australia Post AFL Multicultural Program Ambassadors." http://www.aflcommunityclub.com.au/index.php?id=638

Akermanis, J. 2010. "Stay in the Closet, Jason Akermanis Tells Homosexuals." *Herald Sun*. http://www.heraldsun.com.au/sport/afl/stay-in-the-closet-jason-akermanis-tells-homosexuals/story-e6frf9ix-1225868871934

Aly, W. 2010. *Quarterly Essay 37 What's Right?: The Future of Conservatism in Australia*. Vol. 37. Collingwood, Vic: Black Inc.

Angelico, T. 1993. "Wellness and Contemporary Australian Racism." In *Contemporary Racism in Australia, Canada and New Zealand*, Vol. 2, edited by J. Collins, 237–258. Sydney: University of Technology.

Australian Associated Press. 2013. "Majak Daw Allegedly Subjected to Racist Abuse." *ABC News*. http://www.abc.net.au/news/2013-05-13/majak-daw-allegedly-subjected-to-rascist-abuse/4684880

Australian Institute of Health and Welfare. 2011a. *Australia's Welfare 2011*. Canberra: AIHW.

Australian Sports Commission. 2000. *Harassment-Free Sport: Guidelines to Address Homophobia and Sexuality Discrimination in Sport*. Belconnen: ASC.

Blainey, G. 1991. "They View Australia's History as a Saga of Shame." In *Blainey: Eye on Australia*, edited by Flinders Flinders. Melbourne: Schwarz and Wilkinson.

Burdsey, D. 2011. "Strangers on the Shore? Racialized Representation, Identity and In/Visibilities of Whiteness at the English Seaside." *Cultural Sociology* 5 (4): 537–552.

Burdsey, D., and S. Gorman. 2014. "When Adam Met Rio: Conversations on Racism, Anti-racism and Multiculturalism in the Australian Football League and English Premier League." *Sport in Society*. [ahead-of-print] 1–11. doi:10.1080/17430437.2014.976007

Cazaly, C. S. H. 2013. "Playing the Game: The Experiences of Migrant-Background Players in Australian Rules Football." PhD thesis, School of Historical and Philosophical Studies, Faculty of Arts, University of Melbourne.

Channel 9. 1983. "Bob Hawke Americas Cup iview." *Channel Nine*. https://www.youtube.com/watch?v=BFw7iIvCFpo

Cooper, A. 2014. "Former St Kilda Footballer Stephen Milne Avoids Conviction, Fined $15,000 over Indecent Assault." *The Age*, November 18. http://www.theage.com.au/victoria/former-st-kilda-footballer-stephen-milne-avoids-conviction-fined-15000-over-indecent-assault-20141118-11ot8v.html

Dampney, J., and C. Noakes. 2013. "O'Brien Slams McGuire for On-Air Gaffe." http://www.afl.com.au/news/2013-05-29/obrien-slams-mcguire-for-onair-gaffe

Davies, L., M. Beck, and B. Read. 2004. "Rugby League Club Fined." *The Age*. http://www.theage.com.au/articles/2004/04/28/1083103549947.html

Demetriou, A. December 9, 2005. "The Glue that Brings Us Together: Combating Racism in Sport." https://www.humanrights.gov.au/sites/default/files/content/racial_discrimination/whats_the_score/pdf/afl.pdf

Department of Immigration and Citizenship. 2007. "Fact Sheet 2: Key Facts in Immigration." In *Department of Immigration and Citizenship*. Canberra: DIAC.

Dugald, J. "Tiger, Tiger Burning Bright: The Tiger Family" [cited December 2, 2014]. http://www.richmondfc.com.au/news/2013-07-12/tiger-tiger-burning-bright-the-tiger-family 2013.

Flanagan, Martin. 1985. "Football Wizards with Their Own Black Magic." *The Age*, May 29, 39.

Gardiner, G. 1997. "Football and Racism: The AFL's Racial and Religious Vilification Rule." In Discussion Paper No. 6, Koori Research Centre, Monash University, Melbourne.

Gardiner, S., and R. Welch. 2011. "Football, Racism and the Limits of 'Colour Blind' Law: Revisited." In *Race, Ethnicity and Football: Persisting Debates and Emergent Issues*, edited by D. Burdsey, 222–236. New York: Routledge.

Goodwin, R. 1984. "Immigration Policy Questioned." *Warrnambool Standard*, March 19.

Gorman, S. 2008. *Behind the Play: Football in Australia*, edited by P. Burke and J. Senyard. Hawthorn: Maribyrnong Press.

Gorman, S. 2011. *Legends: The AFL Indigenous Team of the Century*. Canberra: Aboriginal Studies Press.

Gorman, S. 2013. "Michael Long's Letter." In *Telling Stories*, edited by T. Dalziell and P. Genoni. Melbourne: Monash University Press.

Hage. 1998. *White Nation: Fantasies of White Supremacy in a Multicultural Society*. Annandale: Pluto Press.

Herald Sun. Taxi Driver on Protest in Melbourne April 29, 2008.

Hooper, C. 2008. *The Tall Man*. Camberwell, Vic: Penguin Group Australia.

Hunter, B., and K. Jordan. 2010. "Explaining Social Exclusion: Towards Social Inclusion for Indigenous Australians." *The Australian Journal of Social Issues* 45 (2): 243.

Judd, B. 2008. *On the Boundary Line: Colonial Identity in Football*. North Melbourne: Australian Scholarly Publishing.

Klugman, M., and G. Osmond. 2013. *Black and Proud: The Story of an Iconic Photo*. Sydney: NewSouth.

Macintyre, S. 1999. *A Concise History of Australia*. 2nd ed. Melbourne: Cambridge University Press.

Mares, P. 2007. "Reassessing the Tampa." In *Yearning to Breathe Free: Seeking Asylum in Australia*, edited by D. Lusher and N. Haslam, 58–59. Annandale: Federation Press.

Marr, D. 2006. "Truth Overboard: The Story that Won't Go Away." *The Sydney Morning Herald*, February 28.

May, C. R. 1984. *Topsawyers, the Chinese in Cairns, 1870–1920, Studies in North Queensland History; No 6*. Townsville: James Cook University.

Murphy, Padraic, and Richard Sproull. 2004. *AFL Club in Hawaii Gang Rape Claims*. The Australian Online 2004 [cited May 5 2004]. http://www.theaustralian.news.com.au/common/story_page/0,5744,9474501%255E2702,00.html

Niall, Jake, Martin Blake, and Peter Ker. 2003. "Footballers Behaving Badly." *The Age Online*, June 18.

O'Brien, S. 2014. "Lumumba Should Not Resign over Gay Graffiti Slur." http://blogs.news.com.au/heraldsun/seewhatsusiesays/index.php/heraldsun/comments/lumumba_should_not_resign_over_gay_graffiti_slur/

Paradies, Y., L. Chandrakumar, M. Frere, M. Kelahar, and I. McDonald. 2008. "Racism in Australia." http://www.socialjustice.unimelb.edu.au/Research/EconomicCostRacismAustralia.html

Quayle, E. 2008. *The Draft*. Crows Nest: Allen & Unwin.

Reading, C. L., and F. Wien. 2009. *Health Inequalities and the Social Determinants of Aboriginal Peoples' Health*. Prince George: National Collaborating Centre for Aboriginal Health.

Reynolds, H. 2003. *North of Capricorn: The Untold Story of Australia's North*. Crows Nest: Allen & Unwin.

Ritchie, D. 2010. "Ian Roberts Slams Jason Akermanis over Gay Comments." *The Courier Mail*. http://www.couriermail.com.au/sport/ian-roberts-slams-jason-akermanis-over-gay-comments/story-e6frep5o-1225869354626

Rodd, C. P. 2007. "Boats and Borders: Asylum Seekers and Elections, 1977 and 2001." In *Yearning to Breathe Free: Seeking Asylum in Australia*, edited by D. Lusher and N. Haslam. Sydney: Federation Press.

Rucci, M. 2012. "Adelaide Recruiter Matt Rendell Quits over Racism Row." *Herald Sun*, March 16.

Ruddell, T. 2008. "Albert 'Pompey' Austin: The First Aborigine to Play Senior Football." In *Behind the Play: Football in Australia*, edited by Peter Burke and June Senyard. Melbourne: Maribyrnong Press.

Soutphommasane, T. 2013a. *Don't Go Back to Where You Came From*. Sydney, NSW: University of New South Wales Press.

Soutphommasane, T. 2013b. "How Best to Tackle Racism, Australian Style." *Sydney Morning Herald*. http://www.smh.com.au/comment/how-best-to-tackle-racism-australianstyle-20130818-2s4ui.html

Stephen, M. 2010. *Contact Zones: Sport and Race in the Northern Territory, 1869–1953*. Darwin: Charles Darwin Univesity Press.

Swan, J. 2014. "Changes to Race Hate Laws Would 'License Public Humiliation of People because of Their Race'." *The Sydney Morning Herald*, March 18.

Tatz, Colin. 2001. "The Dark Side of Australian Sport." In *The Best Ever Australian Sports Writing: A 200 Year Collection*, edited by David Headon, 554. Melbourne: Black Inc.

Tatz, C., and P. Tatz. 2000. *Black Gold: The Aboriginal and Islander Sports Hall of Fame*. Canberra: Aboriginal Studies Press.

United Nations Permanent Forum on Indigenous Issues. 2005. "Millennium Development Goals and Indigenous Peoples with a Focus on Goal 1 to Eradicate Poverty and Extreme Hunger, and Goal 2 to Achieve Universal Primary Education." Paper read at Fourth Session of the UNPFII, 16–27 May, at United Nations Headquarters, New York.

Victorian Multicultural Commission. 2008. "About Us." http://www.multicultural.vic.gov.au/web24/vmc.nsf/headingpagesdisplay/about+us

Wilson, C. 1991. "Some Footballers Get Abused for More than Just the Colour of Their Jumper." *The Age*, August 24.

Overarching findings

Sean Gorman, Dean Lusher and Keir Reeves

Overview

The issue of racism in the Australian Football League (AFL) is one that has been officially recognized since 1995. Since then, the AFL, the AFL Players Association (AFLPA) and the AFL clubs have been bound by the rules of the code, specifically Rule 35, to deal with racism, racial and religious intolerance and racist abuse, as well as other forms of vilification, when it has arisen. The most recent player-to-player vilification incident occurred in 2011 and involved Western Bulldogs forward Justin Sherman and Gold Coast Sun defender Joel Wilkinson. Despite the problems that many had with Sherman's suspension, which still allowed him to play with the Western Bulldogs reserves side, what was very marked was the speed of the process from the lodgement of complaint to the suspension. This would seem to indicate that when it comes to such matters, the AFL is serious about dealing with racial vilification and it wanted to send a message to all the clubs and players. In the weeks and months after the incident, what became quite evident was the damage Sherman had sustained to his reputation as a professional athlete: his 'brand' is tarnished from here on. Furthermore, the overarching message from this incident as it related to the AFL was that racism in any form is wrong and it will not be tolerated.

The main aims of this project were to assess the ways that AFL players have engaged with the education programmes and professional development offered, and how they understand issues of race, racism, ethnicity and difference within the professional environment of elite football in the AFL, and by association, the everyday. The reason for this is the length of time that has passed since Michael Long made his stance in 1995 and the resources that have gone into educating the players on these matters. What this book is seeking to provide is an understanding of the efficacy of those programmes in educating professional elite athletes about racial and religious issues within the AFL and also the athletes' everyday lives and extended communities. This is important given that the AFL has become an international and national leader on this issue and its corporate and community standing is heavily connected to by Rule 35 and its associated programmes. The prime focus of this project was to find out:

1. What has been learned from the AFL's education programmes and professional development, collectively and individually?[1]
2. How have AFL players engaged with the anti-vilification programmes, and what do they understand racial intolerance to be?

With these aims, we were able to both survey and interview the players on a wide range of racial, ethnic, gender and cultural issues, not just those they encounter in the AFL but also in their day-to-day lives. To do this, a range of examples were used in the interviews to get the players to honestly engage with the topics, which related to community harmony, reconciliation and multiculturalism. The responses to these interviews were then compared with their survey responses. This was done to get a clearer understanding of how each player understood and engaged with the induction and education programmes that had been conducted by the AFL and the AFLPA around these issues. Further to this, an understanding of each of the clubs' cultures and how the players themselves dealt with the internal workings of their clubs when it came to issues of race, ethnicity and gender were explored.

What did we ask and who did we speak to?

What did we ask?

The research on which this book is based involved both survey and interview components. The survey can be divided into (1) standard survey questions, which ask about attitudes and opinions to certain issues (e.g. race and gender), and (2) social network survey questions, which ask about personal interactions within the team (including who do you trust? Who do you have differences of opinion with?). Then there was (3) the interview component, where in-depth questions were asked about issues related to Rule 35. In the sections that follow, we provide substantial detail on each of these three aspects of the research, including what we asked, how we went about it and what we found overall through each type of analysis.

In Appendix 1, we list some example survey questions we asked of the players and club staff members. You will note that there are some very specific personal questions asked. To some players, the questions seemed offensive or annoying, and to others, they were funny or irrelevant. But in the main, most players and staff responded with honesty, took time to provide their responses and engaged very well with the survey.

Who did we speak to?

Nine clubs from the AFL from a range of states across Australia were involved in the research. All players were male, though staff consisted of both males and females. As required for all university research involving people, we applied for and received Human Research Ethics Clearance approval before conducting our research. We collected our data between January 2011 and May 2013. All participants provided written informed consent[2] to participate. It is important to note that the ethics requirements include that individual players and clubs are not to be identified in any reports, including this book. Throughout this book we have, on occasions, removed identifying data in order to respect the agreement we have with the clubs, players and coaches. To keep the identities of individuals and clubs confidential, we provide pseudonyms for each of the clubs involved. The AFL clubs that participated were given one of the following alphabetical names to keep their identities anonymous: Abacus, Bravo, Charlie, Delta, Echo, Foxtrot, Gecko, Hornet and Igloo Football Clubs.

We note that while many people will wonder which club is which when reading this book, to think about these issues in that way is perhaps to miss the point of this research. What we have in this book is an insight into the club cultures of half of the competition, and what we will show is the many similarities between AFL clubs on a range of issues, but also that clubs have particular aspects of their culture that differ. It is important to understand the consistency and also the variability, and what this tells us, rather than 'I think this club is X, and that club is Y'. The authors of this book will not engage in speculation about the identities of the clubs or the individuals who provided data for this project, and we have had to omit, on occasions, some interesting information for the sake of protecting the identities of individuals and clubs as was promised to all participants at the outset of this research. To do otherwise would be to break the confidentiality that was entrusted to us by the participants.[3]

The survey consisted of a pencil and paper questionnaire that was individually completed in a 30-minute group setting at the club in the presence of the research team. Within each of the nine clubs, we have data on the vast majority of the players, in some cases very close to 100%. This high participation rate per club is very important in particular for the social network analysis (SNA), where we are trying to get a bird's eye view of the club *as a whole* and how everyone within it interacts with one another. A total of 363 players completed the survey, of which 41 were Indigenous. Characteristics of the players were that they were single (66.4%), Anglo-Australian (75.2%), Catholic (35.3% – although 42.1% did not respond to the question about their religion) and on average were 22.2 years of age. The average level of experience of the group was 45.6 AFL games played; some players (36.4%) were not currently working or studying in addition to playing football; 29.2% were concurrently studying at university/TAFE; and for the majority of players (86.8%), secondary schooling was their highest completed level of education. As noted, in most cases the survey was completed by virtually all of the players in a team, though in some clubs the top-tier[4] players were unavailable to us. In the surveys, we asked questions about people's backgrounds, such as how many games they have played, and where they grew up. We also asked players about their views on Indigenous Australians, how well the AFL is doing with regard to multiculturalism, to what degree they feel included and supported by their club and their attitudes towards women, gay men and violence. Furthermore, the survey had a social network component to it, in which, for example, we asked players and staff to nominate people they were friends with, trusted, saw as leaders and also those they had differences of opinion with (which we will explain in detail below).

There were 66 coaches/other staff who also completed the survey. Our focus in this book is primarily on the players, especially in regard to their social networks, because players are the primary agents that Rule 35 is directed towards,[5] but comparative analysis on survey responses plus information from interviews of coaches/other staff is included in this book.

Ninety-nine participants completed an interview, 88 of whom also completed the survey. Of these interviewees, 88 were players[6] and 11 were coaches. Importantly, we note that of the nine clubs, only six took part in both the surveys and interviews, leaving three clubs who only did the survey. (These are the last three club cases studies in this book.)

Standard survey questions

The survey included standard and social network questions. We focus on the standard questions in this section (e.g. what factors predict positive attitudes towards Indigenous people?). In the next section, we examine networks of relations between players, which enabled us to analyse how networks and responses to the standard questions go together (e.g. are players who are trusted more likely to be higher in experience, such as having played more AFL games?). Examples of the survey questions are included in Appendix 1. The results are based on answers provided by players only.

Individual responses to the survey data were analysed using standard statistical analyses, such as linear regression, which give an overall picture of respondents as a group, and analysis of variance (ANOVA), which compares groups of people (such as club versus club, or Indigenous versus non-Indigenous players). In these analyses, we are looking at what characteristics of individuals might predict certain attitudes (e.g. is being in the AFL system longer associated with less racist attitudes?). In addition, we can also see if there are differences on average from one club to the next regarding certain attitudes (e.g. do players at Club A have less racist attitudes than players at Club B?). These are very standard sorts of analyses that are usually conducted on survey responses. Importantly, all effects we mention here are statistically significant results, meaning that these effects are the key or significant effects.

Individual factors predicting attitudes to race, ethnicity, masculinity and other club issues

Individual factors that are important to issues of Rule 35 are as follows. Analyses here group all players together across clubs to see which individual-level factors are associated with various attitudes about social issues and perspectives about the club.[7] With regard to attitudes about Indigenous Australians in general, players who were significantly more likely to have positive attitudes were, not surprisingly, Indigenous players. Furthermore, players from higher socio-economic backgrounds were more likely to have positive attitudes about Indigenous Australians. In regard to attitudes about Indigenous AFL players (e.g. Indigenous players train hard), the older players wereless likely to endorse positive statements about Indigenous players. Furthermore, older players also perceived that most others in the club were less likely to endorse such statements about Indigenous players.

On issues of masculinity, we have a number of interesting effects. Players who strongly identify with the club are significantly more likely to be homophobic (e.g. gay males sicken me because they are not real men). In regard to idea that masculinity is tied to sexual success with women, or what we call 'playboy' attitudes (i.e. a real man never says no to sex – see Appendix 1 for further example questions asked), Indigenous players are more likely to endorse playboy views. On the issue of strict gender roles (e.g. a woman should expect to do most of the childcare), older players were more likely to endorse strict gender roles. However, more experienced players were less likely to endorse strict gender roles. As there is a very strong correlation between age and experience, what these effects jointly suggest is that the longer you are in the AFL system, the less strict, or rigid, your attitudes about gender roles will be. Finally, on strict gender roles, players who were working as well as playing football were less likely to believe in such strict gender roles.

On more general issues surrounding the club, players who feel included and supported by the club are those who strongly identify with the club, those who are seen as 'best players' within the team, as well as those who are working as well as playing AFL. With regard to the club understanding the needs of its players, again people who identify strongly with the team are significantly more likely to believe this. However, as players get older, they are less inclined to think that the club understands their needs. On the issue of family inclusiveness at the club, players who believe in statements such as 'My family feels comfortable participating in club functions' are the 'best players', players who have completed a university degree, or players who strongly identify with the club. However, players who are significantly unlikely to endorse such views are younger players and Indigenous players.

Differences between clubs

This set of analyses compares the players in each of the nine clubs, to look for differences in average scores between them on a range of factors. The differences we mention are statistically significant differences as determined by the use of statistical tests.[8] We mention here only clubs that are different, so if a club is not mentioned then it is not different from other clubs. With regard to standard demographic data, players in the Delta Football Club (Delta FC) had significantly lower socio-economic status (SES) than players from the Bravo Football Club (though no other clubs differed on SES). Delta FC had significantly more players from city (as opposed to rural) areas than any other club. Furthermore, Delta FC players were significantly more likely to say that their club is inclusive of family than the Foxtrot Football Club. The Echo Football Club was more likely than other clubs to answer questions about Rule 35 correctly (e.g. what best characterizes Rule 35?). On the issue of how well the club deals with its players, the Charlie Football Club players scored significantly lower than just about all of the other clubs. Hornet FC also had more players working as well as playing football than any other club. Apart from this, on all other demographic or background factors such as age, experience, studying, marital status, number of Indigenous players in the team, level of education and more, there were no differences between the clubs.[9] From this perspective, most if not all of the clubs have very similar background characteristics or profiles to one another.

On issues of race and ethnicity, we found that views on whether the AFL had not stamped out racism or truly recognized multiculturalism were significantly different between Charlie FC, whose players strongly believed this to be the case, and Foxtrot FC, whose players did not believe this to be the case. Importantly, with regard to negative attitudes about Indigenous Australians (e.g. Aboriginal Australians receive more welfare money from government agencies than other Australians), players at Igloo FC did not agree with such views, and on average Igloo FC was significantly different than players at Abacus FC and Gecko FC, who were more likely to endorse such statements. For attitudes about Indigenous players within the AFL (e.g. Indigenous players train hard), we found significant differences again: players at Abacus FC and Echo FC were less likely to endorse such statements than players at Bravo FC, Charlie FC and Igloo FC. Finally, on issues of masculinity relating to strict gender roles, homophobia or violence, there were no differences on average between player attitudes between clubs.

Differences between Indigenous and non-Indigenous players

We also examined differences between Indigenous and non-Indigenous players. There were no significant differences between these two groups of players on a range of factors such as age, experience, being nominated by teammates as a best player, feeling welcome at the club, leadership roles, knowledge of Rule 35 and many views on masculinity. However, there were also some marked differences. Indigenous players had significantly lower SES backgrounds than non-Indigenous players, and were also more likely to be religious than non-Indigenous players. There was a trend towards Indigenous players being more likely to give an interview in this research, and though this effect is not statistically significant, it does suggest that Indigenous players were perhaps more inclined to have their voice heard. In any case, Indigenous voices are not under-represented in this research, which is important.

On issues of race and ethnicity, there are a number of significant and not unexpected effects. First, Indigenous players are less likely to feel that the AFL has stamped out racism in the game or truly recognizes multiculturalism than non-Indigenous players. Second, Indigenous players were much more likely to agree with statements such as 'Indigenous players train hard' than non-Indigenous players, indicating a more positive view of Indigenous AFL players. Third, Indigenous players were much more likely to be pro-Indigenous than non-Indigenous players (as noted through Indigenous players' greater endorsement of statements, such as 'Indigenous Australians are disadvantaged on a range of issues including lifespan, jobs, education and housing'). However, on anti-Indigenous attitudes (e.g. Aboriginal Australians receive more welfare money from government agencies than other Australians), there were no differences in the views of Indigenous and non-Indigenous AFL players. Fourth, compared with non-Indigenous players, Indigenous players were less likely to feel that the club was an inclusive environment for their family and were less likely to be studying, but were more likely to get both of the Rule 35 questions correct. On issues of masculinity, Indigenous players were more likely to endorse playboy attitudes than non-Indigenous players.

Differences between players and coaches/other staff

Finally, for the standard survey questions, we compare players and coaches. In terms of background, intuitive differences between the groups include the fact that coaches/other staff were older, had played more AFL games, were more likely to have a university degree, were more likely to be from a rural (as opposed to urban) area, were more likely to be married, were less likely to be Indigenous and were less likely to give an interview. Regarding thoughts about the club, coaches/other staff that we surveyed were less likely to think that the club was a family-inclusive environment and also less likely to think that the club understands their needs.

With regard to issues of race and ethnicity, coaches/other staff were much more likely to be positive about Indigenous Australians in general than players, but were less likely than players to think positively about Indigenous players, scoring significantly lower on statements such as 'Indigenous players train hard'. On issues of masculinity, compared to players, we found that the coaches/other staff were less likely to be homophobic, less likely to endorse strict gender roles, less likely to endorse violence and less likely to endorse playboy attitudes.

Social network survey questions

An important aspect of this research was the use of SNA to examine social relationships between players in their clubs. SNA is not often used in the analysis of sporting teams, but we hope to show through this book that an analysis of the relationships (i.e. network ties) between players in a team gives us a unique insight into the culture and social dynamics of AFL teams. In this section, we briefly describe in an intuitive (rather than a technical) way how we approached the social network data, before giving an overview of our SNA findings. For those who are more technically minded and interested, there are substantial technical details related to the SNA provided in Appendix 2.

Importantly, we note that some of the results for the SNA differ to the analyses of the surveys above, and this is to be expected, because they are measuring different things. The standard statistical analyses in the previous section measuring differences between groups, or look for a profile regarding what characteristics, are associated with certain attitudes or beliefs. In contrast, the SNA results show us how social relationships are associated with certain characteristics, including things like playing ability, experience or attitudes towards Indigenous Australians. So the social network analyses specifically examine social ties, whereas the standard statistical tests do not. We use a combination of network visualization (i.e. network diagrams, or network maps) and statistical network models to understand the club networks, which we explain in more detail below.

Social network analysis (SNA)

To gain a detailed understanding of club culture, we have used SNA because it allows us to understand the complex social relations between players in a team, including the reasons why some players are popular, some are not, and the informal social rules that shape the social networks within the team. When we refer to social networks, we are not talking about social networking via social media (such as Facebook or Twitter). Rather, we are talking about the actual social relationships between people that happen in day-to-day life, such as friendship, advice, trust or even who people argue with. Friendship, advice, etc., are particular types of social relationships or social interactions that we engage with frequently with other people. We are not forced into these relations, but rather we choose who we want to be friends with, who we might make new friends with, who we might stop being friends with because someone who has done us wrong or whether we continue friendships for a long time with someone we only see very occasionally. Social network relations are informal relations, which differ from formal social ties such as being someone's boss/subordinate/coach. While these formal ties are written into the fabric of an organization, informal ties like friendship, trust and advice are unspoken relationships. But, through careful questioning by researchers, these unspoken social ties can be made explicit, and this research has done just this in order to understand the patterns and implications of the informal social relationships within teams.

By formal definition, SNA is a set of techniques that focuses on the 'relationships among social entities, and on the patterns and implications of these relationships' (Wasserman and Faust 1994, 3). 'The unit of analysis in network analysis is not the individual, but an entity consisting of a collection of individuals and the linkages among them' (Wasserman and Faust 1994, 5). Therefore, 'a social network is one of many possible sets of social relations of a specific context – for example, communicative, power, affectual, or exchange relations – that links actors within a larger social structure (or network of networks)' (Emirbayer and Goodwin 1994, 1417).

The ways that informal social ties are structured in a club give us great insight into how that club operates. It gives insight into the informal rules and 'ways of doing things' that are particular to that club. Networks represent informal connections between people. Often these are unspoken and may be seen differently by people on different sides of the relationship. For instance, player 'John' may say that player 'Chris' is his friend, but 'Chris' may not consider 'John' his friend. Figure 1 demonstrates this difference in view, because the arrow points from John towards Chris (representing John selecting Chris) but there is no arrow going from Chris to John, indicating that Chris does not see John as his friend. If he did, there would be arrows in both directions.

Sometimes network ties form due to the presence of other network ties. For example, consider the case of someone buying you a coffee or a beer. Regardless of that person's characteristics (well, in most cases anyway) or how well you know them, you are likely to buy them a coffee or beer in return in the future due to the social rule of reciprocation.

John   Chris

Figure 1.   People and directed friendship network ties. In this example, John nominates (or chooses, or says) that Chris is his friend, with the arrow pointing from John to Chris to represent this.

Likewise, in social relations like friendship we often see reciprocation occurs – not always, but very often (look, for instance, at Figure 6 and see how many double-headed arrows there are – quite a few). In addition, there are other examples where ties come about due to the presence of other social ties. Think of the common phrase, 'a friend of a friend is a friend'. This suggests that I become friends with you because we share a friend. Or think of another phrase, 'an enemy of an enemy is a friend'. In this case, a tie can come about between you and me if we both dislike the same person – thus, a social relationship forms due to the *absence* of social ties between others (or the presence of a negative tie to others).

So, social network ties can arise between people due to properties of the social network (i.e. the presence or absence of others social ties). This is important because we need to control for these tendencies for network ties to form due to other ties (known otherwise as network self-organization). By controlling for these tendencies, we can then examine, in a more principled fashion, reasons why network ties form that are associated with the particular qualities of people – for instance, because they are Indigenous, or anti-violent, or racist, or homophobic.[10] And this is the real power of examining networks within AFL clubs: it gives us the ability to understand how the individual qualities of players affect the social relations of players in teams, and how the structure of the individual qualities and social ties shapes the culture of the team.

Importantly, we used sophisticated and cutting-edge social network models for our analyses (called *exponential random graph models* or *ERGMs*: see Lusher, Koskinen, and Robins [2013] for a detailed background to these models). These are state-of-the-art models for analysing network data and give us considerable insights into what drives these networks and how social relationships are formed, structured and maintained.[11]

Important network structures

There are three important features we wish the reader to understand regarding how network ties are associated with the individual qualities/attributes of people in a network.

- There may be some people who are very *active* due to certain individual-level attributes.
- There may also be people who are *popular* due to certain individual-level attributes.
- There may be *similarity* effects, such that one person is more likely to have a network tie to another who is similar on a certain individual-level attribute.

People who are *active* are those who *send* many network ties to others (i.e. they nominate many others) due to some particular quality or attribute. These activity effects mean that people *with particular qualities* send more ties than other people within that same network. For example, players who are younger may make more friendship ties within the team. In essence, younger players may be trying to befriend many other players in the hope that some of these friendships will 'stick'. This represents an activity effect of younger age (Figure 2).

Figure 2. *Active* people send more ties due to individual qualities.

People who are *popular* are those who *receive* many ties (i.e. who are nominated by many others) due to some particular quality or attribute. Such popularity effects mean that people with *particular qualities* receive more ties than others within the same network. As an example, players with more experience (such as having played more AFL games) may be more likely to be trusted than other players. As such, this represents a popularity effect of greater experience (Figure 3).

The popularity effect *is a very important network effect* with regard to understanding the culture of a network. We know that popular people within a network are advantaged (Bavelas 1950; Freeman 1977, 1979). Being popular (or in network terms, being central) within a network means that you are more valued within that network than others. In the context of an AFL team, players who are popular network choices (i.e. many people choose them as friends, or trust them, or think they set the culture) give insights into the characteristics that are valued within that team. If best players are popular (or central), then they are likely to be highly valued. The same is true if more experienced players are also popular friendship choices or people who are trusted. In the case of players who are central and hold pro-(or anti-)Indigenous attitudes, their views are more likely to be given value and sway within the team. They are players who are most likely to shape the *culture* of the team – that is the unwritten, unspoken values, beliefs and practices of the team.

A third effect is the *similarity effect,* in which the person sending the tie has the same (or similar) individual quality of the person that receives the tie (i.e. the person the sender has nominated). So, in this case, the sender and the receiver of a tie have the same (or similar) qualities to one another, which we know colloquially as *birds of a feather flock together* (and in the field of SNA as homophily). As an example in an AFL team, we may find that players high in ability (the so-called 'best players') may choose other 'best players' as friends. Or younger players may choose other younger players as friends, or older players select older players (Figure 4).

Similarity effects can represent separation into subgroups within a network. For instance, if we find a similarity effect for experience, this means that not only less experienced players may choose to associate with other less experienced players, but also more experienced players may associate with other more experienced players. So, similarity effects suggest a division into groups based upon a certain individual-level characteristic.

In summary, it is these three network effects – *activity, popularity* and *similarity* – that we focus on in our analyses of the social networks of players in AFL teams that are presented in detail in the next nine papers in this collection.

Figure 3. *Popular* people receive more ties due to individual qualities.

Figure 4. *Similar* people more likely to send ties due to other with similar individual qualities to themselves.

Specific social networks questions and what they represent

Within the nine AFL clubs, we have survey information on almost all of the players. As noted, this is very important as it gives us the bird's eye (or aerial) view of the team as whole, and *the overall pattern* of how each of the players interacts with the others. If we sampled only a few players, then we are unable to get the overall network picture of the team. By getting close to all players within the team – best players, experienced, young, rookies – we get a fuller picture of the team as a whole, the structure of social relations and the culture of the club. This is because not only we have network data on almost every player, but also we have details on each and every player including their background, their attitudes to race/ethnicity, to masculinity, as well as what they think about their club and the AFL more generally. Combining both their background and attitudinal details with their social network responses, we can see if certain people *within each club* are more (or less) likely to be popular due to their attitudes or personal characteristics. To be very explicit, are Indigenous players popular as friends or marginalized within a team? Are players who are racist towards Indigenous players popular or marginalized within the team? Are players who are homophobic popular or marginalized within the team? The importance of this is that the attitudes of popular people may be seen as the norm within the team and may represent the cultural values of the team, regardless of whether most people agree with these attitudes or not. As such, the connection between what people think and how popular (or prominent) they are within the team is of great importance to club culture, to what is the 'accepted way of doing things' in the team.

Players were asked about three general types of social relationships (i.e. social networks) that they are involved in with other players in the team. We spend a brief moment explaining what each of these represent and provide an example.

Explanation of sets culture network

We begin by examining the cultural leadership networks, or the *sets culture network*, in which players identify who sets the culture within the team. We asked players to indicate 'Who do you think sets the culture at the club?' (see Appendix 1 for list of all network questions asked). This sets culture network does not give us a formal network as such, but rather the players' *self-aware analysis* of those within the team who have an influence over the culture of the team. This helps define the team in regard to the behaviours and attitudes that are acceptable and unacceptable within it. Sets culture gives us player awareness of a team's cultural values and reflects players' explicit acknowledgement of who they know influences them. These sorts of networks tend to have only a few people nominated, which most people agree on. In other words, this is a network that represents who players are aware of as having influence over them. Hence, we are interested in the attitudes of the people chosen as setting the culture, because we know from SNA research that people who are central are privileged within their network (see Bavelas 1950; Freeman 1977, 1979). The views of central people are likely to be important to 'culture setting' and can be seen as dominant within the overall club. An example of culture

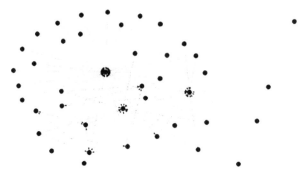

Figure 5.   Example network of 'who sets the culture'.

setting a network is given below. You will note that it is a very hub and spoke-type design, like a set of interconnected cogs. Most people are choosing a very few individuals. What is clear is that if some of these players left the club (e.g. retired, were transferred, delisted) the central and influential people within the network could change very quickly (Figure 5).

Explanation of friendship, trust and after-hours networks: informal, unspoken social influences

The next set of networks is informal social relations that tap into the unspoken and implicit ways of doing things within the club. These networks are friendship, trust and socialize with, which give insights into informal, unspoken team cultural values. In our view, these are *the fundamental* networks to investigate the team culture of the players.[12] They represent social ties that incorporate an emotional investment, and, by their nature and also by their structure, they are highly interconnected. This means that they are quite difficult to change quickly, as opposed to the hub and spoke *culture-setting* networks, which are centred on a few people who, if they left, would dramatically alter the network. The loss of a few people in the friendship, trust or after-hours networks may not necessary radically alter it. These networks are more likely to be implicit and unspoken influences that players may not be aware of. There are indeed similarities between these networks and, thus, much overlap, which is why we have grouped them together. But there are subtle differences between them that mean that they are not interchangeable for another. For instance, it is one thing to be friends at the club ('at work') but it may be another thing to socialize with one another after work (in the 'after hours'). An example of a friendship network is given in Figure 6. What is evident is that social ties are much more evenly arranged than the sets culture network. There are also plenty of triangles ('a friend of a friend is a friend'), which is a very common feature of many human social networks.

Explanation of difference of opinion network and funny network: contested boundaries

Two final networks are examined to understand issues of the boundaries, fissures and unacceptable behaviours and attitudes within the club. These were the 'difference of opinion' network and 'funny' network. We group two final networks together because there is overlap in the fact that they both deal with contested boundaries, though these are two slightly different networks in some ways. In simple terms, the 'difference of opinion' network could be seen as enforcing boundaries, whereas the 'funny' network could be seen as where boundaries are pushed. In either case, both networks allow the possibility to highlight the issues at these boundaries.

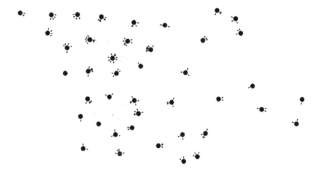

Figure 6.   An example friendship network of players in an AFL club.

The 'difference of opinion' network gives insights into informal, spoken or unspoken, team cultural values that may be supported and which people may also go against (i.e. players may have differences of opinion with others who hold attitudes counter to the majority or the influential players within the team). This difference of opinion network can show fissures or strains in the team. An example of a difference of opinion network is given below. You can see that it is quite sparse compared with the friendship network, as people tend to have fewer 'negative' social ties than they do 'positive' ones (such as friendship) (Figure 7).

In addition, we have the 'funny' or humour network. The phrase 'only joking' is often made when someone says something that another finds offensive. Humour can be used therefore to test the boundaries of what is and is not acceptable. The 'funny' network gives insights into slippage areas or contested spaces and boundaries where players attempt to gain prominence through the use of humour.

Social network analysis (SNA) results

These results for the social network analyses are summarized in the next three tables in this section, and they give overviews of results for the different types of networks for each of the nine clubs surveyed. It is in the following papers, paper "Abacus Football Club (doi:10.1080/17430437.2014.1002975, in this collection)" through paper "Igloo Football Club (doi:10.1080/17430437.2014.1002983, in this collection)", that each club will be presented as a case study and considerable detail about each club's culture and the opinions of the players regarding these issues is provided. What we shall see in this section

Figure 7.   Example 'who you have differences of opinion to' network.

and in the papers that follow is that while there are indeed similarities in the ways that clubs operate, there are a range of ways that these clubs differ, and differ particularly with regard to issues of race/ethnicity, multiculturalism and masculinity. Presented in Tables 1–3 are overall summaries of the project to give some indication of the similarities and differences between the clubs.

Sets culture network: summary across all clubs

As a reminder, by using SNA we are looking at how social network ties are related to the individual characteristics of players, and so these analyses are not only complementary but also different to the standard statistical analyses we have presented. In addition, these tables are a summary only, and there are other effects for each club that can be found in the case study papers (paper "Abacus Football Club (doi:10.1080/17430437.2014.1002975, in this collection)" through paper "Igloo Football Club (doi:10.1080/17430437.2014.1002983, in this collection)").

With this in mind, Table 1 shows the following:

- In most but not all clubs, players who set the culture are best players and are experienced players. These are separate and independent effects for ability and experience, so a player does not need to be one of the best players *and* one of the most experienced, but simply being either means he is more likely to set the culture.
- Only one club (Igloo FC) has culture-setting players who are more likely to be supportive of Indigenous AFL players (e.g. Indigenous players train hard). At Foxtrot FC, the culture-setting players are not pro-Indigenous but, instead, anti-Indigenous. Within Delta FC, Gecko FC and Hornet FC, there are subgroup splits in the culture-setting players, suggesting variability of opinion around Indigenous issues. Furthermore, in Charlie FC, Indigenous players selected other Indigenous players as setting the culture, but such endorsement of Indigenous players was not made by non-Indigenous players.
- There was also contention around whether the AFL had been successful in eradicating racism, with culture-setting players at Hornet FC believing it had, and culture-setting players at Abacus FC mixed in their feelings on this issue.

With respect to issues of race and ethnicity, the network diagrams for each club are also helpful in understanding where Indigenous players are located within each club with respect to setting the culture of their team. Figure 8 shows the position of Indigenous players within the culture-setting networks for each of the nine AFL clubs. Due to issues of identifiability we do not indicate which club is which here. What is very clear is the following:

- In all but one club, AFL players in general are very unlikely to nominate Indigenous players as people who set the culture of their team. This points to a lack of voice of Indigenous players within most teams with regard to team culture.

Despite the SNA data showing the lack of Indigenous players voices in AFL clubs generally the network structures themselves are of these culture-setting networks are quite informative and varied. In some clubs, there is a concerted core of people which it seems most players in the team agree that they set the culture. In other clubs, there seems to be less agreement on who sets the culture. In addition, some individual players nominate everyone in the team as setting the culture (indicated by arrows from them to all other players, indicating an attitude of 'we are all responsible for the culture') but often these individuals are not selected by other players, or by very few.

Table 1. Summary of SNA results per club for *sets the culture* network[a].

Player attributes	Club								
	A	B	C	D	E	F	G[b]	H[b]	I[b]
Playing ability	+	+	+	+	+	+	+	+	+
Experience	+	+			+	+	+	+	+
Supportive of Indigenous Australians				Subgroups				Subgroups	
Unsupportive of Indigenous Australians				Subgroups		+			
Supportive of Indigenous AFL players			+	−					+
Indigenous player segregation									
AFL is a successful multicultural organization	Subgroups						+	+ / −	
Playboy							Salient		
Homophobia	−				Salient		−	−	
Strict gender roles					Salient	−	+		Salient
Violence	+				Salient		Salient		

[a] Dark grey (+) = players selected as setting the culture score high on this (e.g. experience) or endorse this attitude (e.g. homophobia); light grey (−) = players selected as setting the culture score low on this (e.g. experience) or endorse this attitude (e.g. homophobia)/dis-endorse; salient = issue present but not prominent; subgroups = subgroups exist in team which have differing views on this issue.

[b] We have no interview data from these three clubs.

Table 2. Summary of SNA results per club for *trust, friendship and after-hours* network.

Player attributes	Club								
	A	B	C	D	E	F	G[a]	H[a]	I[a]
Playing ability									
Experience		Subgroups	Subgroups		Subgroups	Subgroups		Subgroups	
Supportive of Indigenous Australians		Subgroups			Subgroups	Subgroups		Subgroups	
Unsupportive of Indigenous Australians					Subgroups			Subgroups	
Supportive of Indigenous AFL players					Subgroups			Subgroups	
Indigenous player segregation					Salient	Subgroup			
AFL as multicultural success							Subgroups		
Playboy	Salient								
Homophobia		Salient		Salient					
Strict gender roles		Salient		Salient					
Violence				Subgroups					Salient

Note: Dark grey(+) = players selected as setting the culture score high on this (e.g. experience) or endorse this attitude (e.g. homophobia); light grey(–) = players selected as setting the culture score low on this (e.g. experience) or endorse this attitude (e.g. homophobia)/dis-endorse; salient = issue present but not prominent; subgroups = subgroups exist in team which have differing views on this issue.
[a] We have no interview data from these three clubs.

Table 3. Summary of SNA results per club for *difference of opinion and humour* network.

Player attributes	Club								
	A	B	C	D	E	F	G[a]	H[a]	I[a]
Playing ability (best players)	+ / −	+	+	+	+	+		+	+
Experience	Subgroups		−		+		Subgroups	Subgroups	
Supportive of Indigenous Australians							Subgroups	Subgroups	
Unsupportive of Indigenous Australians									
Supportive of Indigenous AFL players		Subgroups							
Indigenous player segregation		+ / −							
AFL as multicultural success	Subgroups		Subgroups	+			Subgroups	+	
Playboy			−			−			
Homophobia			Salient	Subgroups					Salient
Strict gender roles					Salient	−			Salient
Violence					Salient	Subgroups			Salient

Note: Dark grey(+) = players selected as setting the culture score high on this (e.g. experience) or endorse this attitude (e.g. homophobia); light grey(−) = players selected as setting the culture score low on this (e.g. experience) or endorse this attitude (e.g. homophobia)/dis-endorse; salient = issue present but not prominent; subgroups = subgroups exist in team which have differing views on this issue.
[a] We have no interview data from these three clubs.

In returning to masculinity attitudes that players hold:

- Homophobia was important in two clubs among the culture-setting network, with Abacus FC and Gecko FC having culture-setting players who were pro-gay in their views (i.e. the negative signs in Table 1. For both of these clubs mean that culture-setting players are *not* homophobic).
- Hornet FC also had culture-setting players who did not endorse strict gender roles, though at Gecko FC, culture-setting players did endorse such strict gender roles, and it was on the radar at Igloo FC.
- Endorsement of violence varied among clubs and seems quite prominent as an issue. Abacus FC endorsed the idea that being a man is related to violence, though Foxtrot FC and Igloo FC did not.

Figure 8.   Culture-setting network for nine AFL clubs (players only; black dots indicate Indigenous players).

- Notably, playboy attitudes were not highly present in who sets the culture at these nine clubs, though at Hornet players who *did not* endorse playboy attitudes were those who set the culture.

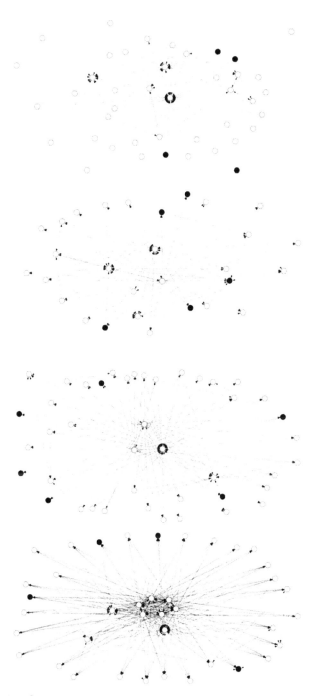

Figure 8. (*Continued*).

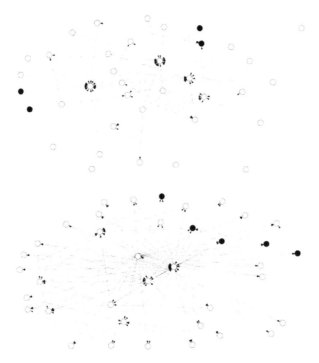

Figure 8.   (*Continued*).

Trust, friendship and after-hours networks: summary across all clubs

In regard to trust, friendship and after-hours social relations, Table 2 summarize the effects for the nine AFL teams.

- Player ability is critical to these social ties, such that players higher in ability are much more popular people to trust, be friends with or socialize with.
- Experience is also highly important, primarily with effects suggesting those with greater experience are prominent, but similarity in experience is also a driving force in these social ties. This is very much to be expected.
- On race/ethnicity issues, again, it is only at Igloo FC that popular players in these networks are those who have positive attitudes about Indigenous players. There are many other clubs that are split in their views on such issues, and at one club (Foxtrot FC), the exact opposite is true. At Delta FC, it is players with strong anti-Indigenous attitudes that are more likely to be trusted. At Echo, Foxtrot and Hornet FCs, there are divisions or subgroups with regard to trust, friendship and after-hours socializing on anti-Indigenous attitudes in which people with similar attitudes are more likely to have ties to another.
- In all but one club, Indigenous players are more likely to be friends with, trust and/or socialize more with other Indigenous players than with non-Indigenous players. This need not necessarily be seen as a failure to make Indigenous players feel welcome in a team; it can also be seen in terms of similarity effects (i.e. *birds of a feather flock together*) that characterize many human social relations. Indeed, we see this desire to socialize with similar others very strongly in clubs in terms of experience. So, the fact

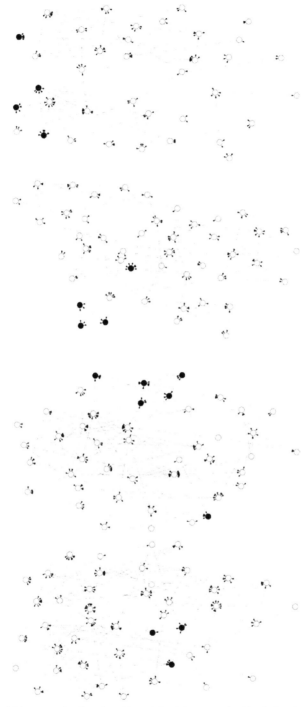

Figure 9.   Friendship networks for nine AFL clubs (players only; black dots indicate Indigenous players).

Figure 9. (*Continued*).

that in one club Indigenous players do not mainly interact with other Indigenous players could be a good thing, in that Indigenous players might feel comfortable within this team. Conversely, this might be a problem in that Indigenous players feel the need to 'integrate' with the team. It is hard to know which of these might be true.

- Interestingly, and as for the culture-setting network, the ways that social network ties were associated with whether the AFL had eradicated racism from the game differed between clubs.

Figure 9 shows whom players chose as friends within their club:

- It is very clear that, in all but one club, Indigenous players are more likely to be friends with other Indigenous players.

On masculinity issues:

- Playboy attitudes are salient but not prominent in these networks.
- Echo FC was the only club in which players who were most trusted were also those who were the most homophobic in their team, indicating a possible culture of homophobia.
- Gecko FC demonstrated that players had social relations with other players who had similar views on homophobia, which results in subgroups of players within the team who have different views on homophobia. For all other clubs, homophobia was unrelated to friendship, trust and after-hours socializing networks.
- Endorsement of strict gender roles and how this is associated with social network ties varies, being salient in two clubs and in another it is dis-endorsed by players who are people choices in these networks.
- Endorsement of violence and who was chosen in networks of friendship, trust and socializing also varied across clubs.

Difference of opinion and humour networks: summary across all clubs

Table 3 summarizes results for the difference of opinion and humour networks in clubs.

- A clear common denominator here is for experience to crop up within clubs for the difference of opinion network, with more experienced players being selected by other players.
- High playing ability was important for who was considered to be funny.
- Again, we see high variability related to attitudes about Indigenous people, Indigenous AFL players and whether the AFL has eradicated racism from the game.
- Issues of race/ethnicity do not feature for difference of opinion for Delta, Echo, Foxtrot or Igloo. On masculinity issues, there are effects for many clubs, but not for Abacus, Bravo, Gecko or Hornet. Together, these two effects suggest that difference of opinion and humour are likely to occur around race/ethnicity or masculinity, but not often both.

Figure 10 presents the difference of opinion network for the nine AFL teams.

***

Overall, from these results of the social network data across all networks and across all clubs, Igloo FC stands out as the only club with a strong pro-Indigenous club culture, and one where masculinity issues are salient but are neither less nor more problematic than at other clubs. Furthermore, the prominent players in the networks at Igloo FC believe that the AFL has eradicated racism from the game. However, not all clubs believe that racism has been eradicated from the game, and this is perhaps not surprising. Rather, it is to suggest that if racism has not been eradicated from society, and it has not, then it is probably a stretch to expect that the AFL has eradicated it from all who are involved with it. And indeed, as results from some of the clubs show, and as can be seen in more detail in the coming papers, some form of racism does still seem to be an issue within some clubs.

This summary is but a taster of more detailed investigation on a club by club basis that we explore in the next nine papers in this collection. For the remainder of this summary paper, we now move away from networks and focus on the interviews where players (and coaches) open up in detail about these issues within their clubs and beyond.

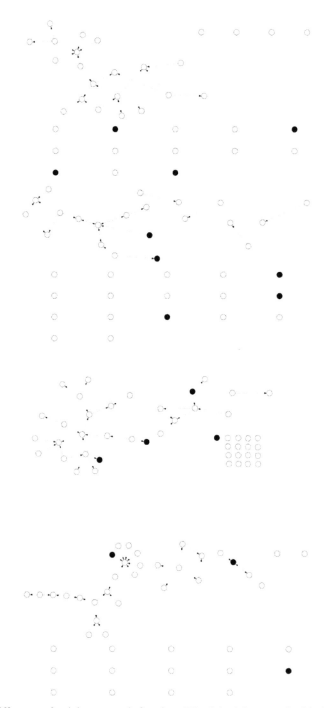

Figure 10. Difference of opinion network for nine AFL clubs (players only; black dots indicate Indigenous players).

Figure 10. (*Continued*).

The interviews

The interviews consisted of a set of open-ended questions (see Appendix 3) focused predominantly on issues of race. This is because it was racism that brought about Rule 35 and because in-depth interviews are lengthy enough (30–45 minutes) without adding other issues, such as masculinity, which could easily have doubled the length of the interview (resulting in fewer people agreeing to participate in this research).

Perhaps the most outstanding feature of the interviews was that all respondents felt that the introduction of Rule 35 was a positive outcome for the AFL. The players could see that it was a hallmark of the code's professionalism and a driver of the inclusive, welcoming nature that the AFL strongly promotes and further evidenced with the Indigenous and multicultural rounds. This was further supported by the vast majority of players who said that they had never heard or experienced any form of racism, either by opponents or by teammates. Aside from the Sherman incident, 10% of players had experienced indirect/direct racial vilification. Of these, two cases involved Italian/Greek players, while the remaining were directed towards Indigenous Australian players. In addition to this, 10% of respondents had heard a derogatory racial term used, but did not recall who it was in relation to.

The majority of respondents who had heard racist vilification did so from the crowd or from experiences in their day-to-day lives. A quarter of players recall hearing/ experiencing racial vilification from the crowd, while nearly all Indigenous players had experienced racial vilification during their everyday lives at some point and while playing. One Indigenous player describes this experience:

> Yeah just things like, 'That like black c …', mainly from the supporters. You know you hear it like mainly in Melbourne, you cop it a bit. Just how do you react to it? Because you don't know where it came from, you just hear it, so it's hard. It's hard to say really what's going through your head at that moment. (Senior Indigenous player)

Another example of how much of an impact Rule 35 had had on the players was when they were asked to comment on how they felt about the Sherman incident, which occurred during the data gathering phase of this research. Of the 99 participants interviewed, just 4 had not heard about the incident. All remaining players were appalled, angered or shocked by Sherman's racist attack on Wilkinson but saw it as an isolated incident. Some of the responses to that incident included:

> To be honest with you, it did shock me … He's paid [a] pretty serious consequence for [it]. (Senior non-Indigenous Player)

> I was pretty disgusted really … it actually makes us footballers look like we're racist towards Indigenous people when we're not! Obviously, he's had a bit of a brain fade or that's just the way he is. (Senior non-Indigenous Player)

> A little bit flabbergasted personally. From my experiences of the AFL, over the last few years, I thought that was gone. I thought it was a thing of the past. [Just] the fact that it happened at an elite level with a guy who's been in the system for so long, who's played with a diverse range of players and he still resorted to use that! I just was flabbergasted. (Non-Indigenous assistant coach)

From these responses, it would seem that the players and coaches have a very strong understanding that the actual use of player-to-player racial vilification is wrong. Further to this, virtually all of the players felt that enough was being done around the issue of addressing racism in the AFL and the elite competition was free of racial or ethnic intolerance. However, this was in contrast to our findings that players had experienced little interaction between Indigenous Australians and non-Indigenous people socializing in their childhoods, growing up and within institutions such as school. This makes the interaction and relationships created at elite AFL clubs with Indigenous and non-Indigenous players all the more important in light of the federal and state initiatives involving reconciliation and coexistence. To put it simply, if Indigenous and non-Indigenous players are meeting one another for the first time in the AFL, then the AFL becomes a much more important instrument for tolerance, harmony and understanding than one might initially think.

This was considered significant given that the players showed a distinct lack of understanding about what reconciliation and multiculturalism were. The vast majority of participants in the research study, including Indigenous participants, did not have a developed or general understanding of what 'reconciliation' meant. Some were able to identify that it had 'something' to do with Indigenous Australians, the Stolen Generations or then Prime Minister Kevin Rudd's 'Sorry' speech in 2008. For example,

> ... To be honest, I linked reconciliation with Kevin Rudd saying an apology. That was certainly a big step, but yeah, I think it is a lot more than that. (Senior non-indigenous player)

In addition, most participants understood multiculturalism to be about allowing 'multicultural' people to play football, or being part of mainstream Australian culture. Many participants did not see how issues of race and racism were experienced differently by people of different cultural or racial backgrounds. For instance, approximately 48% of respondents felt that issues of racism were the same for all people, while approximately 50% felt that they were different. For example,

> You could say they are the same thing, but there [are] different types of judgments about different races and you know in the way they just cop it. Like Muslims cop it a bit now, since the war has been going on. (Non-Indigenous rookie)

> Yeah, I think it's all pretty similar. I don't think Indigenous people get treated any differently to, you know, someone that's a wog, [when] they come over from Italy and Spain ... I think they all get treated the same. (Senior non-Indigenous player)

These types of responses seemed to lend themselves to a distinct sense by many of the players that these concepts were peripheral to the real issues of mitigating racial abuse and vilification, which the AFL already had in hand through the education policies and inductions.

Casual racism

For the majority of Indigenous players and more enlightened non-Indigenous players, issues around casual or nuanced racism still existed.[13] These players had a greater appreciation of racism beyond name calling and insults and could see how more institutionalized issues could, and did, manifest themselves. One Indigenous player reflected on the way that he is treated as an AFL star compared to other Indigenous people or his extended family:

> [They say] nah, nah, nah, he's alright, he's made it, he's done good with himself ... which is pretty shit because it means anybody who hasn't made it to AFL [is a] no-hoper [even] before they've met them. Yeah, it is hard, because, obviously, people recognise who I am and treat me differently because of that. (Senior Indigenous player)

Another Indigenous player voiced his concern about the way that Aboriginal people are still stereotyped:

> Like us Indigenous boys we barely go out that much and if we do, we might have a beer, or have a beer with ourselves because ... we don't want to be getting stereotyped. We're the ones doing this and the ones stuffing up. We're actually here on time, we're doing all the right things that everyone else is doing. But we slip up once, we're the ones that are judged on it. No one else is. (Senior Indigenous player)

In a similar way, a non-Indigenous player reflects on the role that Indigenous players play in challenging stereotypes and institutional racism:

> There are still some pretty deep-seeded issues, with the Stolen Generation. I think politicians have tried to put a few band-aids over massive wounds and expect everything to be okay but, we're talking about massive problems here. Problems that are bigger than our game, but I have no doubt that if Adam [Goodes] gets treated respectfully then what is it that change[s]? Is it the fact that he's wiser, because he's achieved a certain level … because he can kick a piece of leather a long way? Is it because he's one of the most revered footballers of his time or is it because he shows empathy to people and he embraces other peoples cultures as well? I don't have the answer to that. (Senior non-Indigenous player)

Junior football

One of the ways this could be understood further was the reaction of the players when they viewed the footage of Collingwood premiership player Heritier Lumumba (formerly named Harry O'Brien) who recalled how he was vilified in a junior football match in Perth. Lumumba discussed how he left the field and did not want to participate in football any more. He was counselled by his father on how to deal with racial abuse from opponents, with Lumumba stating that his father said, 'No matter what people say, they can't stop you from achieving'. The question was asked: 'How could Harry have responded to racial abuse?' The vast majority of players (90%) replied he had good advice from his father, he could have gone to the coach or umpire to voice his concerns or he could have reacted violently. This reply best summed up these sentiments:

> Oh he could have had a lot of different reactions, a violent reaction. Obviously he chose to walk off the footy field. The best is to just keep playing and ignore it all together or perhaps point it out to an adult or his Dad probably chatted to him about it. It sounds like he learned a valuable lesson and, and yeah, it was a good story I thought. (AFL non-Indigenous Captain)

The remainder of the answers from the player cohort (10%) was more insightful: that the chances of Heretier not continuing and leaving the sport for good were quite possible.

> Harry could have easily, aggressively responded or he could have stopped playing footy and we wouldn't be seeing him at Collingwood. (Senior non-Indigenous player)

The question that this type of response raises is how many players have walked away from AFL football at junior levels because the level of racial abuse was too much? It is a question we and the AFL do not have an answer for.

Many Indigenous players reflected on the Lumumba story stating that they were surprised that he did not respond with violence and that it took a lot of self-restraint, while others discussed what the story said about Australian culture:

> Definitely if they get away with it there, they're going to keep doing it and doing it until someone puts a stop to it and even [if] they're doing it at 10 [years of age] you stop it there and maybe when they're 15, 16 they don't do it anymore. Whereas you let it go from when they're 10 and carry it through to their teens and then they turn into men, and men can be pretty stubborn and don't want to listen to anyone. They carry it for the rest of their lives I reckon. That's how some people are. (Indigenous player)

> I think that education's the key. I think the times that I've been vilified and I talk to the people about what they're saying and how it affects me. They've got no idea, in their mind, how it has affected the person they're calling names or vilifying. I've got no doubt those kids in under 10s don't even know what the words would have meant that they were calling out to Harry but obviously they were told by their coach or their family members to say that to get Harry off his game, 'cos he was a good player. I think that for anyone who does look different or has different beliefs, you know from a certain young age that you are different and unfortunately, in this

country, you put up with a lot of crap. With the vilification code, with our organisation (AFL), what we're trying to do, we're able to fight back and say, 'Enough's enough'. (Indigenous player)

Clubs

During the research, issues about responsibility regarding cross-cultural education were broached. For example, when the players were asked to discuss whether they thought their club was doing enough to create a culturally inclusive and diverse environment, many participants considered it a responsibility of the Indigenous players rather than the responsibility of the non-Indigenous members of the playing group and the club as a whole. Further to this, having Indigenous footballers playing within a team was seen to equate to a more tolerant team/club. For some though, it is not just the presence but also the significance of interaction that was important.

> I think just what the Indigenous guys do, do for themselves is just the best education you can have because they're the best blokes you'd ever meet. (Non-Indigenous rookie player)

> No we're pretty good here .... The Indigenous boys here are pretty good footballers so they, they go through fine. There's no real casualties – if there's clashes with them, it's more personality clashes rather than the fact that they're Indigenous. So there's no racism at all. (Non-Indigenous senior player)

To put this quote in context, an Indigenous player from the same club commented about the cultural awareness of the non-Indigenous players at the club, his teammates:

> I think they [team mates] just sort of worry about it when like the AFLPA and that comes in and talks about it. And then after that I don't think they take much notice. I reckon if we Aboriginal boys told them our stories to them they'd have a freak out a bit. But we don't really talk about it that much. I reckon if they hear it from their own players, from us our experiences that might sort of flick the switch and they might, you know, take more notice of what goes on. (Indigenous senior player)

Conclusion

To conclude, the issues around race and ethnicity, difference and diversity, multiculturalism and reconciliation are things that each club that participated in the project has had to deal with over time and in accordance with the AFL and the AFLPA. Some clubs were better at understanding these things than other clubs for a variety of reasons. Some had younger cohorts of Indigenous players who were still feeling their way and did not fully understand the power of their agency. Conversely, other clubs had very strong and seasoned Indigenous players who were respected members of the club – so their opinions around cross-cultural matters were taken seriously. Others had coaching groups that, while supportive, were under great pressure, making issues associated with Rule 35 not central to team success. For other clubs, racial and ethnic respect was crucial to team unity and on-field success. What was clear is that these are not easy issues to try to address in any organization, sporting or otherwise, because they require individuals to take carriage of complex, ever-changing issues that require constant vigilance, often in the face of great pressure and often with limited resources and time.

The conclusions from the project are these:

- All players understand that vilification of other players is wrong.
- Clubs are highly variable and individual, which create complexity regarding issues of dealing with players of difference.
- Issues regarding nuanced and casual racism are still not deeply understood by the majority of players.

- Understandings of reconciliation and multiculturalism by the players are generally not very sophisticated.
- Indigenous players felt more marginalized from their clubs than their non-Indigenous team-mates.
- Agency to exact club change is not fully understood by Indigenous players.
- Teams with senior players with progressive views were more understanding around issues of diversity and difference.
- Masculinity issues at clubs are variable.
- More longitudinal data need to be gathered.

Disclosure statement

No potential conflict of interest was reported by the authors.

Notes

1. For instance, by the players and clubs.
2. By 'informed consent' we mean that we provided participants with information sheets about the purpose of the research, the sorts of questions that would be asked and how we would publicize the results of their information. We also answered any questions that participants had prior to research commencing so that people were aware of what they were committing to before the research began.
3. Breaking this confidentiality would be akin to a doctor talking to the media about a patient without the patient's consent. It would be both unethical and unprofessional.
4. Older, more experienced players often have different programmes or other commitments and so on occasions at some clubs they were unavailable for the survey. We did, however, get many of these players to participate in an interview.
5. While Rule 35 is primarily for the players, and that is the focus of the book, of course Collingwood President Eddie Maguire's comments came under Rule 35. We shall conduct other analyses elsewhere.
6. Unfortunately, the audio recording for one player was of insufficient quality to be clearly audible, and so his interview was not analysed.
7. For the technically minded, we used multiple linear regression for these analyses.
8. For the technically minded, we use ANOVA to compare clubs, with post hoc tests to examine between which clubs the differences lie.
9. There were some minor differences on these attributes, but due to issues of identifiability at the club level, we have not listed them here.
10. The exponential random graph models (ERGMs) that we mentioned earlier have the capacity to delineate network self-organization effects from the effects related to the attributes of individuals within the network (known as actor-relation, or actor attribute, effects).
11. These models were developed by Frank and Strauss 1986; Wasserman and Pattison 1996; Robins, Elliott, and Pattison 2001a, 2001b; Robins, Pattison, and Wang 2009; Snijders 2011; among others.
12. In the field of social networks, these are commonly asked network questions, more generally too, in organizations, schools or communities, because they represent important social ties that people have.
13. Casual or nuanced racism could be defined as a joke or an off the cuff comment not intended to offend. See Eddie McGuire story (Tim Soutphommasane opinion editorial).

References

Bavelas, A. 1950. "Communication Patterns in Task-Oriented Groups." *Journal of the Acoustical Society of America* 22 (6): 723–730.
Emirbayer, M., and J. Goodwin. 1994. "Network Analysis, Culture, and the Problem of Agency." *American Journal of Sociology* 99 (6): 1411–1454.

Frank, O., and D. Strauss. 1986. "Markov Graphs." *Journal of the American Statistical Association* 81 (395): 832–842.

Freeman, L. C. 1977. "Set of Measures of Centrality Based on Betweenness." *Sociometry* 40 (1): 35–41.

Freeman, L. C. 1979. "Centrality in Social Networks Conceptual Clarification." *Social Networks* 1 (3): 215–239.

Lusher, D., and R. Ackland. 2011. "A Relational Hyperlink Analysis of an Online Social Movement." *Journal of Social Structure* 12 (4). http://www.cmu.edu/joss/content/articles/volume12/Lusher/

Lusher, D., J. Koskinen, and G. Robins. 2013. *Exponential Random Graph Models for Social Networks: Theory, Methods and Applications*. New York: Cambridge University Press.

Robins, G. L., P. Elliott, and P. E. Pattison. 2001a. "Network Models for Social Selection Processes." *Social Networks* 23: 1–30.

Robins, G. L., P. E. Pattison, and P. Elliott. 2001b. "Network Models for Social Influence Processes." *Psychometrika* 66: 161–190.

Robins, G., P. Pattison, Y. Kalish, and D. Lusher. 2007. "An Introduction to Exponential Random Graph (p*) Models for Social Networks." *Social Networks* 29: 173–191.

Robins, G., P. Pattison, and P. Wang. 2009. "Closure, Connectivity and Degrees: New Specifications for Exponential Random Graph (p*) Models for Directed Social Networks." *Social Networks* 31: 105–117.

Robins, G. L., P. E. Pattison, and S. Wasserman. 1999. "Logit Models and Logistic Regressions for Social Networks, III, Valued Relations." *Psychometrika* 64: 371–394.

Snijders, T. A. B. 2011. "Statistical Models for Social Networks." *Annual Review of Sociology* 37 (1): 131–153. doi:10.1146/annurev.soc.012809.102709

Wasserman, S., and K. Faust. 1994. *Social Network Analysis: Methods and Applications*. 8th ed. Cambridge: Cambridge University Press.

Wasserman, S., and P. E. Pattison. 1996. "Logit Models and Logistic Regressions for Social Networks: I. An Introduction to Markov Graphs and p*." *Psychometrika* 651: 401–425.

Appendix 1. Example survey questions

For the survey, we asked questions that centred on a range of themes that we have put into subtitles below, with specific example questions listed underneath. We have not included all questions for each theme, but rather examples questions that were asked. We used a combination of factor analysis and reliability analysis in determining the themes and the items within them, collating an average score across the items for theme which were then used in the standard statistical tests and statistical network models.

Network questions

- Who are your closest friends at the club?
- Which people at this club do you have different views or opinions to?
- Which people do you most socialize with after hours?
- Who do you trust most at this club?
- Who are the funniest people at the club?
- Who do you think sets club culture at the club?

Racism

There were a range of questions asked about racism which are collated into the following themes. Notably, opinions were separated into pro- and anti-Indigenous attitudes, which indicate that not being positive about Indigenous people is different to negative towards them.

Pro-Indigenous attitudes
- Discrimination against Aboriginal Australians is no longer a problem in Australia (reverse scored).
- Indigenous Australians are disadvantaged on a range of issues, including lifespan, jobs, education and housing.

Anti-Indigenous attitudes
- Aboriginal Australians receive more welfare money from government agencies than other Australians.
- Aboriginal Australians are getting too demanding in their push for land rights.

Biological essentialism
To a large extent, a person's race biologically determines their abilities and traits.

Positive attitudes towards Indigenous AFL players
- Indigenous players train hard.
- Indigenous players in this team are respected like anyone else.

Club support

Club support and inclusiveness
In these questions, we asked what the club does for its members. We also asked how accepted the participant feels at the club.

- My opinion doesn't count for much.
- I feel isolated because of my opinions.
- I feel comfortable at the club.

Club understanding its players
- The club understands my needs.
- The club needs to get better at dealing with players as individuals.
- The club works well together.

Masculinity

In this section, we asked about homophobia, endorsement of violence, anti-femininity and playboy attitudes.

Homophobia
- I am accepting of gay men.
- Gays males sicken me because they are not real men.

Endorsing violence
- It's natural for men to get into fights.
- A man should force the issue if another man takes his parking place.

Strict gender roles
- It is OK for a man to cry in public.
- A woman should expect to do most of the childcare.

Playboy attitudes
- A real man can get any woman to have sex with him.
- Some women are only good for one thing.

Other

There were a number of other themes that we analysed.

Knowledge of Rule 35
- Who was the main catalyst of Rule 35?
    2.1. Chris Lewis
    2.2. Jim Stynes
    2.3. Michael Long
    2.4. Nicky Winmar

AFL as a successful multicultural organization
- The AFL has stamped out racism in the game.
- The AFL truly recognizes multiculturalism.

Religious acceptance
- I feel free to practise my faith/spirituality at the club.
- I am comfortable talking about my faith/spirituality with my teammates.

Family inclusiveness
- My family feels comfortable participating in club functions.

Appendix 2. Technical details and SNA methods

Statistical network models

In this appendix, we provide more detailed technical notes for those interested in how we conducted the statistical analysis of the social network data collected for each of the nine clubs. We applied a particular class of statistical model for social networks called exponential random graph models (ERGM). Originally developed by Frank and Strauss (1986), Robins, Pattison, and Wasserman (1999), and Wasserman and Pattison (1996), these models represent the cutting edge of network tools by which to analyse social networks. Given their ability take into account dependencies of social relations, rather than assume independent observations as standard statistical tests do, ERGMs are seen as the analysis method of choice for cross-sectional network (and thus relational) data (Snijders 2011). For a general introduction to ERGMs, see Robins et al. (2007) and Lusher, Koskinen, and Robins (2013).

ERGMs permit us to test hypotheses about the formation of social hierarchy within teams, including inferences about whether structural effects (e.g. reciprocated relationships) or attribute effects (e.g. player attitudes) are important determinants of hierarchy. These models simplify the analysis of complex social systems, permitting a statistical examination of competing hypotheses about why social ties occur, for instance, or if negative social relations generally occur due to issues of race or are related to other personal or purely structural factors. Models with the ability to include both social network structures and individual-level characteristics have been developed by researchers associated with this Australian Research Council research project (Robins, Elliott, and Pattison 2001a, 2001b). These models enable the simultaneous exploration of social hierarchy, norms, identity, attitudes, player ability, experience and background to see which are important within each team.

Importantly, ERGMs can delineate purely structural network effects from actor-relation effects, as we noted in this paper. That is, some network ties form because of the presence of other network ties. An example is that of reciprocity. I may reciprocate buying you a coffee because you have bought me one in the past, so one tie results because of the other (and this happens over time – one tie happens first, then another occurs because of the first one). Another example of a purely structural network effect is the idea that *a friend of a friend is a friend*. We often introduce one friend to another, and they may then become friends too. As such, it is because we are friends with two different people that they end up becoming friends too. For each network that was analysed, the purely structural network effects of Table A1 (effects 1–8) represent that standard inclusion of effects in our statistical network models, though on some occasions other parameters were also required (as one network can have quite different features to another).

In contrast, sometimes network ties (i.e. social relations) come about due to the attribute of people in those networks. As noted in this paper, people in networks can be popular due to a specific attribute (see effect 11 – the receiver effect in Table A1). Alternatively, people with certain attributes may be more active than others, which is a sender effect (effect 10 in Table A1). Finally, people might select others with similar attributes, which is a similarity (or homophily) effect (see effect 9 in Table A1). We note that for each attribute of a person in the network (e.g. playing ability, AFL experience, pro-Indigenous attitudes, etc.) we include a sender, a receiver and a homophily effect to see how the attributes may relate in different ways to social ties.

As noted, it is the actor-relation effects that are the main focus of this book because we are interested in the ways that social ties result from and thus are associated with the attributes of people in the network. However, it is critical to note that we must include purely structural effects when trying to understand whether actor-relation effects are important. If you do not control for purely structural network effects (otherwise known as network self-organization) then effects regarding the attributes of actors may be overestimated and spurious (Lusher and Ackland 2011). That is, to be sure that network ties have resulted because of attributes of the people in the network, it is absolutely

Table A1. Summary table of purely structural effects and actor-relation effects for statistical network models (ERGMs).

	Effect name	Visualization	Meaning
Purely structural network effects			
1	Arc		Baseline tendency for an advice tie to occur
2	Reciprocity		Tendency toward reciprocation
3	Simple connectivity		Tendency for a simple two-path to connect actors
4	Popularity spread		Tendency for variation in the degree to which an actor receives multiple advice tie nominations
5	Activity spread		Tendency for variation in the degree to which an actor expresses multiple advice ties
6	Transitive closure		Tendency for transitive closure to occur
7	Cyclic closure		Tendency for multiple cyclic structures to occur
8	Multiple connectivity		Tendency for transitive multiple connectivity
Actor-relation effects			
9	Homophily		Tendency for network ties to occur between actors who are similar with respect to an attribute
10	Sender		Tendency for actors with a specific attribute (which may be continuous, categorical or binary) to express network ties
11	Receiver		Tendency for actors with a specific attribute (which may be continuous, categorical or binary) to receive network ties

Table A2.   ERGM estimation results for the trust network for Club Abacus.

Effects	Estimates	Std. err.	t-ratio	
Arc	− 3.04895	1.28303	0.03507	*
Reciprocity	3.368418	0.57617	− 0.02503	*
Simple connectivity (two-path)	− 0.75407	0.66725	0.02401	
Popularity spread (AinS)	0.387807	0.27782	0.02327	
Activity spread (AoutS)	0.043535	0.30807	0.01068	
Transitive closure (AT-T)	0.98097	0.30579	− 0.06612	*
Cyclic closure (AT-C)	− 0.19942	0.2996	− 0.04026	
Multiple connectivity (A2P-T)	0.427473	0.69721	0.02156	
Studying (homophily)	− 0.11139	0.42497	0.0087	
Studying (sender)	0.185051	0.31951	− 0.00194	
Studying (receiver)	0.225854	0.31924	0.01139	
AFL Experience (homophily)	− 0.01192	0.00314	0.05339	*
AFL Experience (sender)	− 0.00193	0.00321	− 0.03863	
AFL Experience (receiver)	0.00783	0.00303	0.05484	*
Pro-Indigenous (homophily)	0.08614	0.10449	− 0.0209	
Pro-Indigenous (sender)	0.044304	0.10302	0.04251	
Pro-Indigenous (receiver)	− 0.06668	0.08866	0.01321	
Anti-Indigenous (homophily)	− 0.07304	0.10264	− 0.05399	
Anti-Indigenous (sender)	− 0.15277	0.09237	0.03439	
Anti-Indigenous (receiver)	0.017777	0.10499	0.03391	
Best player (covariate arc)	1.607391	0.32838	0.06636	*

essential that network self-organization is controlled for otherwise the actor-relation effects may be entirely misleading. The ability of ERGMs to control for network self-organization make them cutting-edge models and the most principled of statistical network models to analyse social network data (Lusher, Koskinen, and Robins 2013).

Network analysis using exponential random graph models (ERGM)

Table A2 represents the output of an ERGM of one particular network, which is an analysis of trust relations in a team. In the analysis, we estimate a model – that is we try to understand the processes by which ties came about in the network by seeing is certain network effects occur more (or less) than we would expect by chance. First, we check that all *t*-ratios for all effects included in the model are <0.1, which in Table A2 we can see is the case for effects. This tells us the mode has converged, or in other words, that the analysis has produced stable parameter estimates that make us confident that the model of the data is a good one.

For if we want to know if an effect is significant, and thus what is driving network ties to form, we compare the estimate with the *standard error (std. err.)*. If the *estimate* is more than double the *standard error* then the effect is significant (which we denote with an '*'). In Table A2, the *arc* effect is negative and significant, which means that we see few isolated ties in our network. However, the *reciprocity* effect is significant and positive which means that we see many more mutual ties than we expect by chance. We also have a significant and positive effect for transitive closure in this trust network, which means that there are many triangles in the network (or many instances of *a friend of a friend is a friend*).

For actor-relation effects the interpretation is slightly different. There is a significant and negative homophily effect for AFL (for continuous attributes, this is actually a *difference* effect) and so what this means is that trust ties are more likely to occur between people who are similar (or have less of a difference in their attributes, and thus a negative difference) in AFL experience. There is a significant and positive receiver effect for AFL experience too, meaning that players high in experience are more likely to receive trust ties (i.e. players high in AFL experience are more likely to be trusted). There are no significant effects related to positive or negative attitudes towards

Indigenous Australians. Finally, there is a significant and positive Best Player covariate effect, which means that people tend to trust people they also nominate as best players (i.e. if I think you are one of the best players in the team then I also trust you).

Table A2 shows one analysis only of trust within a single team. We also ran other analyses regarding trust within the same team but including masculinity attitudes, and then another analysis looking at multiculturalism and so on for a number of issues we were interested in looking at. We could not include all of the issues in a single analysis of trust for one team because there are simply just too many variables and it is difficult to make sense of. However, every analysis of a network we did for a team included all of the *purely structural network effects*, plus also effects controlling for *AFL experience* and also for *playing ability*. We include ability and experience because we expect that they are both important individual-level attributes within a team that will shape who interacts with who, and indeed we find pretty consistently in the analyses that both ability and experience are significant predictors of why people have ties to other players in teams. By controlling for ability and experience (on top of also controlling for purely structural network effects) means that we have great confidence that any effects we find for racism or masculinity or other issues occur above and beyond other explanations, and are indeed legitimate explanations regarding why players interact.

This technical detail may indeed beyond what many readers may want to know. However, those interested in understanding more about the cutting edge and highly principled nature of these network models should consult a detailed book on exponential random graph models by Lusher, Koskinen, and Robins (2013) which may further assist in understanding these models.

Appendix 3. Example interview questions

General Questions

- Where are you from/where did you grow up?
- How would you describe your family background (class, socially, culturally, religious?)
- What was the suburb/town like that you grew up in?
- Did you have any interactions with people from Indigenous or multicultural backgrounds growing up?
- What were those relationships like?
- Did you attend school locally or did you board?
- How would you describe your school experiences?
- What were your favourite subjects?
- What year did you go to?

General football questions

- What was your first experience of football/first football memory?
- When did you first start becoming interested in football?
- Why was this the case?
- How important was football in your childhood?
- Why was it important?
- Was there a significant figure in your junior football?
- Did you have other interests?
- Did you play other sports?
- Why did you concentrate on football?
- In your experience what role did football play in your community/suburb/town?
- If you did not pursue football as a career what would you have liked to have concentrated on?
- Are you aware or can you recall any issues around vilification at a junior level?

Chris Lilley

http://www.youtube.com/watch?v=xKK71W3Ft78

- What are some of the justifications that Jonah uses to call Ben names?
- What is the teacher trying to get Jonah to do you think?

- Do you see any parallels with the footage and the way the AFL have tried to deal with issues around race, ethnicity, religion, women?

The Australian sports commission 'Australian Football – a game for all'

http://www.ausport.gov.au/participating/all_cultures/resources/videos/Australian_Football_-_A_Game_for_all

- What do you think are the main points to Harry O'Brien's story? (Skin colour, identity, food, accent, discrimination, difference).
- What could have been some of the other reactions from Harry? (Violence, abuse, retaliation).
- Why did he not react in another way do you think?
- Do you think that intolerance of any kind can have long lasting consequences or is it just a something people grow out of or get over?

Vilification questions

- We all saw the Sherman suspension earlier this year/last year. What was your reaction when you heard about it? (13 years since the last report – Justin Shermin/Joel Wilkinson)
- Has the AFL done enough to educate players about this?

Past players

- Do you recall the vilification rules coming in 1995?
- What are your recollections of it?
- How did your teammates react?
- Do you think the vilification rules changed the game at all?
- How prominent was vilification before the rules were brought in?
- What are your recollections of it?

Current players

- In terms of vilification what is the hardest thing you have ever heard directed at yourself or a teammate? Where did you hear it? How did it make you feel?
- What things has the club done to engage the players about the vilification rules that are in place?
- Do the rules ever come up in general conversation or only in professional development meetings?

AFL

- Do you think the AFL should play a role in teaching players/coaches about tolerance and prejudice or should it happen in other areas? Where?
- Have there been any issues that you are aware of at your club that the vilification laws have helped deal with?
- Are there ways that you think the vilification rules could be improved?
- Do you think that the vilification rules have meant that more Indigenous and multicultural players are a part of the game? Why?
- Do you think players try and take the ideas behind the vilification rules into other aspects of their lives? How?

Sri Lankan Tour – united we stand

http://www.youtube.com/watch?v=8vZgXglhWoI

- What do you think of the point Adam Goodes makes that he is treated differently to his family?
- What do you think of Brett Kirk's comments on reconciliation in Australia.

- What does the word reconciliation mean to you?
- Are issues of race and racism the same for all ethnic minorities or different for different minorities?

Comments required

It's a business out there, I'd make a racist comment every week if I thought it would help win a game … If they're [Indigenous players] going to get upset by taunts then they shouldn't be playing. We're men not kids. It's no different calling a bloke a black bastard than him calling me a white honky and it only lasts as long as the game. (*The Sunday Age*, August 25, 1991, p. 6)

- What do think about this comment?
- Do you agree that to call someone a 'black bastard is the same as calling someone a 'white honky'?

Get the interviewees to respond to the footage

Mark Maclure
http://www.abc.net.au/mediawatch/transcripts/s2895225.htm

- Was Mark McLure justified in making the comments that 'they ran like they stole something'?
- What was his point do you think?
- Could it (the comment) be seen as offensive? Why?
- Do you think it was offensive or harmless? (Was it a joke).
- Do you have anything to add?

Abacus Football Club

Sean Gorman, Dean Lusher and Keir Reeves

> The Abacus football club is an AFL club that participated in this Australian Research Council project Assessing the Australian Football League's Racial and Religious Vilification Laws to promote Community Harmony, Multiculturalism and Reconciliation. Abacus participated in both the surveys and the interviews. This club and its players and staff have all been deidentified as required by Curtin University's ethics guidelines.

The people at Abacus Football Club

At the Abacus Football Club, the vast majority of players[1] and a number coaching/associated staff fully completed the survey.[2] Nineteen of these individuals also took part in interviews. The dominant religion was Catholic (26%) and the dominant culture was Anglo-Australian (823%). Outside of the AFL, the majority of players were either studying at university (35%) or not working or studying at all (35%); almost all players (91%) had completed secondary schooling.

On measures of feeling comfortable and included at the club, there were no differences between Indigenous and non-Indigenous players, meaning both cohorts felt equally comfortable and included. On the players' knowledge of Rule 35,[3] the majority of players (69%) were neither able to articulate the rule as it is currently stood, or identify who brought it about.[4] Only 5% answered both questions correctly. There were no differences in knowledge of Rule 35 between Indigenous and non-Indigenous players.

Club engagement

The research team received strong support from the player development manager at the Abacus Football Club. The research team felt that there was strong professionalism around the club.[5] There was significant maturity displayed by the Abacus players in filling out this survey. Notably, the senior coach and several assistant coaches were involved in the survey as well. This translated into a modicum of interest by the senior coach who enquired about the availability of the results and commented generally about the value of, and interest in, the survey. As outsiders to the club, we were impressed by the way players, coaches and staff went about helping us with the research project. Overwhelmingly, our feeling of this club was that we were taken seriously, shown respect and that people gave considered answers.

Networks and club cultures

To examine the networks within the club, we used statistical models for social networks mentioned in paper "Overarching findings" (doi: 10.1080/17430437.2014.1002974, in this collection), and explained in detail in Appendix 2 in that paper. These statistical network models analyse network data amongst the players within the Abacus Football Club. We limited our network analysis to players (as we do in all following papers (in this collection) about clubs), as the induction and education programmes around the AFL's Rule 35 are specific to players.

Sets culture network: self-awareness of social influences

At the Abacus Football Club, the players who set the culture (i.e. those players who are popular selections by other players as indicated by the SNA survey) are unsurprisingly those players with greater experience as measured by AFL games played. There is also a similarity effect whereby players choose others with similar experience to themselves as players who set the culture. Furthermore, players high in ability (i.e. best players) are chosen as players who set the culture of team. As seems to be common with all of the clubs we have surveyed, these two characteristics – player ability and player experience – are important criteria when determining who sets the culture of a club. It makes sense that players high in ability are seen as prominent and important because they have high playing 'capital' that relates to the key team objective of winning games. Along this line, players with significant experience are more likely to be valued because experience is deemed a valued commodity when it comes to elite sport. Across the range of networks examined within the Abacus Football Club, experience and ability are not universally valued in every network we investigated but these two factors occur so frequently that we argue that they are highly important player-level characteristics. This makes sense and ties in with our experience of clubs and stories by players about having agency only when they are playing well or are established players at the club. This finding that player ability and experience are highly valued gives us confidence that the data we have collected reflect the reality of what generally occurs within AFL teams.

There are other results of interest for the Abacus Football Club about who sets the culture. What the results indicate is that players who set the culture are not homophobic, but believe that others in the team are homophobic. Additionally, players who set the culture are also more likely to endorse pro-violence views of masculinity (i.e. that it is natural and right for men to use violence). Again, given that controlled aggression is part of the game, this is perhaps unsurprising.

There are no effects on who sets the culture in relation to attitudes towards Indigenous Australians, which means that these 'culture setting' players do not strongly endorse or dis-endorse positive (or negative) attitudes towards Indigenous Australians. This is both for attitudes towards Indigenous Australians generally and towards Indigenous players in the team specifically (e.g. Indigenous players train hard, Indigenous players in this team are respected like anyone else). This means that Indigenous players are not viewed any differently from anyone else by the players who set the culture at Abacus FC. Indigenous players themselves do not feature as culture-setting players within the team.

Furthermore, players at the Abacus Football Club who set the culture are those who are more likely to endorse the club as a family-inclusive environment. Finally, for 'culture setting' views on the AFL's success at achieving multiculturalism and ethnic equality, players see those who set the culture as having very different views from themselves on these issues. Together, this suggests some contestation in the team around how effective the players think the AFL is doing in regards to multiculturalism, and that players are aware of this tension regarding culture setting in the club.

Friendship, trust and afterhours: informal, unspoken social influences

Within the Abacus Football Club, in all three networks – friend, trust and afterhours – best players are more likely to be selected than others, and this is unsurprising. The results for experience were slightly different, such that players high in experience were more likely to be trusted, but neither more nor less popular as friends or popular as people to socialize with afterhours. However, in all three networks, players selected others of similar experience to themselves as friends, people they trusted and people they socialized with.

Beyond these expected effects for friendship, trust and afterhours socializing, we find the following. For all three networks, Indigenous players at the Abacus Football Club are much more likely to be friends with, trust and socialize with other Indigenous players.

The majority of Indigenous players within the team are almost completely separated from the non-Indigenous players in the team, with one non-Indigenous player saying that he socializes with one of these Indigenous players, although his view about socializing is not reciprocated. That is, the Indigenous player who is nominated as someone to socialize with afterhours does not nominate the other player in return, which indicates differing perceptions about whether they do, in fact, socialize with one another. (Such differences about ties are quite common in social networks.) When we look at trust within Abacus FC, we note that the separation of Indigenous players is more pronounced, with a number of Indigenous players mutually trusting one another and completely separated from all other players (i.e. they are not selected as people who are trusted by any of the non-Indigenous players). Additionally, one Indigenous player was nominated by many non-Indigenous players as someone with whom they socialize afterhours, but he was nominated by only one other player as someone to be trusted.

We could view the above results regarding the position of Indigenous players in the afterhours, friendship and trust networks as a failure of non-Indigenous players to make Indigenous players feel welcome, or we could see it as a success in that Indigenous players are providing strong social support to one another. We do not necessarily see this as a good or bad thing. Perhaps coupled with lack of effects regarding the importance of pro or anti attitudes towards Indigenous Australians, we suggest that it might not be an issue, but more simply that people with similar social, cultural and racial commonalities tend to congregate together. The fact that we also see, in all clubs, that players with similar levels of experience are more likely to congregate with one another points to the issue of similarity breeding familiarity, or put another way, *birds of a feather flock together* (McPherson, Smith-Lovin, and Cook 2001).

Importantly though, Indigenous players, like non-Indigenous players, are varied and different people; some are more sociable than others, some have complex issues; some are very adept at crossing cultural boundaries; some are more experienced or older, or higher in playing ability than others. While these results in the network diagrams are interesting, we do not over-analyse them because we know that it is not just being Indigenous that explains everything about that person. Our network models (see Appendix 2 in paper "Overarching findings" (doi: 10.1080/17430437.2014.1002974, in this collection), for methodological details), which look at the overarching patterns of why people socialize with one another, are able to take into account the whole gamut of explanations and provide better insights into how all of these factors operate. Nonetheless, the networks are interesting and informative when considering how certain individuals are included or excluded in the networks we are looking at, and thus how they are connected within the club.

There are several other things to note. Players who are very active in the friendship network (that is who choose or nominate many others as their friends, although they may not necessarily have these nominations reciprocated) are more likely to see the club as a family-inclusive environment. With regard to trust, in addition to the aforementioned effects, players who are most trusted are those who think that most others in the club endorse playboy masculinity attitudes. So players who are trusted do not necessarily personally endorse such playboy views, but they think that most other players do. This may reflect that players who are trusted may be privy to stories from others who 'trust them' around such playboy issues and associated behaviours. However, this may also reflect that trusted players are older (we noted before that trusted players are more experienced, and experience and age are highly correlated).

What is generally absent are players being popular choices as friends, as people who are trusted, or as people to socialize with as having pro- or anti-Indigenous attitudes. What this means is that the attitudes players hold towards Indigenous Australians (whether that be players or Indigenous Australians more generally) are unrelated to who they choose as friends, trust or socialize with. The only effect is that for afterhours socializing: players who nominate many others as friends (but who are not necessarily nominated in return) are more likely to hold beliefs that are positive about Indigenous players in the AFL (e.g. Indigenous players in this team are respected like anyone else).

Difference of opinion network and funny network: contested boundaries

Our results for Abacus FC show that players of greater experience are those with whom the team had a difference of opinion. This is likely to reflect the fact that more senior players might see their role to provide a guiding hand in how things are done in the club. Evidence for this is that more senior players are seen as setting the culture of the club, as noted previously in this paper. One final result for this network is that players are more likely to select others who believe their religion is accepted within the club as people they have differences of opinion with. This may suggest that some players see that they can express their religion freely, though other players may not like them to.

For the network that identifies who the funniest people at the club are, players of high ability are highly nominated at Abacus FC. This may reflect the fact that high ability players now feel enabled (or have the agency) to speak their mind and can 'hold an audience', and/ or that players think they are funny because they are good players, or possibly the fact that they are just funny. Other effects we observed were that players thought that players who were considered funny had similar anti-Indigenous attitudes to themselves. This means that players who are strongly anti-Indigenous think other players who are strongly anti-Indigenous are funny, and also that players who score very low on anti-Indigenous attitudes (i.e. they have a high regard for Indigenous people) think other players who score very low on anti-Indigenous attitudes are funny. So players see others players with similar Indigenous views to themselves as funny. An equivalent similarity effect holds for perceptions of the AFL's success in dealing with multiculturalism. Notably, more senior players were neither more nor less likely to be chosen as players who are funny.

Summary of social networks

The player networks at the Abacus Football Club suggest that Indigenous players within the team keep together mostly. There appears to be no overt racism in the club, such as having popular players endorsing anti-Indigenous sentiments. But likewise, popular players do not endorse pro-Indigenous views either. Regarding differences of opinion, players do not appear to disagree about attitudes towards Indigenous Australians, nor do they disagree with respect to homophobia or other masculinity issues. Yet players who are most trusted perceive that most players in their club are pro-playboy, which may simply reflect an age effect for playboy attitudes (which usually decrease over time) or that these trusted players are confidantes of information about playboy activities.

Yet there are subtle markers that negative attitudes towards Indigenous Australians are present, as noted by the similarity effects in the humour network on such views. This suggests that the type of humour employed within the team might include issues of race and ethnicity. Furthermore, differences in views on perceptions of the AFL's success in dealing with multiculturalism with regards to who sets the club culture also suggest that these are issues of prominence at the club. In all, the network data reveal that there are no overt significant issues of race at this club (i.e. there is *not* a culture of racism), but that there are subtle issues regarding race and ethnicity, and less so homophobia. As noted in paper "Overarching findings" (doi: 10.1080/17430437.2014.1002974, in this collection), the fact that Abacus FC scored significantly lower overall compared to other clubs for questions such as 'Indigenous players train hard' and significantly higher than one club for 'Aboriginal Australians receive more welfare money from government agencies than other Australians' suggests that issues of race are present here that are not in some other clubs.

Interview data

Twenty-two interviews were conducted at the Abacus Football Club. Twenty of these were with the players, including the captain and senior players, middle-tier players and rookies. The remaining two interviews were conducted with the senior coach and his assistant. We would have liked to have interviewed more players but this was logistically difficult, given training commitments and core club activities that the players needed to participate in. Of the players interviewed, three were Indigenous[6].

Given that the SNA provided us with a map of the club's social and professional culture, we were able to pinpoint specific participants to provide a further qualitative layer of information that we could use to compare and contrast the SNA data with. The particular participants we wanted to interview were those players who the SNA identified as setting the Abacus Football Club's culture and those who were seen to have the least impact on it. We then used the coding from the encrypted NViVo database that housed the players and coaches interviews to look at their answers to specific questions we asked relating to a range of issues. This included a player's interactions with people from different racial, ethnic and multicultural backgrounds growing up, their views on the efficacy on Rule 35 in the attracting players from different social and racial backgrounds to play AFL football and two video clips.

The first clip involved Heritier Lumumba (formerly known as Harry O'Brien) of the Collingwood Football Club recounting his junior football experiences when he was vilified and nearly walked away from the game (Australian Sports Commission 2010). The second clip involved former Carlton captain and Australian Broadcasting Corporation (ABC) football commentator Mark Maclure, making a post-game joke about Indigenous players Jeff Garlett, Eddie Betts and Chris Yarran (Media Watch 2010). Garlett, Betts and Yarran were described as 'three little live-wire forwards', such was the impact of their collective games on the night in question. From here, Maclure suggested, due to their output for Carlton on this particular night, that they 'ran like they stole something'. It is worthwhile taking a look at these clips if you have not seen them because they give considerable context to the quotes presented below from the players and coaches. The rationale for choosing these clips was to give the players a chance to respond to examples of overt and everyday racism as well as that which is more nuanced and casual. It is our contention that the racism that Lumumba experienced as a junior footballer and nearly saw him cease playing AFL poses a significant question: how many other players from different racial or ethnic minorities have walked away from the game because the abuse was too much? Another question: how many potential players have chosen another football code or sport to play other than AFL for the same reasons? The answer to this is we will never know. The use of the Maclure clip is to show the ambiguity of casual racism, particularly as it is experienced in the media sphere; it harks back to the McGuire *King Kong* attempted gag. Both of these clips are very useful in determining the answer to a central question of this research: how effective has Rule 35 been in combating issues around racism and racial intolerance, not just in the game but everyday?

Abacus FC established players

Of the three players identified from the SNA as setting the culture at the Abacus Football Club, three players, P72,[7] P78 and P69, were interviewed. This included the captain, P72, the vice-captain, P69, and a senior player, P78. The experiences of growing up and being exposed to different cultures and racial minorities were very different for these three. Player P72 grew up in the country:

> I went to school with a couple of Aboriginal kids. Looking back now, there was certainly racial tension in the town. Sports [are an] important part of your upbringing as a child in rural areas, or it certainly was for me. There was very little crossover in terms of [who played with whom]: the white children, if you want to call them that, would play together, the Catholic kids would play their footy in school and the Aboriginal kids would play together. So there was that divide.

Player P69 grew up in a different state from that of the Abacus football club:

> We've always been exposed to [Aboriginal culture] and haven't treated them [Indigenous Australians] any different to anyone else.

Player P78's upbringing is best described as monocultural (i.e. urban, Anglo and middle-class).

When the players were asked to respond to the Lumumba/O'Brien clip, it was player P69 who provided the most insightful answer and what we would hope to be a preferred reading:

> From my perspective, our game would have been worse off [without him]. We've got one of the great ambassadors of the game that wouldn't be playing AFL footy. One of the great ambassadors for cultural diversity wouldn't be in our game right now because somebody at some stage taunted him about his race instead of embracing it.

Player P78's response was as follows:

> The kids probably saying it and doing it probably because they're scared, intimidated and are just jealous of his ability. Those kids probably don't understand the damage they can do.

Player P72 understood that experiencing racial abuse at that age can have long lasting consequences but did not comprehend or mention that it could curtail a junior aspiration to pursue a football career.

Interestingly, player P78 responded to the question regarding the importance of Rule 35 in attracting players from multicultural backgrounds that appears to be at odds with his response to Lumumba/O'Brien clip:

I'm not sure … [it is] just because of that (i.e. Rule 35). You'd like to hope that it's within schools. We are a multicultural country and a lot of people are taking up the game. It's the Australian game and hopefully it's because it's the most exciting game for kids to play and then they stay involved and they have good experiences through their teenage years and they go on with it.

Player P78's response of 'hopefully … they stay involved and they have good experiences through their teenage years and they go on with it' appears to be at odds with the hostile, racialized reaction to Lumumba's ability, and this might not constitute 'a good experience of the Australian game'. This is exactly where the potential fault lines are in junior and amateur levels. It is how the AFL deals with these things as they arise that will determine if someone stays or leaves the code.

When responding to the question, 'Are the AFL doing enough to educate players?', player P78 relates his answer back to the Justin Sherman incident:

I think they do, but you're always still going to get a handful of guys that will always be risk takers and cross the line because … because it's a heated battle. I'm sure Justin regrets it but that's still not an excuse.

Here we see the acknowledgement that Sherman transgressed with his comment to Wilkinson but there is the qualification; it was 'a heated battle'. Player P78 finally gives a begrudging acceptance that Sherman's action was wrong.

It was player P69 who gave the most insightful answer from the Abacus Football Club:

I have to say yes, I think there's a lot more equality. It's motivating for all communities to try and play AFL footy. I haven't played in any other sports overseas but I could comfortably sit here and say, in an educated way, that I couldn't imagine any other sport being as culturally diverse and as accepting of many different cultures and races and I think it's one of the best parts of our game.

After viewing the Maclure clip from the ABC that referred to Garlett, Betts and Yarran as running 'like they stole something', the senior, culture-setting players of the Abacus Football Club responded. Player P78 considered it a harmless joke:

Those individuals should have a strong enough character that they just fob it off. It's not an issue.

For player P72, there was a more nuanced reading:

I think clearly he's running with stereotypes there, linking Indigenous kids and theft together. That's my interpretation of it. I think it's clearly an unacceptable comment.

And player P69 saw it as a gag that was perhaps 'overcooked':

I think it's a bit like the Ranga[8] taunts that because more people talk about that aspect of it and you can justify saying it. It's just because more people are saying it. It doesn't mean that it's right.

These answers show a range of readings of the clip. Given the potential portent for offence to be taken, it is perhaps surprising that player P78 would suggest that the comment was 'not an issue'. It therefore depends where the player aligns with the main sub-themes of the clip and how they read them, given their upbringing, empathy and interaction with people from minorities, and if they find jokes like these 'funny'. Which poses another question: what are we laughing at? It could be argued that the humour from the clip is derived from the stereotype which may or may not make one laugh depending on how they read the clip.

Abacus FC fringe players

In order for us to make a better interpretation of this 'culture-setting' cohort, it is necessary that we look at the cohort at the other end of the spectrum to see if there is any significant variation. These players are the ones deemed by their peers to be the least likely to impact upon the culture setting of the club and are less likely to be nominated as friends. These players were P81, P80, IP73 and P84. It must be noted that all of these players are essentially fringe players. Further to this, during the data collection at the Abacus Football Club, player P80 was considered by himself and his teammates to have features that were considered somewhat 'exotic'.[9] Player P80 was, however, comfortable with the way he looked and the attention he received or any banter he experienced was not an issue for him.

The backgrounds of these players were varied. Player P81 grew up in another state from where the Abacus Football Club is located and had no interaction with Indigenous Australians but had a great deal of interaction with people from multicultural backgrounds. Both players P80 and P84 grew up in the metropolitan area where the club is located but only player P80 had interacted with Indigenous Australians, stating:

> Pretty much from a young age … I was mates with a couple of Aboriginal kids in the street. I've been around Aboriginal boys and stuff like that my whole life pretty much. (P80)

The Indigenous player, IP73, comes from a country town whereby he claims 'everybody knows everybody … It's pretty relaxed [&] you get on good'. Where things become interesting is the way a player from a multicultural background is viewed by player P81 in regard to the Lumumba/O'Brien clip:

> Some people are probably better at it [handling racism] than others. Some people [teammates] may say jokes you know to [multicultural teammate]. Sometimes he'll just go along with it and play along with it whereas it might hurt him deep down but he just gets good at dealing with and not reacting to it.

Player P80 is somewhat more conflicted, referring to his own features to add further context to the clip:

> It's pretty unfortunate that some little kid, especially at 10 or eleven years old, gets that … I think it's something that you could probably get over. If people might call me something I'll laugh it off or whatever. Like it happens a bit here but I mean it's not really an issue. I find it funny and I might be different to other people [whereas they] really might take it to heart.

For player P84, the connection was not made about the potential for a player who is racially targeted to potentially walk away from the game, whereas for player IP73, who is Indigenous, the markers of difference for him were not just in relation to skin colour but extended to the types of food one eats, which Lumumba/O'Brien discusses.

In regard to the Maclure clip, there was also a range of responses. Player P81 said:

> It's a bit of a light-hearted joke, but some people would take that more seriously than others obviously being Indigenous and I think it's a bit stereotyp[ical] to say that they all steal stuff and they run like they've stolen something. I guess that's a bit of a stereotype and not all Aboriginal/Indigenous people are like that, so it's a bit of a harsh thing to say, but some people take it worse than others.

Player P80 said:

> I suppose that's racist to an extent. That's sort of pigeon-holing them that, that they're sort of like thieves and things like that. He could have said so many different things then but he's probably chosen the wrong one. 'They run like the wind' or something like that. I mean if there were three white fellas I don't think he would have said they've run like they've stolen something. If he did, then that's justified. I reckon it was probably a bit more light-hearted, a bit of a joke. I didn't think it was offensive.

Player IP73 responded:

I did [find it offensive] cause we're all not the same, you know. We all don't … go out and steal things and that. You know you always see Indigenous people always in the bad books. On the news and that when something bad [happens], you know burglaries … or drinking issues. I reckon it was offensive.

And for player P84:

I don't think it's a reference to [the] stolen generation I think it's more so that there's a stereotype that Indigenous people steal and that they're poor. It's making a generalisation because of their race. Yeah, it's wrong. I suppose if you steal something you're going to be running away from wherever you've stolen pretty quick, so I think he's just trying to say they were running quick, but it's the wrong metaphor to use.

Further comments

In order to understand the complex nature of these issues as they relate to the Abacus Football Club, we have provided a mixture of responses that we found insightful. Senior player P69 understood and appreciated the process of education as an elite footballer as follows:

I was filling out my CV yesterday and, in the skills and past experiences, I wrote I've done X amount of sessions conflict counselling, racial vilification and cultural diversity and I'm proud to say that. I am up to speed on what's right and what's wrong and what our game's about. I think the values in our game could be, if they were portrayed in society, it would be a much more harmonious environment.

Player P71, a middle-tier fringe player, reflected on the research questions and examples as they related to Indigenous and multicultural players:

It gets pretty confronting doing all this stuff. You never think of it in this depth I guess in your day to day unless something comes up that you're involved with. This just makes you sort of really think about things in their eyes.

For player P72, the captain, the issue around participation and vilification at a junior level was something that he had not really contemplated before:

To think that kids might not have played AFL because they were worried about being discriminated against or vilified is yeah, just a thought that never really entered my head as a kid or much as an adult.

By extension, another senior player, P86, was able to make the connection to family upbringing, personal choices education and community:

It's a basic respect thing. That's something that's been bred into me well before I started to play footy. But, you know, I do think we can be drivers of it in the community. Make it seen to be because obviously in the lower levels of football still it [racial vilification] happens rampantly I would say.

Conclusion

In looking at the Abacus Football Club holistically in relation to the data collected it is possible to draw the conclusion that casual banter about identity and jokes about difference seem to be occurring. While this is alluded to from the summary of the SNA surveys earlier in this paper it would seem clear that this is occurring from the answer that player P81 mentioned in relation to a multicultural teammate:

Some people [teammates] may say jokes you know [to multicultural teammate]. Sometimes, he'll just go along with it and play along with it whereas it might hurt him deep down but he just gets good at dealing with and not reacting that way to it.

This clearly shows that racialized banter is occurring. It is difficult to gauge the level or type of banter that is occurring or, indeed, how the addressee is dealing with it. Given that these clubs are all elite sporting organizations and competition is the key to success, it is anyone's guess as to how the addressee would handle this banter if the team is winning and he is contributing to team success or, conversely, if the opposite is the case. If the addressee is feeling pressured to perform and a day-to-day situation occurs where racialized banter is the norm, this then makes for an environment that could potentially turn toxic quickly or a player's mental well-being could deteriorate to the point where he needs to seek counselling or possibly want to retire. Another example of this is where player P80 critically reflects on his 'difference' as the source for racialized banter, contextualized in relation to the Lumumba/O'Brien clip:

> It's pretty unfortunate that some little kid, especially at 10 or eleven years old gets that … If people might call me something, I'll laugh it off or whatever. Like it happens a bit here but I mean it's not really an issue. I find it funny and I might be different to other people [they] really might take it to heart.

That player P80 concedes 'it happens here a bit' may also account for the data around the friendships and trust networks specific to the Indigenous players at Abacus Football Club and their unwillingness to perhaps put themselves into a social situation whereby a 'joke' could lead to offence. This, combined with the situation that 20% of the players interviewed have had limited or no interactions with people from different cultures, creates the sense that work around this space needs to be increased.

Disclosure statement

No potential conflict of interest was reported by the authors.

Notes

1. We do not specify the number of players per club because of issues of identifiability.
2. More people actually participated, but only these numbers provided usable data. By 'usable', we mean that the data they provided were not incomplete; there weren't substantial portions of the survey where answers had not been provided, as was the case for some individuals at this club and also other clubs. Where significant amount of data was missing or clearly fabricated (e.g. every response was 'strongly agree', even when some of these responses contradicted one another), we excluded surveys from the analysis.
3. This was based on two multiple-choice questions: Which of the following best describes the AFL's rules against vilification? Who was the main catalyst of Rule 35?
4. On the front of the survey was the famous image of Nicky Winmar with his jumper lifted in 1993. A large majority of players, both at this club and at others, selected Winmar as the instigator of Rule 35, which is incorrect. Additionally, most of the errors regarding the scope of Rule 35 related to players who thought it was only about racism, not covering others kinds of vilification.
5. The research team's experience of AFL teams in the past is that they can display a range of behaviours that can range from conviviality, austerity, boisterousness, arrogance and rudeness. Players behave differently when the head coach is around, and are generally more playful, relaxed and conversant in the coach's absence. During the survey, the coach was present for most of the time and this does make a difference to how seriously the survey is taken. In other clubs where the coach was not present, quite different dynamics were present.
6. As noted previously, not all players who were surveyed were also interview, or vice versa.
7. All players and coaching staff were assigned a number from 1 to 99. All Players will have a capital P before their number and all Indigenous players will be assigned IP before theirs.
8. A 'Ranga' is Australian slang for a person with red hair, as in orang-utan.

9. The term 'exotic' is used to foreground that the player's physical appearance was noticeable to his teammates who made reference to it. It was his experience that some of the banter that he had engaged in was in relation to how he looked.

References

Australian Sports Commission. *Australian Football – A Game for All* 2010. Belconnen, ACT: Australian Sports Commission.

McPherson, M., L. Smith-Lovin, and J. M. Cook. 2001. "Birds of a Feather: Homophily in Social Networks." *Annual Review of Sociology* 27: 415–444.

Media Watch. 2010. *Unsporting Commentary on the ABC's Grandstand*. Melbourne: Australian Broadcasting Commission.

Bravo Football Club

Sean Gorman, Dean Lusher and Keir Reeves

The Bravo football club is an AFL club that participated in this Australian Research Council project Assessing the Australian Football League's Racial and Religious Vilification Laws to promote community harmony, multiculturalism and reconciliation. Bravo participated in both the surveys and the interviews. This club and its players and staff have all been deidentified as required by Curtin University's ethics guidelines.

The people at Bravo Football Club

Only players from the Bravo Football Club (Bravo FC) and no coaching/associated staff participated in the survey. Ten of the players participated in interviews. The dominant religion within Bravo FC was Catholic (47%), and the dominant culture was Anglo-Australian (64%). In their lives beyond football, the majority of players were studying at university (62%); a lesser proportion were not working or studying at all (31%). Almost all players (89%) had secondary school as their highest level of completed education, while the rest had also completed a university degree (11%).

With regard to the club environment, Indigenous and non-Indigenous players felt equally comfortable and included. Players' knowledge of Rule 35 showed that the majority (51%) were neither able to articulate the rule as it is currently understood, nor identify who instigated its inception, and only 7% responded correctly to both questions. Indigenous and non-Indigenous players did not differ in their knowledge of Rule 35.

Club engagement

Bravo FC had a professional appearance from the perspective of the research team, and the way the players filled out this survey reflected this. However, despite being invited to participate, no senior coaches, assistant coaches or other staff participated in the research. The senior coach was present while the survey was completed by the players. Feedback from one player to the research team highlighted his discomfort in completing the survey because he felt that there were many complex issues that a survey cannot adequately address.

Networks and club cultures

We will look at the three sets of network relations for the Bravo FC.

Sets culture network: self-awareness of social influences

For the sets culture network, players high in ability (i.e. the best players) as well as players high in experience (i.e. played many AFL games) were seen as setting the culture. Players also tended to select other players with similar attitudes to themselves with regard to the club being a family-inclusive environment. Finally, players who nominated many others as setting the culture were more likely to be inexperienced players, and also perceived that most people in the club were not homophobic. Again, like Abacus, at Bravo FC there is no association between who sets the culture and attitudes towards Indigenous Australians. This means that these culture-setting players overall vary on whether they endorse or dis-endorse positive (or negative) attitudes towards Indigenous Australians, and as such there is no consensus among culture-setting players on these issues.

Friendship, trust and after hours: informal, unspoken social influences

In the friendship network, Indigenous players cluster together, and they are also connected to non-Indigenous Australians. The other reasons for friendships are the standard ones, such that players choose as friends others with similar levels of experience to themselves, or those high in experience. In addition, best players were also much more likely to be chosen as friends. Finally, there was an effect related to attitudes towards Indigenous Australians such that players chose as friends others with similar views to Indigenous Australians as themselves.

With regard to whom players trusted, once again there were very clear and strong effects for best players and players high in experience, who were much more likely to be trusted than other players. Indigenous players were significantly more likely to trust other Indigenous players. Furthermore, players who identified strongly with the club were more likely to be trusted. With respect to issues of masculinity and trust, there were a number of smaller but interesting effects. Players more likely to be trusted were those who perceived that most others at the club believed in strict gender roles. In addition, those who were trusted were those who were perceived by others to disendorse the idea of masculinity being associated with violence. Notably, both of these effects for trust *do not* relate to the personal attitudes of these players, but rather indicate that trusted players hold certain perceptions of most others at the club. What this most likely indicates is that trusted players appear to be picking up cues on what the dominant view held by most others within the club on certain issues is. This may be because the trust others have in them means that people disclose more things to them, or possibly because they are more finely attuned to attitudes and beliefs around the club. Finally, players who were trusted were more likely to believe that the club was an inclusive environment.

The major effects for the after-hours network at Bravo FC are that popular choices for players to socialize with are those players high in ability and also those players with similar levels of experience to themselves. Further, Indigenous players are much more likely to say they socialise with other Indigenous players.

The difference of opinion network shows that players with more experience are more likely to be selected than other players. In addition, players are more likely to have differences of opinion with other players with similar levels of experience.

Who players considered funny was the last network we examined for Bravo FC. Experienced players were more likely to be seen as funny. Indigenous players were more likely to nominate other Indigenous players as funny. Furthermore, those players who thought that the AFL had not stamped out racism or truly recognized multiculturalism were also seen as funny. Furthermore, players also thought funny players were people with different views from themselves on the issue of multiculturalism. Finally, our analyses indicate that players thought that others who had different attitudes from themselves on Indigenous players within the team (e.g. Indigenous players train hard, Indigenous players in this team are respected like anyone else) were funny.

Summary of social networks

As at the Abacus club, at Bravo FC there are clear indications that both playing ability and experience, whether it be in regard to high or similar levels of experience, are important characteristics that shape who players interact with. We would expect this within a professional football team, and so the presence of these effects gives us confidence that the data we have are valid and reliable. A notable other effect is that Indigenous players tend to have strong bonds within this club, and have high levels of interaction with one another. Furthermore, players who considered the club to be an inclusive and welcoming environment were more likely to be seen to set the culture and more likely to be trusted. Similarity effects (i.e. selecting people with similar views to oneself) for attitudes towards Indigenous Australians and Indigenous players within the team were present in the friendship networks. Such similarity effects suggest that players congregate in smaller subgroups with people with similar views to themselves. However, players found people who had very different views from themselves on attitudes towards Indigenous Australians and Indigenous players to be funny, indicating that humour may be a way of engaging with different views on these matters and that there is not a uniform view on these issues. The fact that these effects are present suggests that issues around race are important in shaping and maintaining relationships. Importantly though, there are no popularity effects for these attitudes, meaning that highly selected (or popular) vary in whether they hold positive (or negative) attitudes towards Indigenous Australians, or homosexuality, or other such characteristics. The absence of these effects indicates that there are players who are influential hold varying views on these issues, so there is no overarching team cultural expectation to endorse (or dis-endorse) various views about race and masculinity within the team. However, there is a difference on some of these attitudes, and players separate into subgroups based upon such views. Our conclusion is that attitudes towards race shape people's social relations within this team, but that there is no club culture that either supports or denigrates attitudes about Indigenous people.

Interview data

At the Bravo FC, 10 people in total were interviewed. They were two coaches, the senior coach and one of his assistants, and eight players, five of whom were senior members of the team, including the captain, and the remaining three were junior players. Two of the players were Indigenous, with one being a senior player. Despite the small cohort of people interviewed at the Bravo FC, it was felt that the data received provided perhaps one of the richer insights into the clubs we looked at. The reason for this was perhaps the strong representation of senior players we interviewed: these players had been in the AFL system for some time, were seen by the team as the players who set the culture and were the most trusted at the club, as indicated by the social network analysis (SNA). As with the Abacus Football Club, and all the other clubs we interviewed, we used the same coding analysis with NVivo to draw out specific themes from the video clips and examples we used when interviewing the players and coaches. The players in this cohort consisted of P66, IP58, P64 and P67.

Bravo FC established players

Childhood experiences

The childhood experiences of this cohort of senior players ranged across a variety of backgrounds. For P66, there were no discernible experiences of 'diversity' he could recall. This was despite having a background in the suburbs of an Australian city. For IP58, the situation was somewhat different, which also foregrounds the importance of sport and the social capital it provides for people from different backgrounds:

> I didn't really see myself as Aboriginal. I didn't know what 'Aboriginal' was until I went to high school and people were picking on me. So that [was] the sort of community I come from. I think through my sport at school it definitely made people accept me more than I might have been elsewhere. (IP58)

P64 lived and studied both in the city and the country, which meant that his experiences were varied:

> There were a lot of different cultures but probably not a hell of a lot of Aboriginals in [city]. It was probably more when I was in Year 7 and through primary school I went to school with a lot of Indigenous boys back in [regional centre]. (P64)

P67's childhood experiences could be characterized as not only urban and middle class but also culturally quite varied nonetheless:

> It's probably one of those suburbs where there are pockets of quite affluent people and the private school sector and there are pockets of just your normal battlers really trying hard to make ends meet and kids that go to the local public school. So I think it's a real mixed bag. Very multicultural I'd say, a very strong Italian, Greek and that sort of ethnicity. Playing footy was sort of mixed bag: we had a lot of Lebanese, Italians and then we had the real country boys from [names country towns]. There was the private school kids that got mixed in and a lot of Indigenous boys were there too. I think we were exposed to all walks of life. (P67)

Lumumba/O'Brien clip

Having viewed the Lumumba clip, it was perhaps P67 who gave a preferred reading:

> He [Lumumba] could have had hatred towards the kids that done it to him, or, even worse, if the kids were whatever the race they were, he could have had a real hate towards that general race and then have a real chip on his shoulder. He could have thought, 'Why would I play this game if I'm going to cop this? I'll go maybe play a game where people of a similar culture plays'. (P67)

The thoughts of P66 were perhaps the opposite of this position:

> He could have blocked it out and continued on. He could have been the bigger person in the situation. Obviously, he had done nothing wrong, so he didn't have to feel as though he had to react, in the way he did, he could have just kept playing .... (P66)

The thoughts of the senior Indigenous player were quite salient, given that he connected the individual incident with the macro features that the AFL through Rule 35 is trying to address:

> I think the biggest thing for me was that he obviously realised, from a young age, that he was different – different culturally, different looking – and thought that it was okay to be different. To have a step-dad that gave him such great advice was fantastic. Whether it's his coach or whether it's family members, you need it [support] otherwise it can be very hard. Vilification can hurt a lot. I've got no doubt those kids in under 10s were calling out to Harry but obviously they were told by their coach or their family members to say that, to get Harry off his game, 'cos he was a good player. I think that for anyone who does look different or has different beliefs, you know from a certain young age that you are different and, unfortunately, in this country, you put up with a lot of crap. With the vilification code, and with our

organisation [AFL], what we're trying to do, we're able to have a fight back and say, 'Enough's enough'. (IP58)

P64 said:

> Well there are plenty options. He could have fought. He walked off, which was probably a good thing. He decided to make a stand, as a kid. He could report it to an umpire, he could report it to his coach. I do think it [vilification] can have long-term effects. To have repeat occasions where they're vilified when they enter the football field might have long-term effects and something that they carry around with them. It would seriously affect them. (P64)

'Running like they stole something'

Among the senior cohort of players at the Bravo FC, there were two distinct groups, with P66 and P67 having very similar perspectives regarding the Mark Maclure clip and P64 and IP58 sharing very similar views. P66 said:

> It's very harsh to suggest that Mark Maclure was implying what people think he's implying ... If they put up three guys with white skin and if they said the same thing, nothing would be said. I think it's a very fine line to suggest that he's being racist, in that remark. I see it as these three are three of the quickest blokes in the AFL. I think he's being complimentary [but] I can see how it can be misconstrued because of the word 'stolen' – because there's a stigma attached to that with Aboriginal people. (P66)

P67 commented:

> If anyone stole something, they'd be running like the wind to get out of there. It's what the other people think that's made this a storm in a teacup. If I knocked something off from the milk bar, I'd be out of there quick too. I think if you asked all the players on our list, they'd just go, 'Yeah, whatever'! (P67)

IP58 saw things somewhat differently from his senior teammates:

> 'Cos [sic] it was a joke does it make it right? I didn't take it as a joke but I guarantee a lot of people would say, 'Oh, he was just joking. That's okay', but it's not. I'm sure these three guys would have got phone calls from numerous people telling them about what Mark Maclure said on [the] ABC, and that would have made them feel like shit. So he found a way, through media, to vilify these three boys and make them feel like shit and because of what he said. Yeah. I've got no doubt he would have said stuff like that many times, at a barbeque, with his friends, about Aboriginal people or other nationalities and making jokes about it and that's why he thought, or didn't think, and just said it and thought it would be okay. He was saying that all Aboriginal people have to go out and steal things, that's why we run so fast ... because we have good practice from running around and stealing stuff. (IP58)

P64 saw the clip this way:

> I think he should know better, that's my feeling. He probably can say it because he might just be saying that they can run fast to get away from the law, or whatever, but he should know better and that's my feelings. It's inappropriate. I think he's saying that they're extremely elusive and quick but you can make that same point in a completely different way. I was initially shocked and taken back by it. You've just got to be smarter than that. (P64)

The fact that in the SNA results we see that there is not strong endorsement of attitudes about Indigenous people and players in either a positive or a negative way sits comfortably with the fact that across these senior players there are split views on this issue. In a way, the views held may potentially cancel one another out in the context of the whole club. As such, what may end up happening is that the group may drift into subgroups. We note again that there were similarity effects (i.e. selecting people with similar views to oneself) with respect to players' attitudes about Indigenous Australians and Indigenous players within the team in both the friendship network and the humour network.

Bravo FC fringe players

We will now take into consideration those players who have less impact on the culture setting, friendship and trust networks of the Bravo FC. As indicated by the SNA, these players are the ones deemed by their peers to be the least likely to impact upon the culture setting of the club and less likely to be nominated as friends. These players were P60, P61, P59 and IP65. As with the other clubs, these players are essentially fringe players due to their junior player status or diminished status as second-tier players.

Childhood experiences

P60 did not grow up in Australia but his experiences before coming to Australia were essentially multicultural.

> For me, I didn't see any Indigenous [people]. For us, there was a lot of Asian cultural backgrounds, like there was a lot of people from India, Sri Lanka, China and all that type of thing. (P60)

For P61, who did grow up in Australia, the experience was different again:

> I had lots of friends who were all different nationalities. I had a good friend who was a Torres Strait Islander, who was living where I was. We were pretty close friends. I've had lots and lots of friends from all different cultures and that sort of stuff. (P61)

P59 grew up in the country where football and sport were central to his experiencing different cultures and people:

> Just outside of [town name] [they put] government housing up for the Indigenous and we used to go to school with them. Grew up with a lot of them, fighting in the younger school days and the more we got to know each other, play more footy with each other, we then became friends. Definitely a lot of Indigenous people in that area. There was obviously a lot of theft and crime in the town from the younger generation, the older [Indigenous] generation were part of the footy club and they were trying to steer the younger guys in the right [direction] and into the footy club. (P59)

This is what IP65 recalls:

> Well, growing up there was nothing wrong with the white culture and the black culture. I think a lot of people just got on, made good friends. I don't think there was that much trouble in [name of town], racial-wise. (IP65)

Lumumba/O'Brien clip

There was a range of responses from the cohort from the Bravo FC to the Lumumba clip. P60 had a good understanding of the Lumumba issue, but indeed all three of the rookies recognized that Lumumba could have walked away from the game:

> He started noticing [that he was] different, like how people started treating him [differently] and discriminate against him. Obviously for him, he started noticing as he got older, saying with his mother and his accent and that type of stuff and just the fact [that in] footy, that probably happens a lot. He could have just said you know, 'Stuff this. I want to do something else where there won't be so much racism'. (P60)

P61 was able to see similar themes, echoing P60:

> I mean, growing up, the younger generations, when you're at school and stuff, it is definitely a lot harder for different cultures, you know. He could have just reacted and hit the guy and punched him. He could have just stopped and just walked off the field and not kept on playing. Even after his dad said to him, all those things, because some kids just can't take it. (P61)

P59 said:

> Obviously [he] could have retaliated and made the situation worse [or] not continue[d] with the sport. That's probably one that happens a lot. [There are] probably two things that could have [happened: he] could have walked away from the game and found something that was not on that level [or] retaliated and made the situation worse. I guess it's all depending on the individual, how they cope with the situation or if they can put it behind them and be strong enough to move on. (P59)

'Running like they stole something'

The Mark Maclure clip was something that P60 had not seen previously. This was his response:

> No, it's pretty bad. He probably wasn't thinking at the time. You can't really say that. I reckon that's clearly racist. [He] probably [should have] just have said something way different, just to explain their athletic ability: you know, they're really fast and they really know how to read the game. (P60)

IP65 had similar views:

> I think it was a racist taunt. I think the other guy [Drew Morphett] instead of laughing about it and saying, 'You can't say that', he should have said, 'Hold on a minute, you're being racist right now'. He should have realised that. I reckon it was meant as a joke but he doesn't understand what he really said and doesn't realise what impact it could have on them three boys. I reckon it was offensive. (IP65)

P61 said:

> He was just pretty much saying that Aboriginals always steal stuff. He was referring to that and didn't really take [it] back either. It's definitely offensive but he's obviously said it as a joke. Yes, he's just said it as a joke. He obviously wasn't thinking but I definitely think it was an offensive thing. (P61)

P59's perspective was:

> He's definitely pigeonholing them into their race and that's what they're known for or saying, 'That's what they're all like'. Well, I guess if you are to steal something, then you're going to get out of there as quick as you can, so you want to be running quick. They all have got pace and it could [have been] a throwaway line, but the way I first saw it or first heard it was he was referring to their culture. I can definitely see it as [a] joke, but I can also [understand it if] one of these guys was to take offence. (P59)

It is interesting that all of these players deemed not to dictate the culture of the club are much more unified (or uniform) in their views on the prompts provided for them to open up about race. The fact that they can articulate racist remarks and identify the strong impacts that racism can have in driving people away from AFL indicates a depth of knowledge about the issue that is edifying given the education around these issues in the AFL.

Interesting comments

In general terms, the comments made by IP58 summed up a great deal of what his journey had been like. He shared some very personal information, which provided a great insight for the project as to what it was like to be a high-profile elite sportsperson who is also Indigenous. Initially, he talks about the lack of agency and confidence that young Indigenous players have in speaking out:

> I think the vilification act [Rule 35] is really supportive but I still know quite a lot of our players, Indigenous boys, who don't put their hand up and say, 'This has happened'. [At] every Indigenous [All Stars] camp, we talk about it and you still have four or five players who

put their hand up at the conference who don't put their hand up after a game after being vilified. It still happens, it's still out there. (IP58)

IP58 went on to talk about bigger issues at play regarding the status that elite sportspeople occupy and the stereotypes that they have to endure and negotiate:

> I hear it all the time that, I'm one of the good ones, because I've done something for myself ... 'Nah, nah, nah, he's alright, he's made it, he's done good with himself', which is pretty shit – because it means anybody who hasn't done it, made it to AFL or made anything of their lives, they're just putting them [down] as [an] outcast, or a no-hoper or anything like that, before they've met them. It is hard, because people recognise who I am and, therefore treat me differently because of that. One thing that annoys me, even more on top of that, is that people have this idea, in their head, about footballers in general. Then they meet me for half an hour and they're surprised that I am who I am. In the way that I'm nice, I'm well spoken, I can articulate my opinion, and that annoys me because all I ever wanted was to be treated the same as everybody else, but that's just the way people view the situation and have that mindset in their head. (IP58)

Conclusion

What is perhaps the most salient theme to emerge at the Bravo FC is the difference between the senior and the junior players. All of the junior players interviewed had good awareness of the rules and were able to tap into specific critical themes that we wanted them to discuss. They were able to deconstruct different clips and quotes we gave them, which would seem to indicate that the message that the AFL and the AFLPA have instilled in the players through the induction and education programmes has worked. Maybe this is because they were young and fresh to the AFL system and wanted to seem like they were across the themes we put to them. This is not to suggest that some of the senior players do not understand Rule 35 or indeed do not appreciate what it is meant to do, but there did seem that some of the senior players were more myopic about it, particularly P67 and P66. This was evidenced when these same quotes and clips were given to the senior players: their replies were quite different from the rest of the team cohort. This was especially marked when comparing the Mark Maclure clip and the replies of senior players P66 and P67, who felt that what Maclure said was of little consequence: a 'storm in a teacup', P67 called it. This, when compared with IP58, was quite interesting given that these teammates had been together for some time on the team list, had had success as teammates and had attended regular education programmes around these issues.

What makes this even more interesting is that P67 could recognize that the abuse Lumumba had experienced in a junior match had enough potential to drive him away from the AFL forever, but he could not see that the Maclure clip, despite being classified as a joke, was also highly problematic and had the potential to hurt.

Further to this were the contradictions of two senior players acknowledging that the Rule 35 is working but at the same time thinking that certain things are acceptable to say, or that things were not meant in a certain way or that they were simply jokes. This is in contrast with both of the Indigenous players who have an acute experience of both direct and indirect racism and what it feels like to be stereotyped regularly by people who do not know them.

Disclosure statement

No potential conflict of interest was reported by the authors.

Charlie Football Club

Sean Gorman, Dean Lusher and Keir Reeves

The Charlie football club is an AFL club that participated in this Australian Research Council project Assessing the Australian Football League's Racial and Religious Vilification Laws to promote community harmony, multiculturalism and reconciliation. Charlie participated in both the surveys and the interviews. This club and its players and staff have all been deidentified as required by Curtin University's ethics guidelines.

The people at Charlie Football Club

At the Charlie Football Club (Charlie FC), almost all players and eight coaching/associated staff completed the survey. Twenty-four people were also interviewed. The dominant religion was Catholic (24%), though 62% of players did not respond to the question about their religion, perhaps indicating that they are non-religious. Again, the dominant culture was Anglo-Australian (80%). In life outside of the club, the majority of players were either studying at university or TAFE (62%), while those who were neither studying nor working were roughly one quarter (24%). Almost all players (87%) had secondary schooling as their completed highest level of education, and 9% had a university degree.

With respect to issues of feeling included at the club, there were no significant differences between Indigenous and non-Indigenous players. On players' knowledge of Rule 35, most players (68%) were unable to articulate the rule as it is currently understood or identify who was responsible for its inception, with only 7% getting answering both questions correctly. There were no differences between Indigenous and non-Indigenous players in regard to knowledge of Rule 35.

Club engagement

The research team received good support from the Player Development Manager (PDM) at the Charlie FC. The research team felt that there was a good professional outlook from the club about this research project. Maturity was displayed by the Charlie FC players in filling out this survey. Notably, the senior coach and several assistant coaches were involved in the survey as well. Coming into the club, we were impressed by the way players, coaches and staff were open to the project. We observed that Charlie FC took it seriously, they showed respect and people gave considered answers.

Networks and club cultures

We will look at three sets of network relations.

Sets the culture

This club is different to the previous two clubs with respect to the 'sets culture' network. In comparison to the two previous clubs, best players were more likely to be nominated as setting the culture, but, in contrast, the more experienced players were not seen to set the culture. Importantly, Indigenous players were less likely to be chosen by all others as setting the culture of the club. Furthermore, culture-setting players thought that the club's understanding of the needs of its players was not good and that the club did not work well together.[1]

Friendship, trust and afterhours: informal, unspoken social influences

For the friendship network, again it was best players and players of similar experience who were selected as friends. Another important effect was that Indigenous players were significantly more likely to select one another as friends, but, taking this similarity effect into account, Indigenous players were much more unlikely to be selected as friends by all other players (i.e. non-Indigenous players were unlikely to choose Indigenous players as friends). Finally, for the friendship network, players who were popular as friends thought that the club neither understood the needs of its players nor worked well together as a club.

The trust network showed similar patterns to the friendship network. Best players, but not experienced players, were more likely to be trusted. Indigenous players trust other Indigenous players, but, more generally, Indigenous players are unlikely to be trusted by others players (i.e. non-Indigenous players). Interestingly, experienced players are less likely to trust other players, but are not more or less likely than anyone else to be trusted by their teammates.

With respect to the after-hours network, there are few effects. Best players were popular choices for people to socialize with. In addition, Indigenous players were more likely to socialize after hours with other Indigenous players.

Difference of opinion and funny: contested boundaries

When analysing the fissures and strains in the team, there were only two effects. First, more experienced players are more likely to be selected that as people that players had differences of opinion with, which seems to be consistent with the fact that more experienced players appear less valued within this team than others. Second, players who believe that the AFL has stamped out racism in the game are more likely to have conflicting views with other players.

Finally, we examined the humour network. Players who were deemed funny by others were the best players. Notably, players who held low pro-Indigenous attitudes (i.e. more negative attitudes towards Indigenous people) were seen as funny. Indigenous players were very likely to see other Indigenous players as funny, but overall Indigenous players were significantly unlikely to be nominated as funny by others. Furthermore, players who thought that most others in the club held strict gender role views (e.g. players did not believe that it is acceptable if a woman is the major provider in her family) were also seen as funny. In contrast, players who are personally supportive of gay men are also seen to be funny.

Two final effects with regard to humour relate to feelings of inclusion at the club and the level to which the club understands its players. Interestingly, players who feel included and listened to are seen as funny, but, additionally, players who believe that the club does not do a good job of understanding the players are more likely to be seen as funny.

Summary of social networks

There are two striking characteristics of this club. The first is that Indigenous players are very tight-knit on many sorts of relationships. The second is that experience plays a quite different role in the social relations of this team compared with other clubs. Notably, senior players are less likely to trust other players, and the more senior players are selected for differences of opinion. Furthermore, players who believe that the AFL has stamped out racism in the game are also more likely to have differences of opinion with others.

Regarding who is seen as funny, and thus tapping into contested issues within the club, players with anti-homophobia stances are seen as funny, as well as people who perceived most others to hold strict gender role views. People who feel included at the club are also seen as funny, and yet people who do not feel the club understands its players are also seen as funny.

In this club, it does seem that the Indigenous players might have a separate subculture from others in the team. Furthermore, there appears to be little positive influence of senior players and indeed strong differences of opinion with more experienced players, indicating a lack of leadership and drive by those who have been at the club for some time. Best players are also influential, but this club is in stark contrast on a number of features to the previous two clubs.

Interview data

At the Charlie FC, 24 people in total were interviewed. They were two coaches, the senior coach and one of his assistants, and the PDM. There were 21 players, 7 of whom were senior members of the team, including the captain, with the remainder being a mix of middle-tier players and junior players. Two of the players were Indigenous, one senior and the other junior.

As with the previous club (and the remaining clubs we interviewed), we used the same NVivo analysis to draw out specific themes from the video clips and examples we used when interviewing the players and coaches. The players who were deemed through the SNA survey to 'set the culture' were P37, P47, P45, P41 and IP36.

Charlie FC established players

Childhood experiences

Like many players we interviewed for this project, P37 said his experiences growing up in the country town that he was from were very monocultural:

> It was sort of a very, very Anglo Saxon-orientated town. [A] few migrants would have come in over the time, but not a great deal. (P37)

P45's childhood was somewhat different: football and school brought him into contact with a variety of people:

> Primary school probably not as much, but secondary school I was friends with, and in class with, a lot of Indigenous kids. Got along with them because they played footy. I played footy, played against each other and we played together with school. So we used to have a bit of banter and, you know, they were very good [at football] and they were funny [humorous] people. (P45)

IP36's experiences of growing up in a capital city were somewhat different again but he experienced multiculturalism as part of his everyday life:

> The good thing I love about [home town] is the, the multiculturalism. I was lucky to go to a school I had good mates that were Greek guys. Good mates that were Filipinos. I had mates that I just grew up and there was just a whole big group of us that mixed together … Growing up there no matter what culture you're from, you are all mates and that. Black, white, Greek, whatever. (IP36)

P41 grew up in a medium-sized regional centre:

> I played a lot of footy with Indigenous boys and got on with them really well, so I had a couple of close friends that were Indigenous boys. I actually played footy with them so there was no problem. (P41)

P47 grew up in the outer suburbs of a major capital city where interaction with multicultural or Indigenous Australians was limited:

> There probably wasn't much [multicultural interaction] at all. The only time was like a little bit at school, not a whole heap. Through footy, there was probably others playing in different suburbs and different teams that might have had a few. (P47)

Lumumba/O'Brien clip

All of the players identified from the SNA as setting the culture at the Charlie FC responded in the same way to the Lumumba video. They stated that a range of responses could have been employed by Heritier Lumumba, including an escalation of the violence or informing the umpire and looking to him to sort out the issue of vilification. Some even suggested that Lumumba or his father could have even gone higher, to the league officials, to get something done. Interestingly, no one mentioned that Lumumba could have potentially walked away from the game for good.

'Running like they stole something'

Only one of the players interviewed at the Charlie FC had seen the clip of Mark Maclure from the ABC's *Media Watch* programme or had heard of it occurring in the media when it did. He was one of the Indigenous junior players. This was how the senior players from the Charlie FC responded to the Maclure clip. P37 said:

> I reckon that if he had a choice of words again, I reckon he'd change them. He's playing it out like it's harmless but I think you could take it [as] offensive, no doubt. He's making a point that the three boys with their Indigenous backgrounds that they're causing crime and stealing things basically. (P37)

P45 made a similar reading but also contextualized it to the social and professional era Maclure was from. P45 said this by way of showing how far football and the people who play and work in it now have come as a professional organization and as an elite competition:

> When he was playing, it was okay to say things like that. They [older players] weren't educated the way we are. So, if you're educated, you know at a younger age, you know it's going to help you down the track. So he hasn't been educated, so he thinks it's okay. Hearing that, I was surprised. Like, I've done interviews with him [Maclure] a bit and he says what he thinks. I reckon he doesn't think before he speaks. (P45)

The senior Indigenous player at Charlie FC, IP36, made a further connection with social protocols regarding teammates and what is permissible to say and what is not:

> I think he's just stereotyped the colour of their skin. If I was one of those players and a Carlton great said that, [I] would be disappointed. I probably would have asked for a bit more understanding and explanation of what he actually meant. Obviously to make himself sound

like he was funny and having a joke and not thinking that he'd said anything wrong. So he might know them personally and thinks that 'cause [sic] he speaks like that to them, then it's all right to say it on the air. It's just sort of like Mal Brown and his comments: 'I played with Maurice Rioli and all these [Indigenous guys] guys'. They think because they played with Aboriginal blokes, that they're in the clear to say it, but really they're not. (IP36)

This is how P41 responded:

He wasn't right to say it. He's just branding them. Probably come across, he wanted to come across as harmless type of joke but it was probably. Pretty poor what he said. He was saying [it's] in their culture that they steal things. That's what he expected them to do. (P41)

Interesting comments

What became apparent during the interviews with senior players at Charlie FC was how contested and contradictory issues relating to race, racism, ethnicity and difference were when looking at the social interactions, personal perceptions and day-to-day running within their club. For IP36, for example, this came down to the way he and his fellow Indigenous teammates were stereotyped, a situation he felt was unfair.

Us Indigenous boys, we barely go out that much and if we do we might have a beer. Have a beer with ourselves you know. [But] when we do, we're the ones doing this and that and the ones stuffing up. We're actually here on time, you know what I mean? We're doing all the right things same as everyone else is doing. But we slip up once, we're the ones that are judged on it, no one else. (IP36)

Another senior player, P43, who is from a multicultural background, indicated that these issues also became blurred when trying to navigate off-field casual racism in regard to Indigenous teammates.

Certainly the guys are more aware [and] they watch their tongue a bit. Like, even sometimes singing songs. Like, we like a bit of rap music here in the change rooms or whatever and it ends up like 'niggers' and the like. But you don't know sometimes whether you're allowed to sing it if Blackfellas are around. We'll go 'fuck [indigenous team mate] was there and we were singing that. Is that wrong? Should we go and apologise? Or wouldn't he care, we're just singing?' I actually watch it. I'll leave that word out when I'm around the boys just 'cause I don't know if they'd be upset by it. But sometimes you might sing, 'Oh niggers this' and you think, 'Fuck. Hang on. Is that appropriate?' I guess you're not sure sometimes, even though you're not directing it at anyone. (P43)

Charlie FC fringe players

Childhood experiences

As with the senior and more highly regarded players at Charlie FC, the responses from the less highly regarded, fringe players were mixed and illuminating. Players P51 and IP55 had no interaction or experiences with Indigenous or multicultural people, respectively, that they could recall. This was despite P51 growing up in the outer suburbs of a capital city and IP55 growing up in a major regional centre. P50, who grew up in regional Australia, had different experiences.

I played with a few [Indigenous guys] in under age and stuff like that and that's about it. I've got a mate back home [who is] Indigenous and he's just the same as all of us. Like, you would never think anything different. Which is good, 'cause we all grew up in the same place, everything's the same. (P50)

P38 grew up on a farm in the country. His recollections of growing up and interactions with Indigenous Australians are:

Not so much. We had, from memory, one Indigenous family. [I] certainly played sport against other small country towns that were mainly Indigenous towns. We played in a football competition where there were nine towns being part of it and two of the towns were predominately Indigenous Aboriginal people. (P38)

In contrast to P38, P42 grew up in an inner suburb of an Australian city. He had this to say about interactions with Indigenous and multicultural Australians growing up:

I never really thought about it. I suppose you get in the middle of the suburb in [name of suburb], you've got the Arabs and that sort of community. You go to [name of suburb], you've got the Asians and Italians everywhere. It was pretty multicultural. Didn't really have too much to do with Indigenous Australians within the area. But it was certainly a multicultural area and I remember my best mate in the first couple of years in primary school is [ethnic background]. So yeah, it's certainly diverse. (P42)

Lumumba/O'Brien clip

As with the senior cohort of players, the junior players found the Lumumba clip a rich text from which to consider issues around agency, discrimination and its consequences. When asked if he felt that racial vilification could have a significant legacy, P51 responded by saying:

I reckon it could have lasting consequences. As he said, he didn't want to play football again at that stage and if no one had spoken to him, he probably wouldn't or might not have. [He] might have taken a couple of years to take it back up or get confidence back out there I guess. (P51)

P50 said:

[Maybe] he thought, 'If I just walk off and just quit footy altogether, it's not going to happen again'. By just walking away, maybe the perception the other people would have [had was] something's gone on there, [because] you don't just walk off. [It] might make other people think differently about how bad they actually hurt him. (P50)

P38's perceptions around racial vilification and the possible reactions there could be were:

Some people would get violent, physical. Some people would do what he did [and] storm off the field and never wanted to play the game again, which is quite frightening as someone that wants to promote the game. [It's frightening] because if every person that gets racially vilified doesn't play the game, [players like] Harry O'Brien would not be playing in the AFL. Majak Daw wouldn't be at the Kangaroos. There are people that we wouldn't see at AFL clubs now and the game wouldn't be growing and developing the way it is. If people are going to be vilified and not take up the game, then we're not going to see people from other ethnic backgrounds or from other diverse backgrounds play the game. (P38)

Again, as in the Bravo Football Club, the more junior players readily picked up on the fact that racism may cause people to choose other sports and walk away from AFL. This does suggest that the younger cohort of AFL players is more informed about the importance of dealing with racism. It would seem to indicate that the education programmes that have been developed over time, and how often they are reinforced and the messages contained within them, are working.

'Running like they stole something'

In regard to the Mark Maclure interview, it is interesting to see how the junior players engaged with the themes of the clip. P51 said:

It's probably more [a] stereotype than anything, but you can't really say that. [It] probably just labels them [Betts, Yarran, Garlett] more than anything. He was joking when he said it, but I could see [them] being offended by it, by the comment. (P51)

P50 was quite critical of the Maclure comment but also made a value judgement about what Maclure may think more generally about Indigenous Australians:

> He shouldn't be saying that because some people have the impression [that] Indigenous people steal cars and all this kind of stuff and if you asked any one of those three how would they feel, they'd take it pretty hard. He obviously thinks that's acceptable to say that. I reckon it's a bit offensive because that's obviously the impression that he may have on Indigenous people outside of footy as well. (P50)

IP55 said:

> That's stereotyping and straight away that's the first thing that came to the top of my mind just about Aboriginal people: they stole something [and] they run pretty much. It was offensive towards me. (IP55)

P38's comments were insightful and related back to another high-profile incident in the media involving Rex Hunt:

> I think there are other analogies he could make. I think he probably chose the worst possible one to say. I mean Rex Hunt also made one about Leon Davis being as black as a dog. That was just as bad. You don't refer to that about someone's skin colour. You don't draw any analogies of that, but this is very interesting. In fairness to him, if there were four live-wire forwards and one was white, I don't know if it would have had the same impact. Because people are assuming they're actually thieves. To me it's very racist [but] up for interpretation. (P38)

P42 provided somewhat of a contrast to the majority of his teammates:

> I actually don't [think] there's anything wrong with it because I've worked with young kids who have been Indigenous, Caucasian, Asian and they steal anything they can get their hands on. You can see why people would think they run like they've stolen something because they're Indigenous. I wouldn't take it like that. I don't actually find offence in that comment, but I can understand why people would. If anyone steals something, they're going run pretty quick, so that's what I sort of thought. I didn't have a problem with it. (P42)

Interesting comments

Perhaps two of the most interesting comments from this cohort of players at Charlie FC were made by both P50 and IP55. They related to way that Rule 35 has provided a sense of social and cultural safety, which they perhaps felt was not there for players from diverse backgrounds in the past. It also links with the issues raised by the Daniel Southern story in the introduction. P50 said:

> Well, I think it's good having young Indigenous or multicultural people come in and think, 'Oh well, what if I come in and play? What are other people going to think of me?' It's not just because they've got the rules [Rule 35] to protect them but I think it just gives them a bit more confidence, especially now that we're getting more and more [people from different backgrounds] that play. It just gives them more confidence to be able to come in and want to do it and not feel like they're different. (P50)

IP55 said:

> To an extent, I'd say, yeah, I think Aboriginal players feel more [and] not just Aboriginal players but other ethnic groups feel more comfortable playing without stuff going on which Harry O'Brien did [and] said [he] didn't want to play anymore So, it's less worry about that stuff going on [and] just being able to play football. (IP55)

Conclusion

From the interviews, it would have to be concluded that there are no major issues that the research could find at the Charlie FC regarding racism or religious or cultural intolerance.

However, in the opinion of senior Indigenous player, IP36, socializing amongst the Indigenous cohort was scrutinized unfairly by the club. This is consistent with the findings of the SNA surveys, which showed that the Indigenous players were very tight-knit and, as a consequence, may have become quite conspicuous when they socialized. This became an issue for IP36, as it seemed to heighten his sense of himself (and his Indigenous teammates) feeling as if they were being monitored even when they were having a few beers after hours. This, he felt, was unfair, as it stereotyped them.

The other interesting theme that was brought up with the Charlie FC that was not raised by players or staff we interviewed at other clubs was how the types of music played (e.g. rap music) by the players could potentially cause problems. As indicated by P43, if the lyrics were taken out of context or used in a way that was misinterpreted, this would possibly constitute a contravention of Rule 35. This seemingly benign example shows how casual racism coupled with the everyday sites of the professional athletes' training regime can become very important in the ways racial themes and masculinity issues are understood and dealt with. It is by identifying these behaviours and the everyday spaces they occur in that the issue of intolerance or prejudice can be further interrogated, as the players are able to read more sophisticatedly as to what these things look like and mean. Just as an issue of vilification as it currently stands in the AFL can extend beyond race and religion to include someone's sexuality or physical appearance, so too can the spaces and the actions, *the where and the what*, also be investigated. In this way, it is not just player-to-player vilification on the field that needs to be considered, but also other less obvious examples that can be seen to potentially have impact on a player's welfare and well-being also.

Disclosure statement

No potential conflict of interest was reported by the authors.

Note

1. See Appendix 1 in paper "Overarching findings" (doi:10.1080/17430437.2014.1002974, in this collection), for the examples of questions asked in the survey.

Delta Football Club

Sean Gorman, Dean Lusher and Keir Reeves

The Delta football club is an AFL club that participated in this Australian Research Council project Assessing the Australian Football League's Racial and Religious Vilification Laws to promote community harmony, multiculturalism and reconciliation. Delta participated in both the surveys and the interviews. This club and its players and staff have all been deidentified as required by Curtin University's ethics guidelines.

The people at Delta Football Club

The majority of players and three coaching/associated staff from the Delta Football Club completed the written survey. There were 11 people interviewed. Of the players, the dominant religion was Catholic (31%); and Anglo-Australian was the dominant culture (69%). Almost all players (90%) had completed secondary schooling.

On measures of feeling comfortable and included at the club, there were no differences in ratings between Indigenous and non-Indigenous players, meaning that players from both groups felt equally comfortable at their club. Questions relating to players' knowledge of Rule 35 demonstrated that about one third of players (36%) could neither articulate the rule as it is currently understood nor identify who brought it about. However, 43% of players answered one of the two questions correctly, while 21% answered both questions correctly, more than that at other clubs. Finally, there were no differences between Indigenous and non-Indigenous players in knowledge of Rule 35.

Club engagement

As at some other clubs, the research team received strong support from the player development manager (PDM) at the Delta Football Club. Players were attentive and receptive to the research. The PDM focused very strongly on the Indigenous angle of the research even though the research team described the project more broadly than this to also foreground the multicultural importance of the project. The senior coach was absent, as were several assistant coaches, though the PDM and more junior coaching/support staff completed the survey. The players were subdued but showed interest in the research and completed what was asked of them, respectfully.

Networks and club cultures

Self-awareness of social influences: sets culture network

As a reminder, this network captures player self-awareness of those people whom they consider to have an explicit influence on them. With regard to culture setting, as with other clubs, it was the best players who were nominated more than other players. Additionally, there were a few other factors that were important for being selected as setting the culture at Delta FC. Players who were supportive of Indigenous players in the AFL (e.g. Indigenous players train hard) were unlikely to be seen as setting the culture. Players selected other players who had similar attitudes towards Indigenous Australians as themselves (whether positive or negative) as those who set the culture.

Friendship, trust and afterhours: informal, unspoken social influences

There are only two important effects for the friendship network at Delta FC. First, as with other clubs, best players are more likely to be chosen and so are popular people to have as friends. Second, above and beyond this effect, there is a similarity effect for Indigenous players, indicating that Indigenous players are much more likely to choose other Indigenous players as friends.

Regarding trust relations within Delta FC, overwhelmingly best players are more likely than others to be trusted, which is the dominant effect in the analysis and on par with other clubs. Additionally, Indigenous players are more likely to trust other Indigenous players. Again, this effect has been found in other clubs. Leaders within the club were not more (nor less) likely to be trusted than other players. However, these are a myriad of effects that suggest that issues of race and masculinity are of importance within this club with respect to who the players trust. Notably, players who scored higher than other players in anti-Indigenous attitudes were also more likely to be trusted. With respect to masculinity, players also trusted others with very similar views to themselves regarding masculinity and the use of violence. Finally, players who thought that most other players at the club did not endorse adherence to strict gender roles (e.g. perceived that most players would not agree with the statement 'a man should not cry in public') were more likely to be trusted.

For the afterhours network at Delta FC, best players were more popular choices than other players to socialize with. Furthermore, Indigenous players are much more likely to socialize afterhours with other Indigenous players. Players are more likely to socialize afterhours with players who hold similar views about the connection between masculinity and violence as themselves.

Difference of opinion and funny networks: contested boundaries

Differences of opinion within Delta FC were confined to the following. Players were both more likely to have differences of opinion with others in respect of attitudes about adherence to strict gender roles (e.g. a man should not cry in public). In particular, differences of opinion about this were between players who held very different views about what they perceived most others at the club endorsed. We interpret this effect as players differing over accepted norms of behaviours within the club with regard to masculine behaviours.

For the humour network, Indigenous players were unlikely to be selected as funny players overall. However, Indigenous players were much more likely to select other Indigenous players as funny. Together, these two effects suggest segregation between

Indigenous and non-Indigenous groups with regard to who they think is funny. This is not surprising, given other separations between these two groups on other networks we have studied. Interestingly, players who personally endorse playboy attitudes (i.e. a real man can get any woman to have sex with him) are more likely to be seen as funny. Again, this points to masculinity attitudes being used to gain social capital within the club by *point-scoring* through the use of humour.

Summary of social networks

There are clear patterns in Delta FC that being a good player makes you prominent and popular amongst your teammates. Furthermore, Indigenous players tend to stick together with regard to friendship, trust, socializing afterhours and who is seen as funny. What is interesting is that anti-Indigenous attitudes are present within the team such that players who are more likely to be trusted are those who hold more negative attitudes towards Indigenous Australians. This effect happens in combination with Indigenous players being more likely to trust one another, and indicates divergent views with regard to trust within the team. It highlights possible tensions and sub-group splits within the team. However, for the difference of opinion and humour networks, networks that we considered to best give insights into tensions, attitudes towards Indigenous Australians – whether generally or in the AFL – were not seen as important. In contrast, a range of masculinity effects were important for these two networks, as well as others. Indeed, playboy attitudes, violence attitudes and the adherence to strict gender roles were all delineators of who players had social relations with. That sometimes these effects seemed contradictory seems to indicate that there are not clear club cultures around these issues, but that nonetheless attitudes towards masculinity, and to some degree race, are drawn upon in different contexts (i.e. in different networks) to build relationships with others. However, the lack of coherence in attitudes, apart from the recurring importance of best players, suggests that the club culture is in flux or not well defined on these issues.

Interview data

At the Delta Football Club, 11 people were interviewed. They included the senior coach and the PDM. Of the players interviewed, two were Indigenous. Unlike the other clubs, however, the players interviewed were mostly junior and middle-tier players. However, the vice-captain was also interviewed, in place of the captain, who was receiving treatment. The players who were interviewed were IP22, P21 P26, P28, P29, P34 and P25.

Childhood experiences

IP22, who comes from a regional centre, had positive interactions with people from the non-Indigenous community, mainly consisting of experiences from both school and playing sport:

> At [my] school in [regional centre], the Aboriginal population dominates the non-Indigenous. But [that's] not to say that we don't get along with each other, 'cause I've [got] non-Indigenous friends as well. I interacted with non-Indigenous people as well [at] school.

P21, who comes from the outer suburbs of a capital city, also had good interactions with people from other cultures and backgrounds both at school and in sporting clubs:

> We had a very multicultural school. In my class, if there was [sic] 20 kids, probably five were actually Australians, that come from Australia. There was all different type of races in the school and also in the footy club.

Interestingly, P21 went on to specifically talk about a friend of his from a Sudanese background who was part of his football club and the struggles he had in playing the code:

> He wouldn't be able to play away games and he wouldn't be able to get lifts to training. His family were struggling, which was pretty unfortunate. That's why footy is such a great sport – because of its togetherness. We loved [Sudanese team mate]. He was a part of our team. I reckon he just loved that environment that we had at the footy club but we never really saw his family or anything.

P26 also grew up in an outer suburb of a capital city:

> In the early years, no [interactions], but then probably more African [and] Sudanese coming through [at school]. Definitely Italian and Lebanese and Greeks were definitely present in the community. In terms of Indigenous, there's not that many at all in [suburb]. Like school and things like that were just generally just Australians.

P28 grew up in a capital city and in a working class, suburban family environment:

> We had like a few boys from Italy all the way through school and a lot of people from India. So some of my best mates weren't Australian. I guess when we were bought up we [thought] everyone's the same, on the same level and no one was treated differently. Coming through the ranks with football there was obviously a lot of the Aboriginal boys and a lot of them are great mates of mine.

P29 came from the outer suburbs of a capital city, and sport and school were the main place he came across people of difference, but by and large his experiences seem to be quite monocultural:

> I went to school with people from different backgrounds and that and playing football and sports growing up made me come across a few people from different backgrounds but mainly Australian people. Not too much multicultural people from different descents.

P34 came from a large regional centre. He said succinctly:

> All my best friends are Indigenous.

P25 grew up in regional area where he was exposed to a number of different groups:

> I've grown up most of my life always playing with an Indigenous person or someone from a [multicultural background]. Indigenous boys are very exciting players and they're, you know, a joy to play with. They're very quiet but you know they really are good to get to know when you get talking to them. They're just like us. They're great blokes.

Lumumba/O'Brien clip

As with the other clubs, there were a range of responses to the Lumumba clip. P21 felt that the potential for Lumumba to exit the game forever and the potential for any further issues were very possible:

> I guess that's the main point of it [the clip] was how hard it was for him coming from a different background, moving to Australia. I couldn't imagine how he dealt with that. I mean, if he had of stopped playing footy, you never, you'd never see Harry O'Brien the way he is today and I guess it's a credit to him and his Dad the way they handled it.

P26 also had a similar perspective on the potential dangers of Lumumba leaving the game for good, given the racial abuse he received:

Obviously he [Lumumba] didn't really understand that he was different so he thought he was just a normal kid playing footy in under tens. He could have fought them or something like that. Obviously, like he said, he could have shied away and never returned to football.

P29 felt that the issues around vilification are of an ongoing concern in the lower grade junior competitions. He also made connections with mental health and well-being around the issues of vilification:

No one should really have to go through that you know. He's no different to any other sort of kid out there playing [and] just enjoying his footy and certainly at a junior [level] that shouldn't be tolerated. He could have easily just given up football and not played. He could have [developed] depression. You'd find there'd be a lot of cases of people who are vilified would probably just give up footy because it's probably the easy option. You wonder how many other players of different descents have actually given up football because of similar circumstances. You look at Harry O'Brien and Nic Naitunuai and guys like that and what they bring to the game and how special it is our game. It is a great thing.

P33 was very matter-of-fact in his assessment of the clip:

I think it's pretty sad that a ten year old gets racially abused.

P23 was also able to appreciate that the vilification that Lumumba received was something that could possibly have long-term detrimental consequences:

Yeah, I reckon at such a young age where you haven't really developed [as a person] you don't know how to handle those type things. It would have damaged [his] self-esteem a fair bit but obviously, with his father there to help him, he's come out of it pretty well.

This is how P25 saw the clip:

Playing on the footy field and if they're sledging him [by] bringing racial stuff into it, that's crossing the line. [I] definitely feel for him just how he didn't want to play again. [It] is pretty heavy.

'Running like they stole something'

Like many interviewees for the project, none of the players at the Delta Football Club had seen or heard of the Mark McClure clip before. This is how IP22 responded to it:

I don't reckon he should have said it. It's just sort of the wrong thing to say. There's a lot of other ways he could have said it. Is he saying that because they're Aboriginal? It's pretty stupid that he said it that way. I wouldn't like it. I'd like to ask him what he was thinking when he said it. Yep, I wouldn't like it at all.

P21 saw the clip this way:

[He is implying] they steal [and] it's just not true. I mean not everyone's like that. He shouldn't have said that. That's basically being discriminate (sic) against them. I mean, I can see if one of the Indigenous people from the community came out and had a crack at him for saying that. I would agree with them because he shouldn't have said that. I think he meant it to be a gag but he could have put it a better way. He shouldn't have said it. He could have just said something better than they've stolen something. But I don't, I don't think he meant to be offensive. No way.

P26 felt that McClure had overstepped the mark:

I think there's definitely different ways in which you can say something, like, 'They're on fire', 'They zip around' or something like that. To classify it as that is probably not the best thing to do, I don't think. I think [it] stereotypes the community, Indigenous people. This isn't obviously my opinion, but the stereotypes of them [Indigenous Australians] robbing people and things like that you don't want to really go there and mix it up where it's just no-go zone.

P28 felt similarly:

> I think he might have stepped over the line there. I don't think he was trying to be offensive.
> It was just a bit of a joke that went off the rails. Like, obviously he was trying to say that,
> obviously, they had a good game and, you know, he probably just said it the wrong way.

P29 was able to link McClure's comment to previous ones made in the media relating to
Indigenous players and skin colour:

> I think people understand what he was getting at and he's probably going down the wrong path.
> That's on the verge of racism because unfortunately you know some Indigenous people do
> have that reputation of causing trouble or getting into trouble and you know [it's] just blaming
> the black person. I think he's definitely treading a fine line there and probably going down the
> wrong path. I remember Rex Hunt actually called Leon Davis something similar to that and he
> got crucified for that, so I don't think it was much difference in what he sort of said there.

P33 wondered if the comment would have been made if the identity of the 'live-wire
forwards' was different:

> I think it was probably inappropriate there because there's obviously a connotation with
> Aboriginals and crime. I don't think anyone would have blinked an eyelid if he said it about
> three young Caucasians.

P35 made a bigger connection regarding vilification around sexuality and the problems
that name-calling can cause more generally:

> I reckon it's not as bad as calling him a name. Like, he's not meaning it in that way but it
> offends a lot of people, I suppose, without him probably even knowing it. I suppose you have
> other instances where I think Stephanie Rice on a tweet said something like, 'Suck on that,
> faggot', so that automatically attracts things from the gay community and they obviously take
> to heart those words. So I think Aboriginal people would have taken that to heart and I suppose,
> as I've said before, it's not fair to be saying something like that and being associated with that.

P23's reaction to the clip and what was said was as follows:

> Is he being racist because he's saying, 'Oh, Aboriginals steal things'? I don't think he should
> have said that. They might feel disrespected through it I guess. I don't think he should have
> said it. It is a bit of a harmless gag, but you don't know how those boys are going to take it.

P25 made a general link to the media and the ways Betts, Garlett and Yarran have been
labelled in the past – specifically the novelty of having three small Indigenous forwards in
one side. Then P25 analysed what McClure had said:

> I remember them being called Santa's little helper back in the day when Setanta [O'hAilpin]
> was playing with them. I think it [McClure's comment] was one of those heat of the moment
> things, but I don't think it's a good way to put it. I [think] he's suggesting they've stolen stuff
> in the past or something like that. Or they're renowned for stealing things. A bit of a harmless
> gag that probably wasn't intended to hurt anyone.

Interesting comments

After interviewing the players at Delta Football Club, two different sets of answers from
two players stood out. The first was from IP22 who discussed issues around the education
processes that the AFL and the AFLPA provide. While this project did not focus on issues
of vilification arising from abuse by spectators, it is interesting to draw similar connections
with what Heritier Lumumba discussed about walking away from the game and what IP22
and his father did one day at the football.

> [I think] they've done enough to educate the players but sometimes I think, like, supporters they
> need to be educated. Because the players get educated on it. I reckon sometimes it's the fans in

the crowd as well that need to be educated more about it. I remember I went and watched a Richmond game with my Dad in Melbourne probably three years ago and Jarrod Oakley-Nicholls [Indigenous Richmond player] was playing and we were sitting down and we heard people a few rows behind us racially abusing him, not out loud but just talking to themselves. Me and my Dad sort of just looked at each other. We just sort of thought, 'Oh shit'. It was an awkward situation. Like me and my Dad ended up leaving at three-quarter time because it was starting to get a bit bad – like they were starting to yell. So we just got up and left. (IP22)

IP22 went on to say that he felt that Indigenous players needed to speak up more about what things impacted on them and where they have come from socially, politically and economically:

I reckon if the Aboriginal boys told our stories to them [non-Indigenous team mates] they'd freak out a bit. But we don't really talk about it that much. But I reckon if they hear it from their own players, from us, our experiences, that might sort of flick the switch and they might take more notice of what goes on.

In contrast to IP22, P34 makes some interesting comments that could be read as being contradictory. The initial question that P34 was asked was, 'Has the AFL done enough to educate players around vilification?' P34 replied:

There are still a few guys that say things that don't really understand, so it probably could do with a little bit more [education] just to help people to understand. Because I've lived in an Aboriginal community [and] you don't know what it's like until you're there. It's easy to judge from down south in Melbourne say or Perth, but you don't understand how hard their [Indigenous Australians] life is. If people just go for a trip up to Darwin and go and have a look at what it's actually like, they'll understand.

With this in mind, P34 then made this comment regarding the McClure clip:

Yeah, I think it's a fair comment. They're obviously three pretty quick players. He didn't mention anything about their race or anything like that. There's nothing to do with their skin colour, so it's a fair comment. Nothing offensive about that at all. I wouldn't find that offensive.

Conclusion

From the interviews conducted at Delta Football Club, it would appear that there is a general consistency amongst the players and the answers given to the research questions could be deemed as being preferred answers. This would indicate that the education given to the players has gone some way to providing for them perspectives that are open to difference and acknowledgement that diversity is something that is well understood and recognized. From the data and feedback we got, this would then seem to indicate that the environment of the Delta Football Club is culturally safe but one where improvements can also be made. In saying this, the SNA data suggest that there are some sub-groupings and that Indigenous players are more likely to interact with each other. This could indicate several things, namely that the relationships between the Indigenous and non-Indigenous cohorts are not as developed as the AFL would like it or that this is the natural order of things and that people within those cohorts are comfortable in them.

As we have found with the more culturally inclusive clubs involved in this project, namely the Bravo and Igloo Football Clubs, it is how they are able to incorporate difference into their team structures and beyond that enable long-lasting and sustainable benefits to be realized. This is easier said that done, given the pressure to compete and have on-field success in the elite AFL. Further to this, for culturally specific programmes to be run successfully at any AFL club, these things need to be resourced correctly and the right people need to be in the right roles for the programmes to run effectively. The AFL clubs are not all resourced evenly as internal revenues and membership numbers differ meaning some programmes can be run. The divide between the rich and the poor clubs coupled with the AFL's desire for equalization presents numerous dichotomies in this regard. This makes the social and cultural cohesion of the playing group vitally important because if the playing group is able to interact in a mutually respectful and professional manner then this would be a starting point for on-field success. This is not to suggest that all sides that have not had success have internal cultural or racial problems, but rather that on-field success generally starts with the rapport and trust a team has off it.

Disclosure statement

No potential conflict of interest was reported by the authors.

Echo Football Club

Sean Gorman, Dean Lusher and Keir Reeves

The Echo football club is an AFL club that participated in this Australian Research Council project Assessing the Australian Football League's Racial and Religious Vilification Laws to promote Community Harmony, Multiculturalism and Reconciliation. Echo participated in both the surveys and the interviews. This club and its players and staff have all been deidentified as required by Curtin University's ethics guidelines.

People at Echo Football Club

At the Echo Football Club, virtually all players but no coaching/associated staff completed the survey. Although the senior coach did agree to be interviewed and several times were organized for this to take place, it unfortunately did not occur. Of the players, Catholicism was the dominant religion (32.6%), though 55.8% of players did not respond to this question, likely indicating that they are not religious. The dominant cultural group among players was Anglo-Australian (71.1%). Outside of the club, about half of players were either studying at university or TAFE (41.9%), while one-third were neither studying nor working (34.9%). Almost all players (90.7%) had completed secondary schooling as their highest level of education, and 4.7% of players had a university degree as their highest education.

With respect to issues of feeling included and supported at the club, Indigenous and non-Indigenous players did not differ in their views. On the issue of player knowledge of Rule 35, roughly one-third (34.9%) were unable to answer either question correctly (i.e. could neither articulate the rule as it is currently understood nor identify who was responsible for its inception), though 41.9% answered at least one of these questions correctly and 23.3% answered both questions correctly. Again, there were no significant differences between Indigenous and non-Indigenous players in regard to the number of questions about Rule 35 answered correctly.

Club engagement

Players at Echo FC participated positively in the survey. Some players had questions and concerns about confidentiality, while other players were keen to see that the results of this research were taken seriously by the AFL. As such, there was engagement by the players in team with the survey. Of course, as was the case with all clubs, some players were exacerbated by the questions and this was notable due to the body language displayed. Yet, the overwhelming feeling from the research team was that players considered the answers they provided. The Player Development Manager at the Echo FC was very good in coordinating the times and places for both the interviews and the survey, and was also apologetic for not being able to secure an interview with the senior coach despite repeated attempts to do so.

Networks and club cultures

Sets the culture: self-awareness of social influences

Regarding who sets the culture at Echo FC, the overwhelming effect is that players with greater experience set the culture. However, there is still also an effect indicating that best players also set the culture. In addition, players who perceive that most others at the club feel the club is an inclusive environment are also more likely to be seen as setting the culture. Notably, Indigenous players are unlikely to select other players as setting the culture, and they themselves are unlikely to be selected as setting the culture by others. This suggests that Indigenous players do not notionally support the concept of culture setting. Finally, differences in views about masculinity are important with regard to those players seen as setting the culture in the team. Players select other players with different views from themselves regarding violence, but also regarding homophobia, as players who set the culture. This suggests contestation around violence, but also around homophobia at Echo FC.

Friendship, trust and after hours: informal, unspoken social influences

For friendship, there is a range of interesting effects pertaining to why players nominate others as friends. Indigenous players are very likely to choose other Indigenous players as friends. Another effect is for choosing others with similar experience, such that players select others as friends who have played a similar numbers of AFL games as themselves. Beyond these effects, players who are studying are more likely to be chosen as friends. Importantly, players are more likely to be friends with players who have similar attitudes to themselves about Indigenous AFL players (e.g. Indigenous players train hard). This indicates that players who believe such statements are friends with others who also believe such statements, and that players who do not endorse such views are likely to be friends with other players who also do not endorse such views. Finally, players who are likely to be highly selected friends are more likely to endorse biological essentialism (e.g. to a large extent, a person's race biologically determines their abilities and traits). This essentialism due to race is not necessarily a bad thing, because people can hold positive views towards a particular group of people and think it is due to something innate. However, essentialism in the case of Indigenous players may take the form of 'natural ability' and 'magic' that is inherent to Indigenous players, rather than perceiving that such skills come about due to considerable hard work and application as well. So there appear to be a range of mixed effects around race, and not at all around masculinity issues, with regard to friendship.

With respect to trust, there are many effects present for Echo FC. First, best players and more experienced players are more likely to be trusted than other players in the team. Indigenous players are very likely to trust one another, but very unlikely to trust other players more generally or to be trusted by other players once the similarity effect was taken into account. Players are also more likely to trust other players with similar anti-Indigenous attitudes to themselves. Notably for Echo FC for trust relations, there were a number of effects related to masculinity. Players who were personally homophobic were more likely to be trusted, and players who thought that most others at the club were not homophobic were more likely to be trusted. Together, these two effects suggest that there are most likely different and potentially polarized views around homophobia. The former effect for personally held homophobia views most likely represents a trust in players with public homophobic views on the issue, whereas the latter effect represents a more nuanced perception by some players that perhaps not all people are homophobic, and because of this perceived awareness, they are trusted. However, the opposite effect for trust is in effect in relation to adherence to strict gender roles: players who dis-endorse the idea that men and women should stick to gender-specific behaviours are more likely to be trusted than others in the team, but also players who perceive that most others in the team do endorse such strict gender roles are also more likely to be trusted. So there are complex effects for adherence to gender roles and to homophobia that differ within the team, highlighting support and disdain of such attitudes from different sections of the team.

For the after-hours social ties at Echo FC, experience was a factor but this time in a different way. That is, players with little experience (i.e. low number of AFL games played) were significantly more likely to be popular people to socialize with. In addition, there were two other effects regarding perceptions of most others in the team with regard to masculinity attitudes. First, players who thought that most others were not homophobic were more likely to select many other players in their after-hours socializing network. Second, regarding who players indicate they socialized with, players choose others who hold similar perceptions to themselves about club norms – in this particular instance, club norms relating to playboy attitudes. Taken together, these effects indicate that less experienced, and thus likely younger, players are more socially active after hours, and that views about homophobia and playboy attitudes are important in shaping these socializing relations.

Difference of opinion and funny networks: contested boundaries

There are a range of effects with respect to the difference of opinion network that include experience, studying, masculinity and also religion, but nothing related to race issues. First, players who are more experienced are more likely to be players that others have a difference of opinion with. Further for experience, players are also more likely to have differences of opinion with players of similar levels of experience, which may reflect the fact that many friendships and interactions are between players of similar experience, and so some of these may also turn into differences of opinion. In addition, more experienced players are likely to nominate a greater number of other players as people they have differences of opinion with.

In respect to masculinity, players who are likely to nominate a greater number of others as players they have differences of opinion with are players who personally do not endorse violence as part of masculinity, and who personally endorse adherence to strict gender roles. Further on masculinity, there are a number of effects relating to player perceptions of what most others in the team do, or else what we could call norms regarding masculinity. Players who are likely to nominate a greater number of other players as people they have differences of opinion with are players who perceive most others as not believing in strict gender roles, endorsing violence as related to masculinity, and who are homophobic. With regard to how comfortable players feel in talking about their religion or spirituality with other players and at the club generally, players who feel comfortable doing this are both more likely to be chosen as someone that many others have differences of opinion with and someone who has many others that they have differences of opinion with. Finally, players who are not studying are both more likely to be those who others have a difference of opinion with, but also people who have differences of opinion with a greater number of others.

There are two effects that relate to who players think are funny at Echo FC. First, best players are more likely to be seen as funny, which is a fairly standard finding. Second, players who endorse biological essentialism are more likely to nominate others as funny. It is possible that this latter effect represents jokes made about issues around race, which appeal to people who endorse biological determinism, but it is difficult to be sure about this. In any case, people who see that race and abilities and traits are largely fixed from birth are more likely to find many others funny.

Summary of social networks

In summarizing the network data, there are a number of themes that arise. The first is that Indigenous players are strongly interconnected within this team, but seem detached to some degree from non-Indigenous players. There are some differences in terms of views about race that shape players' social relations, with biological determinism featuring here. In addition, players trust others with similar views about Indigenous players to themselves. Importantly, there are no popularity effects for any of the networks in which negative attitudes towards race make players very prominent or central in that network, and, as such, this means that there are no strong norms around such negative race attitudes in the team, which is very positive for the club. But there is nonetheless some divergence of views on race among players in the team in the background.

Experience is interesting in this club as well because it is not just that people choose similar others as friends on this variable, but that less experienced (thus presumably younger) players are more likely to socialize after hours, and more experienced players are both recipients and instigators of difference of opinion within the team.

Finally, attitudes towards masculinity seem to be quite pertinent within the club. There is divergence around the issue of violence as part of masculinity with regard to who sets the culture at the club, but also to difference of opinion. Views about strict gender roles are important with regard to who players trust and who they have differences of opinion with. With regard to homophobia, it is an important criterion for selecting who players think sets the club culture, for who players trust, for who players socialize with after hours and for who players have differences of opinion with. In all, issues around masculinity are quite pervasive at this club, and homophobia is supported in this club to some degree but is also somewhat contested. While issues of race are present to some degree, the bigger issue with Echo FC is around masculinity, and, particularly, homophobia.

Interview data

At the Echo FC, 20 people in total were interviewed: 19 players and 1 assistant coach. The senior coach was invited on several occasions to participate and agreed to be interviewed, only to renege. No reason was given as to why this was the case. Of the 19 players who were interviewed, a number were Indigenous, with variability regarding whether they were a senior, middle-tier or junior player. Of the entire player cohort at the Echo FC, four of those interviewed would be considered senior players, including the captain, with the remainder being a mix of middle-tier players and junior players.

Echo FC established players

The players who ranked the highest in trust, culture setting and friendship and were interviewed were IP20, P6, P12 and P13.

Childhood experiences

IP20 grew up in regional Australia. This is what he recalls of Indigenous and non-Indigenous interactions in his childhood years:

> There was a lot of Blackfellas from [town] and a lot of Whitefellas, so every[one] got along pretty well. [It] was a nice little community. (IP20)

P6 grew up in a middle-class suburb of a city. This is his recollection:

> The only real interaction [with multicultural people] I had was probably through sport. Played a lot against [name] Football Club. The Indigenous interaction that I had was probably through the [AFL] football club environment growing up around that. Then there was a bit through my schooling as well. We did quite a bit of Indigenous work in [town]. We had like a school exchange program in [town] but that would probably be the extent of it. (P6)

P12's recollections were also based on a city environment but his family would be considered more working class:

> I played a stack of junior football with Indigenous boys. Where I lived there was actually quite a fair few housing estate homes [and] they were normally occupied largely by the Indigenous. They were always around in my neighbourhood as well. A lot of my good friends when I was younger playing footy were some of the Indigenous boys. (P12)

P13 grew up in an outer suburb of a city that was also working class:

> It wasn't a big area for a lot of multicultural [people], you know. Occasionally you might get a multicultural kid in your class sort of thing, but no, not massive. (P13)

Lumumba/O'Brien clip

The established players of the Echo FC had some interesting responses to the Lumumba/O'Brien clip. This was how IP20 responded:

> Obviously he could have started a fight or some [other] reaction to the other players. Just started fighting or even saying stuff back to them I guess. [He] probably [did] the right thing [and] storm off the field saying he wasn't going to play footy again. (IP20)

P6's response was something he tried to conflate to his own experience given that he had not been vilified at any time during his time in junior or senior football:

> [It] probably could have turned to a physical confrontation or a verbal response. Or he could have perhaps just ignore[d] it. I haven't really been subjected to racial vilification so some people perhaps might be able to tolerate it [and] others they [may] never be able to move on from it. (P6)

P12 also had not experienced any vilification:

> There's a million different things he could have done: maybe whack the bloke that was lipping him, rather than storm off angrily. [He] could have got really upset and emotional. Any number of things. I imagine it would definitely have potential to have a long-lasting affect but I've never really experienced it to a large degree, so it's hard for me to say what effect it would have. (P12)

P13 responded with:

> He found it difficult fitting in sort of thing. And then obviously having to deal with a bit of racism around his football and that sort of made him not want to participate in sport, which is obviously not a good thing. I guess retaliating and fighting is the worst way of doing it so. Maybe he didn't know what to do. Maybe it was the first time he sort of heard that sort of stuff and [it] was unfamiliar to him as to how he could approach it. (P13)

'Running like they stole something'

Responding to the McClure clip, this cohort of players all felt that the intention of the comment was perhaps an attempt by the Australian Broadcasting Corporation commentator to make a joke but an attempt that fell short. For IP20:

> I reckon it sounds pretty racist when you think of it. They're obviously three Indigenous players and [he] could have said anything else but to say something like, 'They run like they've stolen something' just doesn't sound right. I think to Indigenous players, I think it would definitely sound offensive. If someone said that about me, I'd be pretty shattered. (IP20)

P6 said:

> I think it's a little bit tasteless. He's using that phrase to associate the colour of their skin. In terms of their performance, I think he's making an association by how they look and the fact that they're Indigenous Australians rather than what they're actually doing on the field. I'm sure some people thought it was a joke. I'm sure he thought he was just joking around. I can see why some people would take offence to it as well. He's probably having a joke but I think he's making a joke from using race as the joke. (P6)

P12's thoughts on the clip were:

> That's probably bad taste, I would have thought. Obviously that's singling them out for reasons that aren't really acceptable I wouldn't have thought. I wouldn't be surprised at all if those three blokes were pretty pissed off about that. He's saying it thinking it's humorous but again the jokes not about him. [It] came straight off the tip of his tongue and is an indication of his general thoughts, so I would have thought that's come from his beliefs or whatever you want to call them. (P12)

Despite thinking that the comment was not as bad as the others in this cohort, P13 still felt that it was unnecessary:

> I think, you know, he's insinuating something that you know can be offensive to Indigenous people, so I think he's got to probably be a bit more aware of what he's saying. Personally, it's probably a little bit harmless but as I said, there [are] different people [who] take things differently and you [have] got to be aware of what you say. (P13)

Interesting comments

Discussion with the players from Echo FC provided two very interesting insights. The first of these was from P12 who was asked if he felt that the AFL has done enough to teach players about vilification.

> I think that they're definitely very, very clear on it. I think it [the education about vilification] happens from well before you get to an AFL club I would have thought, as a general rule anyway. I mean what Harry [was] saying – I've never witnessed that growing up and as I said we would have had eight, nine, 10 Indigenous boys on our team. I don't think anything was ever said. So I think it [education] happens a lot younger. (P12)

In another interview with a senior player, P4, who was on the cusp of retirement, said that he felt that the AFL and Echo FC still had some way to go regarding education around issues of banter, citing the use of homophobic and sexist language particularly by the Indigenous players at the club. P4 said:

> The only thing I thought to mention was the way in which a lot of the kids relate to themselves and to each other. I'm talking more of what they [say regarding] sexuality. I'm just talking about the way that they talk to each other. I just found it really shocking for a while. I found that the way the Indigenous boys relate to each other has changed and

evolved, which is interesting. For a time there, it was jovial but quite aggressive: constantly referring to each other as 'gay cunts' as a laughing thing. I don't find it offensive; I [just] found it shocking that they would consistently refer to each other that way. I wasn't sure how that came about. They don't have any malice in these comments whatsoever except for the fact that I think it is malicious but they don't realise it affects them whether they know it or not. (P4)

Echo FC fringe players

The cohort that was considered to have less influence over culture setting and considered to be less likely to be trusted or regarded as a friend were asked the same questions. This group consisted of P14, P16, P19, IP3, P1, P2, IP8 and IP10 who were junior players.

Childhood experiences

P14, who comes from a working-class family and who had lived in two states, said:

[I] played in a lot of, a lot of different teams, state teams [with] a lot of Aboriginals. At school, we had an Indigenous program and, like, our school was probably mostly Italians. There wasn't a lot of Chinese; it was either Aboriginal or Italian. (P14)

IP10 recalls:

Mum's family and a lot of friends were non-Indigenous. (IP10)

P19 grew up in the country:

There was one player that was Indigenous in the team. We did a lot of football together and my parents drove him and me to [town] and [town] for football. (P19)

IP3 grew up in a large regional centre and his interactions were mainly with his family or other Indigenous Australians:

For me, it's been mainly with the Indigenous family. I think that's [the same] with all Indigenous families: they are very tight knit and they include not just their immediate family. It's the broader family and I guess that's what makes us so close. I went down to [city] to a boarding school and I had no family, no friends and I guess [I] gravitated to [my] own mob. I found it pretty hard in my first year of schooling there and felt, I guess, a bit left out. (IP3)

P2's upbringing was in a capital city and his interactions with Indigenous Australians were through sport:

I played for a footy club [name] in [state]. All the clubs have, like, regions, like an area that they zoned and so ours was [regional centre], so we had a fair few Aboriginal players from there. (P2)

IP8 grew up in a regional centre:

My dad and my brothers and my sister and my mum we were probably a lot more out there in the broader community than the sort of the rest of my family. I think it was because of my Dad. He knew pretty much everyone in the town and stuff like that and he had a lot of mates that were non-Indigenous and so they really respected him and he [was] liked because he was so well known. (IPI8)

Lumumba/O'Brien clip

This is how P14 responded to the Lumumba clip when asked what he thought were the main themes from it:

There is obviously racial vilification in sport [and] he [Lumumba] experienced it. Like he said he would never play footy again and he had someone who helped him I suppose. I think it's important that you have someone to help you get through it. His father helped him and spoke about ways that he can get around that and now he's playing AFL footy and doing well. (P14)

This is what IP10 thought of the clip:

[I] definitely think [vilification] can have lasting consequences. If you've suffered that your whole life, you're obviously going to see other people and races in a different way. (IP10)

This is what P16 thought could have potentially happened:

[He] could have given up, could have hit someone or hit those kids or reacted violently or gone down a different path. [He'd] remember that for the rest of his life, that incident. Probably remembers more than one, I think. (P16)

P19 said:

They [opposition players] probably don't know any better. They've been taught that way. That's the only way they can attack him. He [Lumumba] might have been in shock because he hadn't heard it before. Might have a lasting impact but it depends on the person and how much they can forget about it. (P19)

P1 felt that:

[He] probably could have very easily hit someone or gotten very physically violent or something, which would have been pretty tough. [He] could never have played footy again. [You would] probably want to be by yourself instead of having to deal with all that. (P1)

P2 said in response:

He felt like he was discriminated out on the field. You've got to be strong to deal with things like that but he shouldn't really have to, to go through things like that really. I think it depends on the person but I think that those people probably [need] to learn to stop behaving like that. They're probably embarrassed now. (P2)

IP8 said:

Those kids are 10 years old, they're 10 and they're all ready having a go at another kid because of his colour. That's a 10 year-old. Imagine when he's 18, 20? (IP8)

P7 felt that:

You know, if you're strong minded you can actually push past that and set your goals and actually achieve anything. I'd say everyone gets things said about them and it might not be racism but it definitely hurts and I suppose it's how you react to it [and] showing that it hurts you, I suppose. (P7)

'Running like they stole something'

When it came to the McClure clip, the players from Echo FC responded in a variety of ways. This is what IP10 said:

Depends how people take it. Some people would be very offended that it's said because they are Indigenous and they would steal something but at the same time you can look at it in a way that if anyone steals something, they're going to run pretty fast. [Laughs] So I don't know what's going through his head and how he meant for that to be seen but at the same time to be safe you might as well not say anything like that. (IP10)

P16 responded in a similar way:

If you stole something, you'd run pretty quickly. But then with the Aborigines, I don't know, it's sort of, like a cliché thing you hear around a bit. I mean I've heard jokes of that sort of stuff. I don't know [if it] was a joke. I guess it's pretty offensive when you realise that it's about Aboriginals. (P16)

IP3 used his answer to incorporate a range of issues that encompassed the framing of Indigenous Australians in a negative way:

> Look, every time they [the media] talk about crimes and homeless people I look on the streets and I see just as much white people as I do black people. It just seems ridiculous to even think that because there are a lot of white people that do the same [steal]. I think it's really hypocritical by them [ABC commentators] to even think that. I didn't like it. I think it just stereotypes Indigenous people and we're all not like that. (IP3)

This is how P1 responded:

> [It] depends on his intention. If he was implying it because they are Aboriginal, then it's probably not right. If he was just that they are fast runners, then it's all right I suppose. So I guess we'll never really know what his intention was. On face value, I personally don't take much out of it, so I reckon that's probably okay. [It] didn't seem to be maliciously aimed or anything like that. It just seemed to be a harmless joke, but I reckon he probably should maybe pick his words a bit more carefully. (P1)

P2 had a somewhat different perspective:

> You can't say that I don't think [laughing]. I don't think it's [okay]. It's interesting that the way he said it in terms of it because I think it had a double meaning. It sort of a back-handed compliment. (P2)

Interesting comments

IP3 was asked if the AFL has done enough to educate players about issues around vilification and he responded by saying:

> I think so, but I guess it's just on the player themselves and how he takes that education and whether he actually takes it on board. It's entirely up to them. They're their own person. If they feel that they need to lower themselves to that level to do that, to put somebody else off their game then, yeah, it's not acceptable I guess. (IP3)

Conclusion

For the Echo FC, we would conclude that the issues around racism and racial and ethnic difference are generally well understood. The majority of the players were able to grasp the themes we put to them in a way that showed that they were able to deconstruct certain scenarios or examples provided to them in a sophisticated way. Like many of the other clubs though, banter and jokes were something that provided a more nuanced insight into the player's perspectives relating to issues of homophobia. In the SNA survey, players who were more likely to be trusted at the Echo FC were more intolerant of homosexuality than other players. This was then to some degree anecdotally confirmed by P4 discussing the use of the terms 'gay cunts' by the Indigenous players in the club, with P4 feeling that this was in some way detrimental to the social well-being of the club and to that cohort of players. The survey data also showed that, like some of the other clubs, Indigenous players were somewhat separate from the rest of the team. There are several ways that this can be viewed: it could indicate a strong sense of solidarity or a preference by players from specific cultural or racial backgrounds to group together and an unwillingness by players from marginal backgrounds to mix with those whose sensibilities or world view is different from their own.

Disclosure statement

No potential conflict of interest was reported by the authors.

Foxtrot Football Club

Sean Gorman, Dean Lusher and Keir Reeves

The Foxtrot football club is an AFL club that participated in this Australian Research Council project assessing the Australian Football League's Racial and Religious Vilification Laws to promote community harmony, multiculturalism and reconciliation. Foxtrot participated in both the surveys and the interviews. This club and its players and staff have all been deidentified as required by Curtin University's ethics guidelines.

The people at Foxtrot Football Club

At the Foxtrot Football Club, many players and coaching/associated staff participated in the survey. For the interviews, nine players and one assistant coach were selected. The dominant religion of players at Foxtrot FC was Catholic (41%) and the dominant culture was Anglo-Australian (76%). Beyond the football field, 41% of players were either studying at a university or a TAFE. There was an almost equivalent number neither working nor studying (38%). Regarding their highest level of education, most players (84%) had completed secondary schooling, while some had also completed a university/TAFE degree (11%).

With regard to whether players felt comfortable in the club environment and felt the club was an inclusive environment, Indigenous and non-Indigenous players did not differ in their views. Players' knowledge of the AFL's Rule 35 showed that about one third (35%) were not able to articulate the rule as it is currently understood, or nominate which player was its instigator. The majority, however, answered one of these questions correctly (57%); only 8.1% responded correctly to both questions. Knowledge of Rule 35 was not different for Indigenous and non-Indigenous players.

Club engagement

The Player Development Manager at Foxtrot FC was extremely supportive of the research and although there were a number of false starts and rescheduling to enable participation in the research, the research team was welcomed with respect and interest in the project. During the survey, there was the usual fun and joking between players, but they took the questions seriously and dedicated time to responding properly. The same is true for coaching and other staff. In the interviews, some people were candid and gave extended answers, while others watched the clock. In this respect, they were no different from any other club. Overall, people at this club took the research seriously and engaged with the researchers in professional manner.

Networks and club culture

Sets culture network: self-awareness of social influences

For the sets culture network, there was a range of factors for which players were nominated as setting the culture in the team. As per other clubs, not only best players but also more experienced players were seen to set the club culture. Additionally, players chose others with different levels of experience to themselves as people who set the culture. Importantly, Indigenous players were significantly unlikely to be selected as setting club culture, and further players holding negative attitudes to Indigenous people (i.e. think that discrimination is no longer a problem or think Indigenous people are not a disadvantaged group) were more likely to be selected as setting the club culture. Interestingly, players who do not see their identity as strongly tied to the club are more likely to be seen as setting the culture, but also players who feel the club does a good job of making people feel welcome, and player who see the club as a family-inclusive environment, are also seen as culture setters. Players are also likely to select others with similar views to themselves in regards to feeling free to express their faith/spirituality as people who set the culture. Finally, players who do not personally endorse violence were seen to set the culture, and also players who perceived that most others in the team endorsed violence were also seen to set the culture. These two final effects indicate that views towards violence are salient and possibly contested among players with regards to club culture.

Friendship, trust and afterhours: informal, unspoken social influences

Regarding the choice of friends among players at Foxtrot FC, as was commonly found in other clubs, players gravitated towards the best players as well as players with similar levels of experience. Indigenous players were very likely to select other Indigenous players as friends. Regarding the view of Indigenous players within the team (e.g. Indigenous players in this team are respected like anyone else), players who did not support such views were more likely to be chosen as friends. However, players who perceived that the norm was that most others in the team *did support* such views of Indigenous players were also more likely to be chosen as friends. This highlights potential disparity between sub-groups of players within the team around the acceptance of Indigenous players within the team.

The trust network has many similarities to the friendship network in that best players and players of similar experience are more likely to be trusted within Foxtrot FC. Furthermore, there is more likely to be trust among Indigenous players. With regard to masculinity, players are more also likely to trust other players with similar playboy attitudes to themselves. Finally, players who feel more comfortable expressing their faith/ spirituality are more likely to be trusted.

The afterhours networks mirrors the friendship and trust network in major ways, notably that people popular to socialize with afterhours are the best players and players with similar levels of experience. Furthermore, Indigenous players are also more likely to socialize with other Indigenous players. Players who do not think that the club is family-inclusive are popular people to socialize with, in contrast to the effect of who sets the culture.

Difference of opinion and funny networks: contested boundaries

The final two network analyses for Foxtrot FC relate to differences of opinion and humour. Notably, there was only one effect for the difference of opinion network. Players who did *not* endorse playboy attitudes (i.e. disagreed with 'a real man can get any woman to have sex with him') were more likely to be people that others had differences of opinion with.

Finally, regarding whom players thought were funny, unsurprisingly more experienced players were more likely to be chosen. The other effects for humour pertained to masculinity attitudes. First, players who did not believe in strict gender role adherence (e.g. It is OK for a man to cry in public) were more likely to be chosen as funny. Second, players who perceived that most others in the club (i.e. the club norm) did not endorse violence attitudes were also seen as funny. Third, players were likely to select as funny other players with very different personal views to violence. Taken together, these effects for humour in relation to masculinity suggest contestation around behaviours of what it is to be a man and express masculinity, particularly in relation to violence and the adherence to strict gender role behaviours.

Summary of social networks

Foxtrot FC shows significant issues around attitudes towards Indigenous people and around masculine attitudes and behaviours. In many other clubs Indigenous players are very likely to congregate in friendship, trust and afterhours relations – as it also happens at Foxtrot FC. However, the other effects of culture setting players holding attitudes that discrimination is no longer a problem or think Indigenous people are not a disadvantaged group are somewhat problematic to say the least. Furthermore, that players who were more likely to be chosen as friends were those who did believe Indigenous players in this team are respected like anyone else is indicative of tensions around race/ethnicity. The lack of network effects around difference of opinion and humour for issues of race suggests that there is not necessarily contestation on issues of race/ethnicity. Rather, Indigenous players within this club appear to be marginalized and less valued than non-Indigenous players.

On issues of masculinity, again Foxtrot FC has a number of issues to note. On a positive note, there are no concerns around the issue of homophobia, such that there are no associations between who players interact with positively or negatively and their views towards gay men. However, the players at Foxtrot FC show that their attitudes towards violence, strict gender roles and playboy attitudes are all important with regard to social interactions within the team. Violence as part of the masculine make-up is important to who sets the culture, but apparently in contested ways, with some culture setting personally endorsing it but others see that it is not the norm. Players are more likely to trust others with similar playboy attitudes to themselves. Notably, players who do not endorse playboy attitudes are significantly more likely than anyone else to be selected, as someone that players have a difference of opinion indicates that such views are not supported within the playing group. What this suggests is a club culture that endorses negative sexual attitudes towards women. In other respects Foxtrot FC demonstrates many similar effects to all others in that playing ability and experience are valued commodities within the team. However, effects around both race and masculinity indicate potential issues with this club's culture.

Interview data

Nine players and one assistant coach from the Foxtrot Football Club were interviewed. There were no junior player interviewed for this club. Of the players two were Indigenous. Due to a clash of treatment times we were unable to interview the Foxtrot captain. Further to this, the senior coach declined to be interviewed but nominated his senior assistant instead. No reason for why the senior coach did not want to be interviewed was given.

Foxtrot FC influential players

The senior players who scored highly in relation to culture setting, friendship and trust were P93, P90 and P91.

Childhood experiences

For P93, who grew up in a capital city, his experiences of interacting with Indigenous and multicultural people were limited:

> No not a lot. [Previous city] probably has got more [Aboriginal people] per capita than [current city] so yeah look I was aware of them but like my High School was pretty much just a white community so not a lot.

For P90, who comes from a small country town, he also experienced a similar situation:

> No Indigenous [people]. There's like a family that lives on a farm nearby. They're like Indigenous but they're not full on like you couldn't just pick them out like. I can't remember growing up with any mates that weren't Australian [read: Anglo].

For P91, who comes from a multicultural family, his experiences were different to that of his teammates:

> I played a couple of seasons with [previous AFL club] and I played with [Indigenous player] while I was there. He was the first Aboriginal person I'd ever met. Then coming to [present AFL club] like [I] got on really well with [names several Indigenous teammates]. You know [Indigenous teammate] is one of my closest friends. I probably didn't have any interaction with Indigenous people until I was about 18 I reckon. As far as other cultures I went to school with lots of Vietnamese kids. I had a pretty good idea of their culture and other cultures as well. I've had lots of interaction with different cultures.

Lumumba/O'Brien clip

Having watched the Lumumba clip, P93 responded by saying:

> He could have just quit right then and there and never went back to football and obviously that's a waste of great talent, which would have been good for us when we're playing him but it's a bit disappointing when you look at it like that. You sort of think 'far out' you don't realise what ramifications it can have on someone until you see things like that.

For P90, this was what he thought in relation to the clip:

> I just thought it was pretty shithouse like I didn't grow up with people like Harry so I didn't really didn't see it [vilification] at all. Maybe because I'm a bit older now I know it's the wrong kind of thing to do but to hear that when he was playing underage footy, that little kids were saying that kind of stuff, was pretty shithouse.

For P91, he made a deeper reading of the clip:

> Like [they're] just saying it because [their] parents have said it. Because you've heard it from somewhere, you've heard it from another kid who's heard it from their parent. It's disappointing to hear it. I don't think ultimately those little kids are racist I just think they don't really have the conception [sic] of what they're saying. I think if he was gifted junior footballer the reason they have been trying to racially vilify him is just because he was better than them and that was probably the last resort.

When asked an ancillary question to the Lumumba clip if racial vilification can have long lasting effects, P91 responded:

Look it depends on the person, it depends how severe it's been. I know my Dad was racially vilified lots when he was a kid and when he was at school. My Grandparents when they came to Australia my Grandfather used to have his shopwindow smashed in all the time from Aussies thinking he was with the Germans [in WWII] and all that sort of stuff. So that stuff can last forever like but it does depend on the person, it depends how severe it is.

'Running like they stole something'

In response to the mark Maclure clip this is what P93 said:

He was trying to get at 'they ran like they stole something' [and] you don't want to get caught. I thought more like 'did that just sort of happen?' I have fun jokes with [Indigenous teammates] and vice versa. I'm sure if I ever overstepped the mark or they ever overstepped the mark we would tell each other you know, I'd be apologetic and so would they. None of it should be taken as humour. It's definitely offensive you know and look it might not be offensive to [Indigenous teammates] but a lot of people listening to that they might find that a lot harder because it's not a joke for everyone you know [Indigenous teammate] might not and other Aboriginal communities might not. And that's where you've got to think well it's not really acceptable.

His teammate P90 had somewhat of a different perspective:

I don't know if I see something wrong with it or not. He probably would have said it if three little white fellas were running around. I think if he backs it up with saying the same comment about white people well then I don't see anything wrong with it. I reckon he was just saying they were pretty quick. It was harmless to me.

P91 was one of the few players from any club we interviewed who can recall it occurring when it did; he said:

I do remember it when it happened. He's definitely not justified I mean it's ignorant that he would even make a joke like that. You know he's a legend of Carlton's. It's a bit of an indication of the times, probably when he played and the attitude then but the attitude of people, of people now it's just disappointing that he said it in a public forum. I would be offended by that and the [other] commentator hears him and says 'you can't say that' Drew Morphett and I'm sure lots of people out there would have laughed at it and said you know that's pretty funny.

Interesting comments

For the more influential players at Foxtrot football club, P93 was very grateful for the amount of education that he had had around these issues:

I reckon the AFL has done a lot. [I've] been in the system now [number] years and do get sick and tired of doing the old meetings and all that. But they really ram home a lot of good information and good knowledge and stuff you know ninety nine percent [99%] haven't stuffed up and haven't said anything so you know that's a great result. Especially when you look at it from larger community if you were to get seven hundred [700] blokes between our ages I'm sure you'd have a lot more stuff ups then what's going on in here. So I give credit to the AFL that they've done their job.

P90 would concur with this teammate, but also added:

I guess it [makes us] aware of what kind impact it can have on people if you do racially abuse them. But yeah I think it comes down do the person you know they're either going to do it or not. I guess they do enough. They probably do too much.

P91 was in no doubt that the AFL led the way when it came to issues of diversity and difference:

From my point of view I think the acceptance of different cultures in AFL footy is as good as it's ever been I reckon.

Foxtrot FC fringe players

Players from the Foxtrot Football Club who were on the fringes when it came to issues of trust, friendship and culture setting consisted of IP92, P94, P96, P99 and IP95.

Childhood experiences

For P94, this was what he had to say regarding growing up:

We've always had Indigenous kids coming around from up north from remote areas visiting the school, staying at our house or we'd be going up there on various trips. So yeah had a fair bit of interaction I suppose from aged about 15, 14 onwards.

IP92 said:

Back home we were pretty cruisey in [town] especially because there was a heap of us and there was a lot of [Aboriginal family names] everyone living in [town]. There wasn't any incidents of racial vilification going that I heard of in [town]. Everyone got on pretty well.

For IP95, his experiences of were slightly different again, but the importance of football as a socializing agent is clear:

When I started going to school [I] didn't go to class because there was no Aboriginal kids in class. So I would skip it. I met friends through football. Like Australian Aussies [Anglo Australians]. I'm still pretty close with a couple of the guys I played [with]. I still keep in contact with them actually.

P96 said:

I did a lot of Indigenous study at school, it seemed like every year we studied Indigenous topics. I went to a school in a [specific European country] community. Like at school it was mostly [specific European country] [people]. That's just where the school was that Mum and Dad wanted to send me to and so the majority was of [specific European country] descent.

Lumumba/O'Brien clip

P94 responded to the Lumumba clip in a preferred way specifically noting the potential for him as a junior player to leave the game. It is also interesting to note P94's position on individual prejudice as a learned response:

Harry could have aggressively responded obviously. Or he could have stopped playing footy [and] we wouldn't be seeing him at Collingwood today. I don't think you could grow out of it [racial prejudice] because surely the reason you are that way is because of how you've grown up and what beliefs you've been bought up with.

IP92 responded similarly:

You know you're playing on a team that's got pretty much all white boys on it and you're the only black dude so you've just got to try and ignore that sort of stuff. Like he said he didn't want to play football anymore because of that stuff.

This was reflected also in the answer by P96:

[He] could [have] turned to violence or things like that. He could have done what he actually said and turned away from football and obviously we'd lose a great player [because of] kids calling him names.

'Running like they stole something'

Turning to the *Media Watch* clip a range of responses were given. This was what P94 said:

> Yeah it's shithouse by Mark Maclure. He was having a go at Indigenous Australians you know. Stereotyping them as you know [as] bad people and kind of lowly scum. Offensive? I would have been if I was them that's for sure.

IP92 also was taken aback by what Maclure said:

> I certainly think that he shouldn't have said that because that's just insulting. Especially hearing that from, you know, [a] great of the game. If he had his time again I'm sure he would have [he] wouldn't have said it but it's just insulting that he said that stuff. I'm sure he's been educated on it now. Blacks [Indigenous Australians] are well known for stealing stuff and that's just the way blacks have been bought up. Oh certainly offensive if he would have said that to me then on air, through the media, I would have pulled him up a little bit I would have thought so. [I] certainly hope I don't hear that again.

P96 could see that Maclure had overstepped the mark but felt that it was up to the individual as to whether they would be offended or not:

> I've said before like white people do steal as well but there's I guess the stolen thing again they've [Indigenous Australians] been accused of things like that before so it makes it more offensive to them. I think it sounded like it was just harmless joke but then again you don't know how people are going to take it.

P99 felt that Maclure comment was, at best, ironic:

> I find it hard that he could have said that and realised it was okay. Point is they were quick. Ironically he was probably trying to compliment them. It doesn't sound like it was said with malice, with any real racial intent but again if I was the player spoken of like that you know, if I was an Indigenous player and that was the first thing that sprung into someone's mind you'd have to ask some questions about that expression. I wouldn't be happy about that one.

Interesting comments

With the interesting comments from the fringe players at the Foxtrot Football Club, IP95 felt that more needed to be done around education of supporters:

> Well it's still happening now with the Majak Daw's. They're giving education to AFL clubs now but you can't educate fans. When Hawthorn played Collingwood there's sixty-five thousand [65,000] so you can't educate sixty-five thousand [65,000] people. You can't get all the Hawthorn fans to do a big education [class].

P99 felt that Rule 35 is an important thing to help protect players and attract new ones, but vilification needs to be more harshly policed:

> I would imagine it's a bigger issue for kids wanting to play. If it helps the younger kids realise they can do it I imagine that would start a whole new generation of kids wanting to play because they don't [get] abused and don't have to worry about feeling different. I'm not sure what else they can do, if you're the kind of person who still thinks it's okay [to racially vilify] I think you don't deserve to be playing in the AFL. It's like telling someone you can't go and bash someone. You can't treat people like that so I think they've [AFL] done enough. The bigger the penalty for these guys the better.

It was perhaps the response by IP95 in regard to the Maclure clip that was the most interesting:

> It's funny because one of my best team-mates [Anglo teammate] he goes 'oh you black bastard' and I say [you] 'white bastard'. We joke around because we're close mates and we know it's not meaning [abuse] but we joke around. [Laughs] I get it [racism] a lot, I still get it now when I'm driving my car. I was driving my car and I pulled up in front of the TAB.

117

I parked and [there] was one copper on this side and one copper on the other side. They said 'who's car is it' and I said 'it's mine'. 'What's your name. Give us your license'. [Gave me] a random drug test. Random breathalyser test and I got nothing and they say 'where you going?' I said home. 'Where did you come from?' Training.

The club doctor gave me a script, [had] and we've gone in there [chemist] and said 'I need to get these drugs'. They said 'we don't sell these here'. It was for Endone. Pain killer coz I had an injury. I told my fiancé[1] and she walked in there and said 'I need a script for Endone' they said 'here of course'. She cut sick[2] at them. I just wanted to get drugs. I was in pain. I just went straight to the next one [chemist] and they knew who I was, the other had said no we don't sell them here because they thought I was a druggie or something.

It's not a really big deal [what Mark McLure said] I'm used to it [racism] that's nothing compared to what people say back where I grew up.

Conclusion

The Foxtrot Football Club interviews provided a great insight as to how the players at that club have taken up the ideas from the education processes around Rule 35. This seemed to be the case especially around the reactions to the Lumumba clip and the Maclure clip where the players were uniformly concerned that Lumumba could have experienced that type of abuse in a junior competition and that he could have easily left the game. Equally, the players seemed to feel that the way Mark Maclure employed the line that he did to describe the play by Yarran, Betts and Garlett was inappropriate and, in most cases, offensive. The exception to this was the response, ironically, was by IP95, who has obviously experienced a lifetime of racial responses to his Indigeneity and felt that Maclure's gag did not offend him as it was 'nothing' compared with other experiences he had had. This criterion is an interesting interpersonal response and could be read as a specific coping mechanism. In comparison to the two other examples IP95 gave involving the chemist not giving him painkillers despite having a doctors script and the police harassing him, the Maclure gag does, on the face of it, appear to be the less offensive. However, when using the example IP95 described of the police questioning 'whose car is this' the insinuation is that IP95 has possibly stolen the car as it appeared too expensive for him to afford. Similarly, IP95 says that the chemist felt that he was a 'druggie or something', the connotation is a negative one as that 'something' could range from a thief to a drug dealer. In this way, while it is understandable that IP95 has created a hierarchy of one negative stereotype over another the simple issue is that they are all essentially the same stereotype. In this way the stereotyping of IP95 whether it is by the police, a chemist or a football commentator as a car thief, a drug addict or the punch line of a gag they are all equally problematic because they all occupy the same socially constructed referent: that being Indigenous Australians are seen as untrustworthy, unreliable and deviant.

Disclosure statement

No potential conflict of interest was reported by the authors.

Notes

1. This player's fiancé is non-Indigenous.
2. *Cut sick* is a slang term for getting mad/upset.

Gecko Football Club

Sean Gorman, Dean Lusher and Keir Reeves

> The Gecko football club is an AFL club that participated in this Australian Research Council project Assessing the Australian Football League's Racial and Religious Vilification Laws to promote community harmony, multiculturalism and reconciliation. Foxtrot participated in the surveys only. This club and its players and staff have all been deidentified as required by Curtin University's ethics guidelines.

People at Gecko Football Club

There were a number of players at the Gecko Football Club who fully completed the survey. No interviews were conducted at the Gecko Football Club. No coaches or ancillary staff completed the survey. Of the players, the dominant religion was Catholic (41%) and the dominant culture was Anglo-Australian (78%). Outside of the AFL, the majority of players were either studying at university/technical and further education (52%) or not working or studying at all (38%), and almost all players (95%) had completed secondary schooling.

On measures of feeling listened to by others and feeling included and understood by the club, there were no differences between Indigenous and non-Indigenous players. With regard to player knowledge of Rule 35, the majority of players (48%) were unable to define the rule as it was currently understood and they were also unable to identify who brought it about. Only one person (2%) answered both questions correctly. On knowledge of Rule 35, there were also no differences between Indigenous and non-Indigenous players.

Club engagement

We had considerable difficulty accessing players and staff at this club. They promised us time and again that interviews would occur, but they didn't eventuate. Only the players participated in the survey, and no coaches or other staff were present, except for the Player Development Manager (PDM). As a result, the players were a bit rowdier than other clubs we had been into where the coaches were present, even if those coaches did not participate in the survey.

Notably, one player at this club asked publicly if he had to do the survey, to which another player replied, 'Why wouldn't you want to do it?' The player who initially questioned his need to participate did actually participate, though he was the first to finish and leave. At the end of the survey, the players left the room with pens and paperwork (such as participant information sheets) all over the place. While everyone else got up and left, one of the Indigenous players in the team helped the researchers clean up the room. Upon leaving the club some players jokingly and sarcastically made racist comments towards the PDM, while looking at and smiling at members of the research team. This was then followed up by more banter, with some of the players saying things like 'Nah, I'm not racist'. In short, this club was quite different from the others we'd looked at; this was perhaps due in part to the absence of senior football department staff at data collection or perhaps the way the players saw themselves.

Networks and club culture

Sets culture network: self-awareness of social influences

For the sets culture network at Gecko Football Club, our range of analyses showed the following. As with other clubs, the best players and more experienced players were highly selected as setting the culture. With regard to the club itself, those who set the culture did not identify strongly with the club. However, those setting the culture felt more comfortable at the club (e.g. are more likely to say that 'Other people listen to what I have to say') but are very unlikely to say that the club does a good job at dealing with players (e.g. 'The club understand my needs').

On issues of race and ethnicity, culture-setting players did not endorse racial essentialism (i.e. biological determinism of traits and abilities). Furthermore, they did not believe that religious beliefs or faith were well accepted within the club. Notably, there were strong differences in regard to the degree to which the club was seen as a family-inclusive environment. Players who were studying were also more likely to be selected as setting the culture.

In regard to masculinity attitudes, there were a number of effects. First, players selected other players with similar attitudes to themselves about adherence to strict gender roles as those who set the culture. Furthermore, beyond this effect for similarity in views about strict gender roles, there was an overarching effect that players who strongly endorse strict gender roles were also more likely to be seen as those players who set the culture. Second, players who were not homophobic were more likely to be culture-setting players. Third, players who thought that most others at the club endorsed playboy attitudes were more likely to set the culture. Finally, players who thought that most others at the club did not endorse violent masculinity attitudes were more likely to set the culture.

Friendship, trust and after hours: informal, unspoken social influences

At Gecko FC, best players were more likely to be selected as friends. Furthermore, players selected other players high in experience as friends, or players with similar levels of experience to themselves. When considering their views on whether the club does a good job of understanding its players and works together well, players chose as friends other players with similar views to themselves and also players who strongly disagreed with these statements. Therefore, at Gecko FC, players who did not think the club supported them well or functioned effectively were popular people to choose as friends.

Trust within Gecko FC played out in the following ways. Best players and more experienced players were much more likely to be trusted. Furthermore, players were more likely to trust others with similar levels of experience. Trusted players were more likely to believe that the club was a family-inclusive environment, and that the AFL has been very successful in its attempts at eradicating racism from the game and truly recognizing multiculturalism. Whether players were studying was important for trust, such that players trusted others who were also studying (thus reflecting a similarity effect for studying in regards to trust). Several other interesting effects were also present with regard to inclusiveness at the club. Trusted players were those who strongly felt listened to by others at the club. Additionally, those players who are more likely to trust others were players who also felt listened to by others. However, players who were trusted were those who did *not* think that the club did a good job of understanding player needs and of working together well. These somewhat contradictory results imply that highly trusted players feel that their voice is heard by other players, but, beyond the playing group, that the club does not understand its players.

In respect to after-hours socializing, again it was best players who were popular as people to interact with after hours. Additionally, players were more likely to socialize with others of similar levels of experience. Notably, there were no effects pertaining to race/ethnicity. However, for masculinity, players were more likely to socialize with other players who had similar views on homophobia (irrespective of whether these were homophobic or non-homophobic), indicating a polarity or sub-grouping of players on attitudes about gay men.

Difference of opinion and funny: contested boundaries

Differences of opinion between players at Gecko FC related to AFL experience and attitudes towards racism and multiculturalism. First, players were more likely to have differences of opinion with other players of similar experience levels; but there was also a general effect that more experienced players were chosen as people with whom one had a difference of opinion. Second, players who were more likely to nominate others as people they had differences of opinion with (i.e. players who were more likely to have differences of opinion with others) were those who did not think that multiculturalism in AFL was a success or that the AFL had stamped out racism in the game.

Finally we look at the perception of humour within Gecko FC. Those most likely to be considered funny by their peers are the best players and also the more experienced players. Players also choose as funny those of similar levels of experience to themselves. The other effects relate to both positive and negative attitudes towards Indigenous Australians. Players are more likely to see as funny those players with similar views to themselves for both pro-Indigenous and anti-Indigenous attitudes. This indicates that humour around race/ethnicity exists at Gecko FC (which was certainly the experience of the research team in collecting these data, as noted previously) but that different sub-cultures are in action, comprising people who have similar views.

Summary of social networks

The Gecko Football Club has a number of features in common with all other clubs: playing ability and experience are valued commodities amongst players and certainly impact the social dynamics of the team on such issues as who is seen to set the culture, who is trusted, who they socialize with and who they think are jokers. These two factors are slightly different for each club but generally do have a large impact on how the social relations of the team are structured.

However, Gecko FC also has a range of interesting findings that relate to race/ethnicity and masculinity, as well as how the players view the club itself. Furthermore, the general approach of the players to the research was less professional and respectful than in other clubs. This may be due to the fact that no coaching staff members were present and so the players were much less formal in their interactions, as they did in other clubs before coaching staff (always the last to arrive) joined the data-collection session. Or it may simply be that this club is different from others. Combined with the fact that over a period of eight months this club promised on a number of occasions to be involved in the interview component of this research project wasn't, our conclusion is that the answer to the question above may be a little bit of both. We do note that while one player was not interested in participating, another player criticized him publicly for not wanting to participate in this research, which is indeed a sign of support for the research but more so the issues it addresses. However, we also note that at another club (i.e. at Igloo FC) we surveyed the players only in the presence of the PDM and the level of respect and professionalism at the Igloo FC was much greater.

With regard to race/ethnicity issues there were some interesting effects. For team culture, the fact that culture-setting players did not endorse biological determinism suggests that the leaders in the team do not buy into ideas of 'natural giftedness' of some races. Jokes were shared amongst players with similar positive and negative attitudes about Indigenous people, indicating potential differentiation along the lines of such attitudes and thus sub-groupings of players on such issues. Furthermore, players who were more likely to say that they differed in their opinions with others were those players who did not think that multiculturalism in AFL was a success and/or that the AFL had stamped out racism in the game. So issues of race/ethnicity are not clear-cut and there is contestation around such issues within the club. Notably, the difference of opinion network and the humour network showed that there were fissures around these issues.

Masculinity is also important in this club. Players who are not homophobic are seen to set the culture (which is encouraging), as also are those players who adhere to strict gender roles. Furthermore, culture-setting players also perceived that most other players endorse playboy attitudes. Strict gender roles and homophobic attitudes also dictated which players socialized together, but masculinity was unrelated to trust, friendship, differences of opinion or humour. In all, masculinity seems to have less influence in this club than others.

Finally, there seems to be a disparity between players feeling listened to and their opinions counting for something (presumably by their peers) and their views on how the club deals with the players. That popular people in the setting the culture network feel more comfortable at the club (e.g. are more to say that 'Other people listen to what I have to say') is unsurprising because they are central and prominent individuals in the team. However, that such players are very unlikely to say that the club does a good job of dealing with its players (e.g. 'The club understand my needs') indicates a tension possibly with coaching staff and the club's administration. That similar findings occur for trust suggests that this is pervasive, as trust is most likely more important than who sets the culture because we are more likely to stick by people we trust than people who may be in leadership roles that could change. The setting the culture networks are configured on a few individuals, which can change radically if people retire or move clubs or captaincy or leadership status changes, whereas the more distributed nature of the trust network, in which there are fewer prominent individuals and a more even spread of relations, indicates that it is harder to change because it would take longer to do so (see Figure 8 in paper "Overarching findings" (doi:10.1080/17430437.2014.1002974, in this collection)). In any case, at Gecko FC, it appears that the players stick together but there are tensions between the playing group and the wider club.

Disclosure statement

No potential conflict of interest was reported by the authors.

Hornet Football Club

Sean Gorman, Dean Lusher and Keir Reeves

The Hornet football club is an AFL club that participated in this Australian Research Council project Assessing the Australian Football League's Racial and Religious Vilification Laws to promote Community Harmony, Multiculturalism and Reconciliation. Hornet participated in the surveys only. This club and its players and staff have all been deidentified as required by Curtin University's ethics guidelines.

People at Hornet Football Club

At the Hornet Football Club (Hornet FC), the majority of players and also coaching/ associated staff fully completed the survey. Due to limitations in resources, we could not interview people from every club that we went to, so no interviews were conducted at this club. Of the players, the dominant religion was Catholic (31%). With regard to cultural background, 28% identified as Anglo-Australian and 51% as Australian (or 79% joining the two groups). Outside of the AFL, the majority of players were either studying at university/TAFE (33%) or not working or studying at all (42%). Almost all players (87%) had completed secondary schooling, and beyond this some had also completed a university/TAFE degree (9%).

On indices of their level of comfort at, and inclusion by, the club, there were no differences between Indigenous and non-Indigenous players. On the players' knowledge of Rule 35, the majority of players (64%) were neither able to state what is in the rule nor identify who had brought it about. Only one player (3%) answered both questions correctly, and there were no differences in the number of questions about Rule 35 answered correctly between Indigenous and non-Indigenous players.

Club engagement

The research team found the Hornet FC helpful. The research project was embraced not just by the players and coaching staff but by a significant number of associated staff at the club. The experience of the research team was that it was a very professional football club. There was some joking around from players but, on the whole, the players took things seriously which may have been due to the number of coaching staff that was in the room. Players were courteous to the research team. The PDM was very accommodating at this club and provided great assistance in facilitating the conduct of this survey.

Networks and club culture

Sets culture network: self-awareness of social influences

Indigenous players predominantly sit on the periphery of this network of culture setters, that is Indigenous players are not seen as setting the culture at Hornet FC. The results of the network models show that best players and more experienced players are likely to be selected as setting the team culture. In addition to this, players who identify with the club are more likely to set the culture. However, and in contrast, another finding indicates that culture-setting players also believe that the club needs to become better at understanding player needs and dealing with them as individuals.

On race/ethnicity issues, players who set the culture do not endorse biological essentialism, and further they believe the AFL has done a good job of recognizing multiculturalism and stamping out racism from the game. Furthermore, players who select others and those they select as setting the culture are likely to have similar anti-Indigenous views, indicating some separation into subgroups on issues of race/ethnicity.

Masculinity attitudes are also important in determining who sets the culture in the club. Notably, players who set the culture do not believe in an adherence to strict gender roles. In addition, culture-setting players do not personally endorse playboy attitudes but perceive that most others at the club do.

Friendship, trust and after hours: informal, unspoken social influences

When examining our network models for Hornet FC friendships, we find that players chose others as friends with similar levels of experience to themselves. In addition, players high in experience are generally more likely to be chosen as friends. Indigenous players were more likely to choose another Indigenous player as a friend. Notably, players who are less likely to think that AFL has eradicated racism from the game were more likely to be chosen as friends. Furthermore, players choose other players as friends who had similar anti-Indigenous attitudes. With regard to the club, players chose others as friends who had similar views regarding whether they felt comfortable and listened to at the club. Finally, there were no effects for masculinity attitudes on friendship.

The trust network at Hornet FC had only a few effects. Best players were more likely to be trusted. Indigenous players were more likely to trust other Indigenous players. Lastly, and in line with the friendship network, players who are less likely to think that the AFL has eradicated racism from the game are more likely to be trusted.

In the after-hours network, Indigenous players socialize after hours with one another. Beyond this, players socialize with others of similar levels of experience. There are no effects for best players. Finally, players are more likely to socialize with other players who hold similar beliefs about Indigenous players in the AFL (whether they are positive or negative) and negative beliefs about Indigenous Australians. Like other clubs, this suggests some segmentation or subgrouping of players on the basis of attitudes about Indigenous people. Notably, the one leadership player (i.e. the captain) does not socialize with any other players in the team. (It is possible he socializes with coaching staff, but such network ties are not shown here.)

Difference of opinion network and funny network: contested boundaries

With regard to differences of opinions among players at Hornet FC, players who others differed with most (i.e. players who were selected by many others) were those who strongly believed in biological essentialism, but also players who were positive about

Indigenous Australians. Again, this suggests two different subgroups of players. Indigenous players do appear to have differences of opinion with non-Indigenous players. So there would appear to be contestation around issues of race/ethnicity in this club.

Finally, humour offers another possibility to examine possible fissures within a team. In Hornet FC, we have a number of reasons that players are seen as funny. First, players see as funny others who have the same level of experience, or those players who are simply more experienced. Those players who identify strongly with the club are more likely to be seen as funny by other players. Additionally, players who identify strongly with the club are also more likely to think that many other players in the team are funny. Together, these two effects indicate that players who have a strong affiliation with the team are both seen as funny and think others are funny, thereby highlighting that humour is connected to the player identification in the team.

Summary of social networks

At Hornet FC, there are a number of interesting effects. Best players are seen to set the culture and are trusted, but do not feature prominently in any other of the networks. Experienced players are also seen to set the culture, but they are not more (or less) likely to be trusted than other players. Rather, experience plays a role in friendship, after-hours socializing and humour, but not trust. This suggests that the best players and the more experienced players are possibly separate groups.

Masculinity attitudes play out in the culture-setting network, but not in any of the other more stable and harder to change networks like trust, friendship or socializing. Clearly, there are only a few people who dominate the sets culture network, so this could be reconfigured quite quickly should a few key players retire or leave. However, the more distributed nature of the other networks (i.e. most people have only a few ties and there is a general absence of people who are highly popular) suggests that the patterns we see are more diffused and would take longer to change. In any case, beyond the acknowledged influences of key players who set the culture at Hornet FC, masculinity does not drive the formation of any of the key networks in the team, so appears not to be important to the culture of this club.

In contrast, there are a number of network effects for race/ethnicity at Hornet FC. Furthermore, these effects are not always in the same direction and do suggest contestation (of beliefs, we do not mean physically) within the team and around race/ethnicity. The split in difference of the opinion network into two apparent subgroups is indicative of this division, and that humour which is seen to be present between people of different views leads to a similar conclusion. The fact that people choose others as funny with similar attitudes to themselves suggests that players share jokes, potentially around issues of race/ethnicity, only with those other players they know to have similar views to themselves. There are no clear or obvious issues of difficulty at this club. However, there are different perspectives around race/ethnicity that are being negotiated by the players in their interactions with one another.

Disclosure statement

No potential conflict of interest was reported by the authors.

Igloo Football Club

Sean Gorman, Dean Lusher and Keir Reeves

The Igloo football club is an AFL club that participated in this Australian Research Council project Assessing the Australian Football League's Racial and Religious Vilification Laws to promote Community Harmony, Multiculturalism and Reconciliation. Igloo participated in the surveys only. This club and its players and staff have all been deidentified as required by Curtin University's ethics guidelines.

People at Igloo Football Club

At the Igloo Football Club (Igloo FC), there were many players but only one coaching/ associated staff member who completed the survey. No interviews were requested by the research team at this club. Of the players, the dominant religion was Catholic (48%), though 40% of players either said 'none' or did not respond to this question. The dominant cultural group among players was Anglo-Australian (76%). Outside of the club, 50% of players were either studying at university or TAFE, and around one-third were neither studying nor working (32%). All players had completed secondary schooling, and a further 13% of players had a university degree as their highest education.

With respect to issues of feeling included and supported at the club, Indigenous and non-Indigenous players did not differ, indicating that both groups felt equally included and supported by the club. On the issue of player knowledge of Rule 35, more than one-third (42%) were unable to answer either question correctly (i.e. could neither articulate the rule as it is currently understood nor identify who was responsible for its inception). A total of 42% of players answered one question correctly, and only 13% answered both questions correctly. Finally, there were no significant differences between Indigenous and non-Indigenous players in knowledge of Rule 35 as adjudged by the number of questions answered correctly.

Club engagement

The experience of the research team was that this was an extremely professional football club. While there was some joking around from players, and they participated in the survey with only the Player Development Manager (PDM) in the room with them (someone who usually does not rank as highly as coaching staff), player banter was kept to a minimum. This is in marked contrast to Gecko FC where respect for the research team and the research was somewhat questionable. More generally, players showed considerable courtesy to the research team. There were indeed smiles and smirks at the questions asked, as was the case at all clubs, but overall there was an air of professionalism that one might experience in walking into a business environment. This club stood out from all other clubs in terms of this very professional manner and approach. The PDM was very accommodating at this club and provided great assistance in facilitating the conduct of this survey.

Networks and club culture

Sets the culture

At Igloo FC, players who set the culture are the best players and the more experienced players. Furthermore, players who feel that their personal views are listened to by others are more likely to be seen as those who set the culture. However, those who believe that the club needs to do a better job of understanding its players as individuals also set the culture. The pattern of these two effects is one we have seen at other clubs.

On issues of race/ethnicity and culture setting, players at Igloo FC strongly endorse Indigenous players within the AFL (e.g. Indigenous players train hard), but notably such culture-setting players also perceive that most other players do *not* hold such views. Culture-setting players are also likely to endorse biological essentialist ideas, such that they believe that one's traits and abilities are determined by one's race. As noted, biological determinism is not necessarily associated with negative prejudice: it can also be associated with positive prejudice (e.g. Indigenous players are naturally gifted and 'magic'). Together, these effects suggest that culture-setting players believe that Indigenous players train hard but also that they are naturally gifted – quite a positive view about Indigenous players.

On issues of masculinity, culture-setting players are those who do not endorse violence. However, culture-setting players perceive that most other players *do* endorse violence, and also perceive that most other players believe in strict gender roles.

Friendship, trust and after hours

An examination of the friendship network at Igloo FC shows that players are very likely to choose other players of similar levels of experience as friends. In addition, players who were studying were more likely to choose other players as friends who were also studying. With respect to race/ethnicity, Indigenous players were very likely to select other Indigenous players as friends. With respect to attitudes towards Indigenous players within the AFL, players chosen as friends were those who personally thought positively towards Indigenous players (particularly that they train hard). However, players who were popular choices as friends perceived that most others viewed Indigenous players negatively. There are no effects for masculinity and friendship.

One of the things that is striking about the trust network at this club is that there were fewer ties than at other clubs. Those who are trusted are the best players, as well as those with similar experience or more experience. In regard to trust and race/ethnicity, Indigenous players were less likely to be trusted, except by another Indigenous player. Trusted players also believe that the AFL has eradicated racism from the game and truly recognizes multiculturalism. Furthermore, players trust other players who have similar attitudes about Indigenous players as themselves, indicating some division into subgroups on this issue. Finally, players are also likely to trust others with very different views on the endorsement of violence.

The effects for the after-hours network were quite simple. First, players socialized with others of similar experience. Second, Indigenous players were more likely to socialize after hours with other Indigenous players. Third, players who were studying were very unlikely to be selected as someone to socialize with, unless it was by another player who was also studying.

Difference of opinion and funny networks: contested boundaries

On differences of opinion, players at Igloo FC had differences of opinion with others who had similar levels of experience. This may be a by-product of the fact that similarity in experience shaped friendships and after-hours socializing, and more exposure to such people may also lead to having more differences of opinion too. The only other effect was for homophobia. Players who perceived that most others in the club were not homophobic were more likely to be targets of difference of opinion (i.e. other players had differences of opinions with people having such perceptions). This last effect implies that a number of players disagree that most others within the club are *not* homophobic.

The humour network is the last network for Igloo FC. There is one player in particular who others consider funny, though there are other players selected as well. Our network results indicate that more experienced players are thought to be funny. Players who feel that the club is a family-inclusive environment are also more likely to be seen as funny, and players choose as funny others with different views to themselves on this family-inclusion viewpoint. As far as race/ethnicity goes, there were no effects other than Indigenous players being very unlikely to be seen as funny. Finally, in regard to masculinity, players were more likely to choose as funny others with different perceptions about what most in the team thought about strict gender roles. Players who perceived that most others in the team endorsed playboy attitudes were also seen to be funny.

Summary of social networks

The only effect for Igloo FC that stands out as problematic is the subgroup division in relation to trust and attitudes about Indigenous players. Other effects related to race/ethnicity are not out of the ordinary – for instance, Indigenous players, as in almost all other clubs, do tend to interact closely with one another. However, it is notable that this is the only club in which players chosen as friends were those who personally thought positively about Indigenous players (i.e. players highly selected by others as friends were more likely to be supportive of Indigenous players – for example believe that 'Indigenous players train hard'). As the friendship network is a key network within teams, this is strong and striking evidence of a culture very supportive of its Indigenous players. Further at Igloo FC, there are not great issues around masculinity, though there are some effects that are important. Notably, players who set the culture do not endorse violence as related to masculinity: that is a positive sign. There are differences of opinion around homophobia, and people who are funny perceive that others endorse playboy attitudes. However, most of these effects for masculinity relate to perceptions about club norms rather than beliefs held by players. For Igloo FC, playing ability and experience are quite prominent, which is common to all of the clubs we surveyed. In short, this appears to be a club without significant issues on masculinity and indeed, through the friendship network, has strong support for Indigenous players.

Disclosure statement

No potential conflict of interest was reported by the authors.

Conclusion

Sean Gorman, Dean Lusher and Keir Reeves

This conclusion discusses some recent examples of racism in AFL in order to explore the question of 'how far have we come in the AFL when it comes to racism?' This paper also discusses what the potential future trajectories are for Rule 35 and the findings from the Australian Research Council Linkage project that this book came from.

Skin in the game

There's enough racism that is just under the surface and it peeps out now and again. Racism to me is a majority and a minority thing. It's easy to be in the majority and say there is nothing. Ask the minority, and they will tell you that there is. – Mick Malthouse (Lowden 2012)

On 28 May 2014, *The Age* ran an article with the headline: 'Racism on the field has all but been eradicated'. The 'author' was someone called the 'Secret Footballer', presumably a current or recently retired AFL player who sat down to pen his thoughts regarding the topic. It is not easy to determine just what racial, ethnic, political or economic demographic the Secret Footballer comes from, given his anonymity, but it could be strongly assumed that the person was not from a minority group that AFL premiership coach Malthouse was referring to. From the opening line, this is strongly alluded to.

... Not once in my football career have I heard or witnessed racism towards a player. Not once. And that stretches back to my time in underage footy where not all the players – or spectators, for that matter could be classed as sensitive new-age guys. I have played with and against Samoans, Italians, Greeks, Irish, Sudanese, and Aborigines and many other races besides. (The Secret Footballer 2014)

The Secret Footballer goes on to say 'hand on heart' that he has not heard anything directly or indirectly in the change room or anything uttered underneath the breath of a player to another regarding one's racial or ethnic heritage. The article then goes on to talk about the recent spectator abuse experienced by Neville Jetta (Melbourne), Majak Daw (North Melbourne) and Adam Goodes (Sydney), stating that these incidents draw the ire of 'leading figures' in the debate enabling 'one more nail in the coffin for racism' to occur. The author rounds the article out by stating that:

each off-season (and to the annoyance of some players), we sit through an afternoon of AFL-run seminars designed to educate us in regards to issues such as racism, and drugs and alcohol ... The lasting message that has stuck with me is that, regardless of what we mean to say, if it is deemed offensive by someone, then it doesn't matter what the intention was, it is offensive. (The Secret Footballer 2014)

The overriding desire of this project has been to determine the efficacy of the AFL's and AFLPA's education programmes directed towards its players. We have wanted to know:

What have the players learned from the education provided? What do the players understand racism and ethnic intolerance to be? How have the players taken these principles into their everyday lives? Despite the annoyance that the 'Secret Footballer' saw displayed during the education seminars by his teammates, and possibly even felt himself, the message that he seems to have grasped is this: Think about what you are saying. Choose your words carefully after consciously assessing a situation and make an educated choice. Get to know your team mates. Ask questions. Become informed. This is opposed to an off the cuff remark, gag or ignorant put-down that has the power to wound, hurt and denigrate. This is the central tenet of the policy from ex-AFL CEO Andrew Demetriou regarding racial abuse and why it is imperative to address it: '[because] it doesn't only apply to football: it's the way we must live'.

Running concurrently to the Secret Footballer's article was a massive debate in Australia in 2014 regarding the potential repealing of 18C of the Racial Discrimination Act. This was floated by the Coalition as a means to address a perceived imbalance regarding free speech in Australia when News Ltd journalist Andrew Bolt was found to have breached 18C in two columns he wrote about the financial benefits and privilege afforded to Indigenous Australians with fair skin. As the debate swirled on talk-back radio and in print media, an extraordinary situation presented itself in Parliament in late March 2014. It was here that Labour senator Nova Peris asked a question of the Attorney General, George Brandis, about the damage such a repeal would have on people from marginalized communities. Peris, an ex-Olympian and an Indigenous woman from Darwin, was clearly talking from life experience and feared that the excision of 18C set a dangerous precedent and could lead to real social harm for so many. The Attorney General replied by saying:

> People have the right to be bigots, you know. People have the right to say things that other people would find insulting, offensive or bigoted. (Harrison and Swan 2014)

In an ironic twist on the Attorney General's position on this 'right', in mid-October 2014, a video emerged of a young man on a Brisbane train abusing a Queensland rail guard. The rail guard, who is of African heritage, asked the passenger to remove his feet from the seat. The passenger responded with, 'Learn some fucking English, 'cause this is Australia. I can't understand you … Do you even have citizenship, you fucken nigger …'. The verbal barrage continued in this vein and lasted for over five minutes. It was a great example of how a bigot, as defined by Australia's Attorney General, was exercising his right to be one. Thankfully both the offender and his friend who filmed the barrage and then loaded it up on a *Facebook* page were charged with creating a public disturbance and fined $400. They also received a huge public backlash that what they had done was not acceptable, with even the Prime Minister labelling it as 'un-Australian'. The public backlash to the possibility of repealing 18C was also immense and in the end the Coalition backed away from pursuing it.

It is from this position one's thoughts must turn to the last reported incident involving player-to-player vilification. It involved Justin Sherman and his racist attack on Joel Wilkinson, with Sherman's career ending prematurely in shame and regret. The AFL have taken the incident and used it as part of their education programme by making a short, five-minute video where Wilkinson is very explicit in what he felt Sherman was trying to achieve in calling him a 'black cunt'.

> I remember being in the room with the captains and the coach and they said to me 'Joel? What do you wanna do?' I remember saying, 'I want something to happen', because I could feel him thinking he was superior to me and he felt like I was worthless. (Australian Football League 2013a)

While player-to-player vilification is seen as a thing of the past despite the Sherman/Wilkinson incident, the notion that the AFL's education process, as the Secret Footballer suggests, has, like a vaccination, eradicated the use of racist language or beliefs cannot be sustained. We only have to recall the Rendell and McGuire comments to perhaps reconsider what racism actually is. Like a biological viral strain, racism takes on different, ever-changing forms. It is not just a word used in a heated exchange or a muffled response to frustration in a situation – it can be many things: an action, a look, a gesture, a joke or an insinuation. In this way, it is no different to sexism or ageism or any of the number things in society that deride, denigrate or make fun of something because it is deemed different, less valuable or unworthy. Take, for example, this reply from a retired Indigenous 200-game AFL player from a previous research project conducted:

> Racism is really disappointing but at the same time I feel sorry for that person who thinks that way. I recall one comment when a [teammate] had his car stolen. He said, 'One of your cousins stole me car'. That, I think, is being racist. How does he know who stole his car anyway? (Gorman 2012, 41)

This response feeds into 'taken for granted' notions or stereotypes of Indigenous transgression and criminality (Mickler 1992, 1998) and is what might be referred to as 'overt' racism. It also aligns itself neatly with the Maclure gag that has been used to elicit responses from the players for this book. There are many other examples that can be used and have been given throughout this book, but the central tenet as to why this situation is problematic is this: it is unnecessarily hurtful and it comes with a history. If racial vilification has been eradicated on the field, then we need to perhaps change our field of view and use the principles learned from that 20-year process and start to look at the internal workings and cultures of the clubs and the abuse by spectators. This is suggested by Gardiner, who explains the rationale for Rule 35 being brought in in the first place:

> In the Australian context, racial abuse of Aborigines comes with a history: a colonial history of violence and dispossession ... So when a white footballer racially abuses a black footballer, that abuse connects to our Australian history; a history that was never a level playing field for Aborigines. And this is not simply a matter of the abuser uttering an anachronism, or of being unconsciously held or fixed by the past. It is about words with the power to wound; words that can open old sores and perpetuate stereotypes – language of bad race relations (Gardiner 1997).

It should be noted that for the player who was told that 'his cousins' stole a teammate's car, the insult was perpetuated not on a building site or in a mining camp or randomly on the street but within the confines of an elite sporting organization, in the AFL – an organisation that should be (and is) trying to, as a condition of its professionalism, improve the welfare, well-being and education of its players for maximum on-field performance, with the fundamental nexus of that improved performance being the quality of the relationships between the players in that club. In this way, AFL clubs cease to be just sites where sport is played; they become centres of excellence. For a player to make a sweeping, stereotypical generalization about the theft of his car to an Indigenous player, a teammate none the less, is both unprofessional and unfair. This becomes even more problematic if the player making the accusation is a senior player or in the leadership group and the player who the insult is directed at is from a marginal group and/or a rookie. Multiple premiership-winning AFL coach and current senior Carlton coach Mick Malthouse responded to a question relating to welfare and development of Indigenous players in the elite AFL:

> You find the player, you then find the accommodation that is required for the player. I'm not talking about housing, I'm talking about having things in place that cater for every type of

player that comes through your door, whether they be indigenous, Irish, Fijian, a country kid coming down from the bush, whether it be a Tasmanian kid that just doesn't like the big life in the main cities, whether it be a shy kid or an extrovert, whether it be a highly educated kid or someone who struggled through school. You have got to have in your football organisation, particularly with the modern game today where there's so much money going through it, it's your responsibility to ensure that you've got things in place that make it an easy passage for that player to come in and feel very comfortable. And where he's deficient, you help. And that deficiency may well be settling into a big city, it may well be that he needs to study to get his year 12, it may well be that he needs a car licence, may well be that he doesn't know how to eat properly because he's never been taught the right skills, it may be as simple as a Skype to his parents who live in Dublin once a week just to give him the opportunity to settle. (Lowden 2012)

It is in these general everyday suggestions by Malthouse of eating a meal and getting a car licence that one can begin to unpack the issues of integration and comfort (or the lack of them) for some players who have entered the elite AFL. One example that comes from a previous research project involved an Indigenous rookie. He opened up about the support he had from his host family, responding with:

My host family is really good. When I first came, it was a bit different. Back home, we don't sit around dinner tables; we don't even have a table at home. I was sitting at the dinner table [at the host family] and I was like scared. I was getting shamed to eat. I was thinking this mob are probably looking at me eat. It probably took a couple of months until I got used to it. At home, if we want a feed, we get the rifle or the fishing line. We don't have lunch-time. (Gorman 2012, 60)

The other example came from a casual discussion with Cory McGrath, who was, at the time, the Indigenous and Multicultural manager at the AFL Players' Association. McGrath recounted a story about an Indigenous recruit who needed his car licence and had met his driving instructor at the club. Being in the city, the instructor asked the recruit if he could make his way down the road and turn right at a bus stop. The recruit tried to comply but drove past the bus stop. The instructor asked him why he did not do as he asked. The recruit replied that he did not know what a bus stop was (Taib 2012, 88).

Given these everyday pressures plus the hostility that can be meted out to players by spectators at games or as public figures in everyday life, the way that an AFL club is able to provide a socially nurturing and culturally safe environment may be the difference between a player staying or leaving. Even then, when measures are put in place, it can perhaps be a 'bridge too far' for some people. The difficulty for this with many clubs is one of resources, the right personnel doing the right jobs within the club, and will. Seeking assistance from outside the club can be problematic for some clubs as they have an unwritten 'in-house' policy where the same systems of dealing with problems are employed as different issues arise (Gorman 2012, 76–77). As players from a variety of different backgrounds are increasingly becoming part of the AFL system, it will take perhaps greater strategic input to ensure that the same formula is not used for different issues, and that creative and innovative methods are employed to address new issues as they arise. But in saying this, there are also long-established fault-lines that can curtail a player's potential even before he gets to the draft.

Im coming for you ... Junior football and racism

Che Cockatoo-Collins was a beautiful footballer to watch. He played 160 AFL games, 85 for Essendon and 75 for Port Adelaide. His first game was a baptism of fire, debuting against the West Coast Eagles in 1994, the side that would take out the premiership that year. Cockatoo-Collins was still somewhat of a rookie when he played in the 1995 ANZAC Day game, when Long was vilified by Monkhorst. Cockatoo-Collins was actually standing right next to the incident when it occurred. This is how he recalls it in a personal interview with Sean Gorman, August 2014:

> I remember Gavin (Wanganeen) was in the same contest, Longie was underneath, and I was over the top. There were a few other people there as well, and what was said was said. It was like a little punch in the nose. It stunned you for 10 seconds and you think, 'Did you just say that?' I looked at Tim Pfeiffer, who's the umpire closest. 'Tim, did you hear that?' we asked him. And he just said, 'Play on.' I knew Tim from SANFL days, and I just thought, 'That's rubbish.' I don't know why, when you don't put up with it in your work environment, then why would you put up with it when you're playing? It was used as a tactic.

Despite being brought up in different parts of Australia and in very different ways, Long and Cockatoo-Collins both experienced very similar responses from a range of people who felt that they were over-reacting to the situation that occurred during the game. During the interview with Sean Gorman, August 2014, Cockatoo-Collins said:

> It was said to me on a couple of occasions, 'Why don't you just not worry about it, because it is distracting you from your football' and I was like, 'Hold on. This is much bigger than football and much bigger than our careers.' I refused to accept that as standard or good behaviour. You have to call it out where it is.

Having a long family history of being politically engaged and being at the vanguard of cultural change with the AFL as a player, it would seem somewhat cruel and ironic that the work that Cockatoo-Collins has done over time came back to revisit him in 2014. Unfortunately, it was through a junior football competition in Queensland involving his eldest son Sachem who was 13 at the time of the incident. It was reported in the *Courier Mail*:

> Former Port Adelaide and Essendon forward Che Cockatoo-Collins is shattered after his oldest son quit the game because of racial vilification … Sachem was racially abused by a boundary umpire in a club game, was allegedly called 'nigger' by the umpire and targeted with remarks he should watch his back. (Fjeldstad 2014)

Cockatoo-Collins was not at the game to witness his eldest son being threatened and vilified, as he and his wife Darlene were driving their two other sons to other football matches on the day in question. In the aftermath of the game, Sachem and club officials rang up Cockatoo-Collins to explain the situation and he became incensed. It appears that Sachem was verbally targeted and physically threatened by the boundary umpire who was affiliated with the side Sachem was playing against. It also appears that the boundary umpire knew Sachem from past matches as he was one of the standout players, not just in the league, but in Queensland, having been selected for the prestigious Flying Boomerangs squad. It appears that the umpire, who is in his forties, had been trying to get under Sachem's skin with general banter. In an interview in July 2014, Sachem recalls the situation like this:

> It was leading into the finals, and we've always had a rivalry with the other team. I tackled a guy and he ended up pushing me. It turned into a big scuffle and the game became a lot more heated. I kept scoring goals and then all of a sudden, the kids on the other team started coming at me with their racial remarks, calling me nigger and stuff. I wasn't too fazed by it, because I was kind of expecting it to come. Then halfway through the third quarter, the boundary umpire came up to me, and he was following me around the field for about 10 minutes. He came up to me, and said, 'I'm coming for you, you dirty nigger.' I wasn't expecting that, so I started to cry. I didn't know what to do. My mum wasn't there. My dad wasn't there. And I was like crying, bawling my eyes out. I got so angry that I was going to go up to him and hit him. Then in the fourth quarter a kid came up to me and he called me a nigger as well. I punched him in the face and then got yellow carded and sent off for the rest of the game.

Of the incident, Sachem said he felt 'intimidated', 'scared', 'confused', 'disrespected', 'upset' and 'depressed'. Despite going to the Australian Human Rights Commission, the Anti-Discrimination Commission Queensland and AFL Queensland, the umpire received only a two-week ban. But in the midst of all of this is the sad reality that for Sachem Cockatoo-Collins, the pathway to an AFL career, one based on an outstanding junior track record that looked so assured and bright in August 2013, has now ceased as he has left the sport for good. What is the AFL's loss is the NBA's gain, as he has thrown his efforts into following in the steps of San Antonio Spurs NBA star, Paddy Mills. In an interview with Gorman, July 2014, he explains:

> Eventually I want to be known around the world for what I can do. I eventually want to play for Australia, which I can't really do in the AFL. That's been a long-time dream for me, to play a sport for Australia.

The whole incident has left Che Cockatoo-Collins bewildered and sad, given that Sachem had two AFL clubs, in the Brisbane Lions and his father's old club, Port Adelaide, very keen to have him be part of their organizations when the time was right. During the interview with Gorman, July 2014, Che explains:

> I know my son. He's not going to play again. It was such a traumatic experience for him. Imagine you're 13, and a fully grown 40-year-old-plus male comes up to you, and is telling you, 'You better fucking watch your back' and he's supposed to be an AFL official. Would that scare you away from the game? AFL Queensland have proven through that incident that they cannot protect my son. And they've proven that they don't care. I can't see him playing club level again. He's already moved on and because he's such a talented athlete, he's had choices. Next year is so crucial because it's where you get to go to the national championships but he's not going to play through a club, which means he's not going to be selected in the Queensland state team. That's a full stop on it. Without that incident, we wouldn't be having this conversation. He'd be still playing right now.

The impact that this situation has had on the Cockatoo-Collins family really does put into perspective the choices Heritier Lumumba made when playing in the under 10s for Rossmoyne Football Club in Perth. This was one of the specific questions we asked of the players and coaches in this project. The thing we were not able to determine (and nor are the AFL) is how many other unaccounted stories are there of gifted and talented boys from different minorities who have walked away from the AFL due to the issues that racism and ethnic intolerance created for them?

Where to from here for Rule 35?

As frustrating as it is not to know who the Secret Footballer is so as to make a more informed reading of where he is positioned according to his club and his experience, the words of the Secret Footballer are consistent with one of the key findings of this project: that on-field, player-to-player vilification has seemingly ceased in the elite AFL. This is a significant outcome, given the many examples when vilification was used as a direct tactic by VFL/AFL coaches and players prior to 1995 to distract, upset and anger players from marginal racial and ethnic groups. Despite some examples (post-1995) where players grappled with the notion that to call someone a name based on religion and skin colour was both morally problematic and illegal in the AFL, thankfully this is something that seems to be firmly in the past. This could be evidenced when we asked both players and coaches to tell us their thoughts and feelings when Justin Sherman abused Joel Wilkinson. Not one player or coach we interviewed tried to explain it away or soften it by saying it was 'in the heat of battle'. The majority were angered by it, with the next most frequent reaction being bewilderment and frustration by coaches and players alike. But although we have shown that while direct on-field racism has been eradicated, there would still appear to be other strains of racial intolerance or stereotyping that need to be addressed. The issue needs to be taken up in the professional development and education of the players, club officials, recruiters, presidents, CEOs, board members and general staff affiliated with all aspects of the AFL industry.

This is to some extent already underway, with the AFL introducing its industry standard process known as the 'AFL Codes and Policies Certificate' in 2013. The programme that underpins this certificate includes a resource that focuses on equality, vilification, community standards and tolerance and has come about from broader feedback from clubs and the players themselves. The programme deals with a wide ranging set of topics affiliated with Rule 35 and focus on vilification, gambling, illicit drugs, performance-enhancing drugs, respect for women, concussion, alcohol and school visits. As the programme structure becomes more streamlined, it will be rolled out to encompass all people who work in the AFL, not just the players. In this way, the certificate provides the fundamental acknowledgment that AFL employees are aware of what the standards are when they commence work in the AFL, whether it is at a club level or in the administration. This seems to be following other governance trends specifically in the UK and the English Premier League (EPL) and the process of 'safeguarding'. Safeguarding covers all clubs within the EPL on issues around social and employment policy, procedures and practices, equity, education and training, implementation and monitoring (see Hedges 2014).

Perhaps the next frontier for the AFL is how it will deal with the seemingly ongoing issue of spectator abuse of players, particularly the abuse that targets a player from a racial or ethnic minority. This was raised in an article that was written in the wake of the 2014 AFL Grand Final, which basically called on the AFL to do more to stop bad crowd behaviour – behaviour that was to some degree exacerbated by a combination of a warm September day, alcohol consumption and a surprisingly boring AFL Grand Final that saw the Sydney Swans (the favourite) outplayed by Hawthorn and the game over by half time. Here is what Erin Riley wrote of the 2014 grand final experience:

> A large group of Hawthorn supporters standing at the back of the bay I was seated in, (were) making sexist, racist and homophobic comments throughout the game. They shouted that Adam Goodes was racist. They referred to Sydney players only by female pronouns – implying, of course, that being female is to be laughable and weak. And when the Hawks led by a large margin in the last quarter, they started chanting, 'Sydney take it up the a––, doodah, doodah'. My experience was not unique. Friends at other points in the ground heard Goodes called a 'black dog'. Others were heard saying, 'That girl was right about you', referring to the incident last year when Goodes pointed to the crowd after he was called an ape. Another chimed in, 'I can definitely see the resemblance.' When I complained to a security guard, he told me that all fans do it and there was nothing they could do. Another person who'd complained shortly before me had been told the same thing, and was visibly distressed. (2014)

So bad was the booing of Adam Goodes by the crowd that two senior and respected sports writers in Martin Flanagan (Fairfax) and Patrick Smith (News Ltd), wrote about it. Flanagan said:

> The booing of Adam Goodes is to be regretted deeply, both for his sake and ours. White Australia can issue as many reasons as they wish as to why they don't like Goodes, but in Aboriginal Australia there is a view that it's because he's spoken out on Aboriginal issues. (2014)

On 29 September, Smith said on SEN radio's 'Hungry for Sport' segment with Kevin Bartlett:

> What I didn't like (from the Grand Final) was the booing of Adam Goodes. I can only presume that the booing is racial – it's the only thing that I could think of why you would boo him that constantly. I think there is a kick-back from the time he effectively reported that girl for racially abusing him. I do think there is a nasty racial undertone to that booing, which is really, really shocking. It ruined the Grand Final in many ways.

By reflecting on the answers provided by both the survey and the interviews conducted during this research project, combined with Malthouse challenging clubs to get better in the recruitment of minorities and their contrast with the Sachem Cockatoo-Collins situation and the Lumumba incident and further framed by the 2014 Grand Final, one can see that the situation regarding vilification more broadly is somewhat complex. Despite the many positive inroads being made through football, there is still some way to go before we can say that the AFL is free of the variety of social and racial intolerance and prejudice that still haunts society more broadly. This also needs to be read in the current context of the numbers of Indigenous players at the top level who are seemingly in a declining recruitment pattern despite two new franchise sides being added to the AFL in recent years. A recent news report suggested that there is a correlation between the decline in numbers and issues of equity and opportunity, which has seen the Indigenous player cohort decline from 90 in 2009 to 68 in 2014. Dr Geoffrey Verrall, the Chair of Training for the Australian College of Sports Physicians said, 'On the premise that this is not a cyclical issue but a consequence of the current system, you'd have to say that there's not as much opportunity for Indigenous people selected in the draft' (Terzon 2014). One would hope, then, that, unlike like Sachem Cockatoo-Collins, the choice young men are making not to go onto play AFL at the elite level is because they believe that they are better at other sports or enjoy more, rather than the direct or indirect abuse they experience because of their skin colour or religious beliefs. More research around this needs to be undertaken in order for it to be better understood.

Findings

These are what we believe to be the salient 'take-home' points of this research:

All players understood that vilification of other players is wrong

The overarching positive message of three years of research into Rule 35 tells us that all AFL players and coaches we interviewed understand that player-to-player vilification is unacceptable and reprehensible. While some players grappled with answering our questions and some, perhaps, felt the examples relating to racial intolerance and stereotyping were of no real consequence, the vast majority of the players and coaches were able to critically engage and gave thoughtful answers around this issue.

As mentioned in paper 'Overarching findings' (doi:10.1080/17430437.2014.1002974, in this collection), of the 99 participants interviewed, only four had *not* heard of the Sherman/Wilkinson incident. All remaining participants were appalled, angered or shocked by Justin Sherman's racist attack on Joel Wilkinson but saw it as an isolated incident. Some of the responses to that incident included the following:

> To be honest with you it did shock me … He's paid [a] pretty serious consequence for [it]. (Senior non-Indigenous Player)

> I was pretty disgusted really … It actually makes us footballers look like we're racist. (Senior non-Indigenous Player)

> A little bit flabbergasted. Personally, from my experiences of the AFL, over the last few years, I thought that was gone. I thought it was a thing of the past. [Just] the fact that it happened at

an elite level with a guy who's been in the system for so long, who's played with a diverse range of players and he still resorted to use that! I just was flabbergasted. (Non-Indigenous assistant coach)

These answers show a level of understanding that not only are these types of comments problematic but also they are definitely a thing of the past and very much an anomaly in the AFL today. This, it would have to be strongly assumed, has come down to the regularity of the education of the players around these issues, the quality of that education and also the continued efforts by the AFL to promote issues around social justice more broadly.

Given the regularity of the professional development of elite AFL players, players do understand what standards they are expected to maintain as a professional AFL footballer when it comes to Rule 35 and the responsibilities they have as professional athletes within the code, their relationships with club officials, teammates, opponents, their club brands and the corporate brand of the AFL. This has come about due to the extensive education programme that deals with Rule 35 and further includes the following:

- AFL Anti-Doping Code;
- AFL Illicit Drugs Policy;
- AFL R&R Policy;
- AFL Gambling Regulations;
- AFL Vilification Policy;
- AFL Concussion Guidelines;
- AFL School Visit Protocol;
- AFL Alcohol Policy.

Clubs are highly variable and individual, which creates complexity regarding issues of dealing with players of difference

As the Social Network Analysis (SNA) has shown, the social fabric of a club can be determined by who sets the culture within a club, who is trusted, who is seen as a friend and who is socialized with after hours, as well as other sorts of social relations. In short, these informal social relations shape accepted and also often unspoken ways of behaving within the club – that is they shape the club culture. Variability in the clubs can come about from the ways that club cultures have been developed over time. However, club cultures are also dependent on extraneous factors that individual players bring to a club regarding their own social, economic, religious, educative, cultural and political backgrounds. Cultures may be enduring in some clubs or change quite rapidly if there are some significant individuals who wield a lot of influence over others. How individual players within the club grow or become more engaged with others within their club, or become more aware of the world around them or deal with the policies, guidelines, regulations and rules of the AFL, will be dependent on club cultures and individual choices.

The fact that clubs do vary significantly has implications for the effectiveness of education programmes. While racism may be an issue at one club, at another it might be homophobia. It may be better to have a targeted education programme around issues that are salient for each team as the best remedy for specific issues at the club in question. However, this would entail more extensive incursions (such was carried out in this project) of all clubs in the elite AFL and greater monitoring of the issues that are present in the clubs currently. For this reason, it is worth considering the move by the EPL around issues of big data and how these are being used to monitor and improve not just game-day outputs of teams but also player recruitment, club compatibility and player well-being.[1]

Issues regarding nuanced and casual racism are still not deeply understood by majority of players

It would seem that players understand direct and explicit examples of racial vilification. Thankfully, many of them have never engaged in this type of behaviour nor have they experienced it directed towards themselves or others. Perhaps the things that stands out from the research regarding vilification is the way that some players still could not see that the probability of Heritier Lumumba walking away from Australian rules football was significant, or that a gag about Indigenous footballers 'running like they stole something' is a big deal. Perhaps senior player P43 from Charlie Football Club, who is from a multicultural background, shows just how complex these things can be to navigate. He demonstrated awareness that a song in the gym can have a potential negative consequence:

> We like a bit of rap music here in the change rooms or whatever and it ends up like 'niggers' and the like. I'll leave that word out when I'm around the boys just 'cause I don't know if they'd be upset by it. But sometimes you might sing, 'Oh niggers this' and you think, 'Fuck. Hang on, is that appropriate?' I guess you're not sure sometimes even though you're not directing it at anyone. (P43)

This example shows how clubs and individuals within them are able to manage these things should they ever become an issue. Maybe consulting with a range of stakeholders to identify what nuanced and casual racism (or homophobia or sexism) can look like and how to address it if it does present as a problem could be a condition of being a professional sportsperson within an elite organization.

Understandings of reconciliation and multiculturalism by the players are generally not very sophisticated

In addition to the players' general lack of understanding regarding nuanced or casual racism, understandings of historic social movements such as reconciliation and multiculturalism were not well understood. Given that the AFL has major themed rounds based around these two concepts, the Indigenous round and the Multicultural round, coupled with the professional development in this space, it seems strange that the answers to the questions related to reconciliation and multiculturalism were not better articulated in the interviews. When one Indigenous player (IP20) of the Echo Football Club was asked what he thought 'reconciliation' was about, he replied, 'No idea, mate, to be honest with you'. Similarly, a non-Indigenous teammate (P2) said, 'I probably thought it was a bit of a black and a white thing'. Another non-Indigenous teammate (P19) said, 'No idea'. This is in contrast to a senior Indigenous player (IP8) of the Echo Football Club saying that reconciliation was 'people respecting what Aboriginal people went through. Especially with the Stolen Generation and realizing that it was hard and that people treat people the same way you want to be treated'. Perhaps a greater understanding of the histories that have brought these two social movements about and how they are manifest within the AFL calendar would assist the players in understanding the significance of them socially, culturally and politically.

Indigenous players felt more marginalized from their clubs than their non-Indigenous teammates

It can be easily seen in the SNA data that Indigenous players are often, though not always, seen as occupying the margins of the social world of the club. Maybe this is a reflection of society and Australian history where Indigenous people have regularly been marginalized and continue to be so. Indigenous players are less likely to feel that the club was an inclusive environment for their family than non-Indigenous players, and are also less likely to feel that the AFL has stamped out racism in the game and truly recognizes multiculturalism than non-Indigenous players. Furthermore, Indigenous players in most clubs are much more likely to associate with other Indigenous players, which can indicate that Indigenous players feel a need to stick together, or alternatively this could reflect the fact that people tend to hang around with similar others (e.g. we often see that players interact with others of similar AFL experience). Finally, in some clubs there are indications that Indigenous players are less trusted than non-Indigenous players. One can only speculate as to why this is the case; it may have something to do with broader societal issues when it comes to stereotyping Indigenous Australians or it may be the internal club culture, which sees these attitudes prevail.

Agency to exact club change is not fully understood by Indigenous players

While it should not always be up to Indigenous people to put on the agenda the treatment of, understanding of and issues facing Indigenous people, understanding how Indigenous people enact change and use their agency to do so is also vitally important to understand. From the SNA results, which demonstrate that Indigenous players are often marginalized within their club, one could conclude that Indigenous players perhaps need to speak up more to avoid this occurring. Perhaps this, along with more proactivity around key dates on the Indigenous calendar, such as National Aborigines and Islanders Day Observance Committee, the encouragement of teammates to take part in the Long Walk, or an invitation to local elders to speak could be a way of empowering players and increasing awareness. This is not an easy thing to do if one is self-conscious or a rookie who simply wants to fit in with his teammates. But for cultural change to occur, potentially tough conversations with key figures within the club need to be had. This might be a case of speaking with the club PDM or asking player mentors within the club, who can provide a conduit to the senior coaches or management, to help raise an issue if this needs to occur. A previous research project showed how one senior Indigenous AFL player reflected on the process of feeling comfortable within a competitive and elite sporting environment.

> When I found my niche, so to speak, I was able to leverage that and discuss the things that I believed in: all my family values, my heritage. I was able to marry that into my professional life. You have to want to fit into the system. Don't shy away from things. Get yourself involved because you need to develop relationships quickly with the club and your team mates because there's a lot of bonding that goes on before you even put the boots on. So being shy or shame does not help. I was scared but I had to find my place and mixing with [senior teammates] helped my career. I gave myself the opportunity to start speaking to them. It's as simple as that. (Gorman 2012, 70)

The additional difficulty is that within teams, we see from the SNA data, sub-groups of players within clubs that are split regarding their support, or lack of it, for Indigenous people and players. Indigenous players may be more attuned to such divisions because issues of race and ethnicity are more visible on their radar, making them uncomfortable about initiating potentially difficult discussions if club culture suggests that such discussion will be unwelcome.

Teams with senior players with progressive views were more understanding about issues of diversity and difference

This follows on, but extends, the notion of agency because it relies on the quality of the interpersonal relationships with senior non-Indigenous players who have progressive views or Indigenous players who have standing within the club and are able to impart cultural knowledge to junior players and club officials and coaching staff. These senior players are able to navigate the complex professional challenges of the elite AFL because they have built up social capital within the organization. The value in this is they can impart to the younger players coming through the pitfalls and the challenges that they will face as professional athletes; they can also further enhance a player's understanding of issues of vilification, homophobia, violence and community responsibility. Recruiting players with football skills coupled with these potential leadership traits could have benefits beyond just winning games and premiership points.

Masculinity issues at clubs are variable

There was strong variability from club to club, and even from one type of network (i.e. sets culture, trust), on gender issues relating to playboy attitudes, the endorsement of violence, homophobia and strict gender roles. In many cases, there were divisions around such issues, suggesting that some players were, for instance, not homophobic while others were. Again, what is clear is that there is much contestation around these issues; we don't see club cultures that are utterly homophobic or misogynistic or promote violence. While we see again and again across all clubs that player ability and player experience are highly valued commodities, indicating that these are AFL-wide valued characteristics, the variability in endorsement of the various masculinity themes indicates a club-specific dimension to such attitudes and thus something that is not endorsed consistently across the code, and this is indeed a positive thing. It is noteworthy, that given all of the hype and negativity predicted to surround any AFL player coming out as gay (i.e. remember Akermanis' comment about destroying the fabric of the club), we see within most clubs little evidence of homophobia. Clearly, attitudes may become more polarized on such issues if a player was to come out. But it is also likely, as in the case of Jason Ball, that players are going to say, 'So what?' and just 'get on with it'. Our data on half of the clubs in the competition clearly show that homophobia in the AFL is just not the big issue in the eyes of its players that it is purported to be.

More longitudinal data needs to be gathered

The novelty of this project is that it is the first of its kind that has been undertaken using an organization like the AFL and analysing a rule like Rule 35. The main strength of this project has been the successful execution of the research programme and it application of a mixed-method approach. This approach has been led by the SNA, which has provided a valuable starting point to see where the potential fault-lines and strengths were in each of the clubs. This helped inform the specific questions for the interviews. It is from this that we know that the data is of very good quality and provides an extensive picture of the ways players and coaches see issues of vilification in the AFL. This book thus provides baseline data that have provided a basic diagnostic of how things are regarding vilification in the AFL. This data is just the beginning for more research of this kind to be undertaken, not just in the AFL but also in other major sporting and business organizations in Australia to help further chart and navigate Australian society through uncertain times where issues of race, ethnicity, sexuality, difference and diversity can be responsibly assessed and reported on.

Conclusion

To conclude, the issues around race and ethnicity, difference and diversity, multiculturalism and reconciliation are things that each club that participated in the project has had to deal with over time and in accordance with the AFL and the AFLPA. Some clubs had a better understanding of these things than others, for a variety of reasons. Some had younger cohorts of Indigenous players who were still feeling their way and did not fully understand the power of their agency. Conversely, other clubs had very strong and seasoned Indigenous players who were respected members of the club – so their opinions around cross-cultural matters were taken seriously. Others had coaching groups that, while supportive, were under great pressure, making issues associated with Rule 35 not central to team success. For other clubs, racial and ethnic respect was crucial to team unity and on-field success. What was clear is that these are not easy issues to manage in any organization, sporting or otherwise, because they require individuals to take carriage of complex, ever-changing issues that require constant vigilance, often in the face of great pressure and often with limited resources and time.

Through the three years of research involved in crafting this book, we have put AFL players and coaches under a microscope regarding issues surrounding vilification. Our analyses show that while obvious problems are understood and direct vilification is deemed wrong by the players, more subtle forms of issues around vilification are not understood. There is certainly more to be done, but if we take a step back and compare the AFL and its players to peoples' homes around Australia, or other workplaces in Australia, or other sporting clubs or groups in Australia, how do they compare? We would have to say that the work the AFL and the AFLPA have done in addressing and educating players around racial issues and vilification has been very good. Given the data from both the SNA and the interviews, this is perhaps summed up by player P69, who said:

> I was filling out my CV yesterday and in the skills and past experiences I wrote I've done X amount of sessions conflict counselling, racial vilification and cultural diversity and I'm proud to say that I am up to speed on what's right and what's wrong and what our game's about. I think the values in our game could be, if they were portrayed in society, it would be a much more harmonious environment.

Disclosure statement

No potential conflict of interest was reported by the authors.

Note

1. See http://www.theguardian.com/football/2014/mar/09/premier-league-football-clubs-compu-teranalysts-managers-data-winning

References

Australian Football League. 2013a. *Making a Stand – Joel Wilkinson*. Docklands, Melbourne: The Australian Football League.

Australian Football League. 2013b. *Rules*. Docklands, Melbourne: The Australian Football League.

Fjeldstad, J. 2014. "Former Power Star Che Cockatoo-Collins' Son Quits Football due to Racist Attacks." *The Advertiser Sunday Mail*, May 31. http://www.adelaidenow.com.au/sport/afl/former-power-star-che-cockatoocollins-son-quits-football-due-to-racist-attacks/story-fnia3v71-1226938416121

Flanagan, M. 2014. "Why Do Footy Crowds Boo Adam Goodes?" *The Sydney Morning Herald*. http://www.smh.com.au/comment/why-do-footy-crowds-boo-adam-goodes-20141003-10ppvf. html.

Gardiner, Greg. 1997. "Football and Racism: The AFL's Racial and Religious Vilification Rule." Discussion paper no.6, pp. 9–12.

Gorman, S. 2012. "What if Indigenous Australians Didn't Play Footy?" *The Conversation*. http:// theconversation.com/what-if-indigenous-australians-didnt-play-footy-5964

Harrison, D., and J. Swan. 2014. "Attorney-General George Brandis: 'People Do Have a Right to be Bigots'." *The Sydney Morning Herald*, March 24. http://www.smh.com.au/federal-politics/ political-news/attorneygeneral-george-brandis-people-do-have-a-right-to-be-bigots-20140324- 35dj3.html

Hedges, A. 2014. "Safeguarding in Sport." *Sport in Society: Cultures, Commerce, Media, Politics*. doi:10.1080/17430437.2014.976010.

Lowden, D. 2012. "In Conversation: Mick Malthouse." *The Conversation*. http://theconversation. com/in-conversation-mick-malthouse-5985

Perth Murdoch University, Western Australia. S. Mickler. 1992. *Gambling on the First Race: A Comment on Racism and Talkback Radio*. Louise St John Johnson Memorial Trust and Centre for Research in Culture and Communication. Murdoch University, Perth Western Australia.

Mickler, S. 1998. *The Myth of Privilege: Aboriginal Status, Media Visions, Public Ideas*. South Fremantle: Fremantle Arts Centre Press.

Riley, E. 2014. "AFL Has a Problem with Racism, Sexism and Homophobia." *The Sydney Morning Herald*, September 28. http://www.smh.com.au/comment/afl-has-a-problem-with-racism-sex- ism-and-homophobia-20140929-10n7pm.html

Taib, N. 2012. "Indigenous and Multicultural Policies in the Australian Football League Players Association." *Journal of Australian Indigenous Issues, Special Issue 'The Politics of Participation: Current Perspectives on Indigenous and Multicultural Sports Studies'* 15 (2): 87–94.

Terzon, E. 2014. "Indigenous AFL Player Numbers Drop Result of 'Equity Issue', Says Sports Physician." *105.7 ABC Darwin*, October 9. http://www.abc.net.au/news/2014-10-09/afl- indigenous-player-numbers-dropping/5796048

The Secret Footballer. 2014. "Racism on the Field Has All but Been Eradicated." *The Age*, May 27. http://www.theage.com.au/afl/afl-news/racism-on-the-field-has-all-but-been-eradicated- 20140527-zrpuc.html

Index

www.ingramcontent.com/pod-product-compliance
Ingram Content Group UK Ltd.
Pitfield, Milton Keynes, MK11 3LW, UK
UKHW010020280225
455677UK00023B/709